# New Product Development

## FOR

# DUMMIES®

# New Product Development

## FOR

## DUMMIES®

### by Robin Karol, PhD, NPDP, and Beebe Nelson, EdD, NPDP

**Foreword by Dr. Geoffrey Nicholson, Vice President, 3M ret.**

BICENTENNIAL
1807
WILEY
2007
BICENTENNIAL

Wiley Publishing, Inc.

**New Product Development For Dummies**®

Published by
**Wiley Publishing, Inc.**
111 River St.
Hoboken, NJ 07030-5774
www.wiley.com

WILEY

# About the Authors

**Robin Karol** is CEO of the Product Development and Management Association (PDMA), a professional society that creates and nurtures a global community in which people and businesses learn to grow and prosper through innovation and the introduction of new products. Robin is an adjunct full professor at the University of Delaware Lerner School of Business Administration, where she teaches courses on the Management of Creativity and Innovation. Robin worked at DuPont for 23 years in various aspects of innovation and new product development, achieving the role of Director of Innovation Processes. A certified new product development professional (NPDP), she received her PhD in Biochemistry from the State University of New York at Buffalo. She has numerous publications and has presented at many conferences and workshops. The Industrial Research Institute (IRI) presented Robin with its Maurice Holland Award for the best paper in its journal *Research-Technology Management* in 2003.

**Beebe Nelson** is Co-Director of the International Association for Product Development (IAPD), a consortium of leading product developers who come together to improve their ability to execute new product development. She has organized, chaired, presented at, and facilitated conferences and workshops in product development, and has contributed chapters and articles in a number of venues. From 1998 to 2003, she was Book Review Editor of the *Journal of Product Innovation Management,* a publication of the PDMA. Beebe is a certified new product development professional (NPDP) and holds a doctorate in philosophy from the Harvard Graduate School of Education. Beebe has taught Philosophy at the University of Massachusetts at Boston and most recently in the College of Management at UMass-Lowell. She chairs the Advisory Council of Partners in Ending Hunger, a not-for-profit organization located in Maine.

# Dedication

We dedicate this book to the members of the PDMA and the IAPD with whom we have worked and learned, and to George Castellion and his Frontier Dialogues. He was willing not to have the answers so that we could all learn together.

# Authors' Acknowledgments

Our number one acknowledgement goes to the hundreds of new product development professionals who have made the practice into a field that we could write this book about. Thank you George Castellion for PDMA's Frontier Dialogues, where we asked each other dumb questions until the answers began to emerge.

Thank you Kemp Dwenger and Dan Dimancescu (yes, those really are their names!) for researching Japanese product development practices and bringing them to the IAPD for us to learn from.

Thank you Merle Crawford, Robert Cooper, Abbie Griffin, and countless other academics for doing the research that enabled us to regularize the practices of new product development. Thank you Clayton Christiansen, Stefan Thomke, Henry Chesbrough, and many others for continually pushing the limits of NPD from your professorial offices.

Thank you Peter Senge for bringing home the systemic nature of new product development, both in your writings and in your association with the IAPD and the PDMA. And thank you Tom Bigda-Peyton, with whom Beebe applied the lessons of "the learning organization" at a number of client companies, including UTC, Corning, Fairchild, and Becton-Dickinson.

Thank you to the product developers and the leadership at DuPont, where Robin learned almost everything she knows about product development with the DuPont Consulting Solutions team. Thank you to the New Product Delivery Support Center at Polaroid, where Beebe worked with one of the most inspiring teams she has ever known.

Robin gives a special thank you to the original PACE(r) team members who struggled with her to understand how all this worked: Eric Schuler, Ken Pausell, Bob Gentlzer, Richard Tait, Greg Ajamian, Edmund Ziegler, and Ed Artz. I would also like to thank Michael McGrath of PRTM (Pittiglio, Rabin, Todd, and McGrath) for the creation of the PACE(r) process, for writing his books, and for being a mentor as I was learning new product development. I also thank Amram Shapiro and Mark Deck for working with the original team at DuPont and training us all.

Beebe's special thanks go to Polaroid colleagues Julie Manga, Karen Anne Zien, Dick Collette, Christina Hepner Brodie, the late Pat McGurty, Carolyn Walker, Catherine Seo, Jim Fesler, and Mark Durrenberger. We were all beginners — none more than I — and working with you was a distinct pleasure. My clients at Polaroid, including Walter Byron and Wendy Watson, provided lots of OJT, and I hope they learned as much from me as I did from them.

I also have some very particular thank you's. Thank you to Bob Gill for our first glimpse of an NPD territory — one that went far beyond the "river of development" — and to the late Bill Ausura for extending that view into the product lifecycle. Thank you to Christina Hepner Brodie, who taught me almost everything I know about customer visits when we worked together at Polaroid and later at the Center for Quality of Management.

Beebe and Robin reached out to many colleagues as they wrote the chapters of this book. The following people talked over content and structure, read drafts, and generally improved what we had to say: Thank you Don Ross of Innovare who helped us with Chapter 5 and with whom Beebe has done many exciting early stage NPD projects, and Rich Albright of Albright Technology Group, with whom Beebe co-wrote the chapter on technology mapping for the PDMA ToolBook2. Thanks to Mike Compeau of Compeau-Faulkes for his help with the chapter on new product launch. Thanks to Scott Elliott of TechZecs for help with Chapter 14 and to Don Hardenbrook of Intel for help with Chapter 11. Thanks to Mike Ransom and Dave Vondle of Eli Lilly for their input into Chapter 16.

Many, many thanks to our Technical Editor, Steve Somermeyer, a PDMA Board Member, a long time member of the IAPD's Steering Committee, and the president of Somermeyer and Associates. Because of Steve's hard work, we don't have to say "the errors that remain are ours." Now they belong to Steve as well.

Beebe particularly wants to acknowledge the IAPD and the IAPD members for an ongoing, high-level course in new product development. This group of companies has, for the past 15 years, been willing to set aside what they know to explore what they don't yet understand, and it has been a fascinating and rewarding experience to work with and for them. I also know that without my clients — David Deems of Becton-Dickinson, Shriti Halberg of Cerner, all the folks at Praxair, Dick Tyler of Bose, Jacques LeMoine of Corning, Jennifer Lee of Globe Union, and, well, I wish I could mention every single one by name — I wouldn't have understood what actually makes NPD work. Thank you all.

The success of the PDMA's effort to codify the knowledge of thought leaders in the field of new product development was crucial to writing this book. Robin wants to thank the PDMA for supporting her with the time to work on this book and for being a resource of information. I want to specifically thank the Board Chair, Hamsa Thota, for his encouragement; Ken Kahn, VP of Publications, for getting me started on this; Gerry Katz, who heads up the PDMA's Body of Knowledge; and all the directors, VPs, and members for being there to talk to throughout this project.

Mike Lewis, Acquisitions Editor at Wiley, held our hands through the contracting process, and Chrissy Guthrie, Senior Project Editor at Wiley, has been unfailingly supportive as we've worked toward the final product. We thank them both.

Steven Haines of Sequent Learning Networks held our hands as we worked through a number of thorny issues. His contribution to our understanding of product lifecycles enlivens many parts of the book. Phillip Clark jumped in to rescue us when we were overwhelmed by Wiley's editing process. Thanks to you both.

We're indebted to April Klimley, Editor of the PDMA's *Visions,* who was always there to lend her mind and heart, as well as a hand, an eye, or an ear. If we couldn't figure out how to do something, or to whom we could delegate it, April always sprang to our sides and pressed through. The book, our readers, and we owe her a great deal.

## Publisher's Acknowledgments

We're proud of this book; please send us your comments through our Dummies online registration form located at www.dummies.com/register/.

Some of the people who helped bring this book to market include the following:

*Acquisitions, Editorial, and Media Development*

**Senior Project Editor:** Christina Guthrie

**Acquisitions Editor:** Michael Lewis

**Copy Editor:** Josh Dials

**Technical Editor:** Stephen Somermeyer

**Editorial Manager:** Christine Meloy Beck

**Editorial Assistants:** Erin Calligan Mooney, Joe Niesen, David Lutton, Leeann Harney

**Cartoons:** Rich Tennant (www.the5thwave.com)

*Composition Services*

**Project Coordinator:** Patrick Redmond

**Layout and Graphics:** Carl Byers, Brooke Graczyk, Denny Hager, Joyce Haughey, Shane Johnson, Heather Ryan, Alicia B. South, Erin Zeltner

**Anniversary Logo Design:** Richard Pacifico

**Proofreaders:** Aptara, John Greenough

**Indexer:** Aptara

**Publishing and Editorial for Consumer Dummies**

**Diane Graves Steele,** Vice President and Publisher, Consumer Dummies

**Joyce Pepple,** Acquisitions Director, Consumer Dummies

**Kristin A. Cocks,** Product Development Director, Consumer Dummies

**Michael Spring,** Vice President and Publisher, Travel

**Kelly Regan,** Editorial Director, Travel

**Publishing for Technology Dummies**

**Andy Cummings,** Vice President and Publisher, Dummies Technology/General User

**Composition Services**

**Gerry Fahey,** Vice President of Production Services

**Debbie Stailey,** Director of Composition Services

# Contents at a Glance

# Table of Contents

# Foreword

· · · · · · · · · · · · · · · · · · · · · · · · · · · · · · · · · · · · · · · · · · · · · · · · ·

*N*ew *Product Development For Dummies.* I would guess that some of my colleagues might be offended at these words. But the fact is that a certain amount of naiveté is an essential ingredient in the process of getting a new product to market. After all, if we know it all, where is the room for discovery? It has been my experience that successful innovators have the characteristic of trying something first to see if it works, and explaining it later. Indeed, even better still, they get someone else to explain it.

This book teaches us the various hurdles to be overcome and the activities required if this endeavour of developing new products is to be successful. Indeed, it is a survival issue for many companies and for countries, including the U.S. A recent study by the National Academy of Science shows that the United States has moved from having a positive balance of payments of $33 billion for high–tech products in 1990, to having a negative balance of payments of $24 billion in 2004.

There are incremental new products, and there are revolutionary new products, those products that change the basis of competition. Developing new products requires creativity — coming up with ideas for new products — and innovation — the process of turning those ideas into something of value.

I use the following definitions:

> "Research and Development is the transformation of money into knowledge. Innovation is the transformation of knowledge into money."

Clearly we need both. This book focuses on the transformation of an idea into something of value — in other words, the transformation of knowledge into money. We cannot be happy with satisfying the customer; we have to reach the next level of delighting the customer. That often comes from products that satisfy a need that the customer did not even know he or she had.

To be successful with new products, an organization must provide an environment that allows innovation to thrive, the resources to get it done, and a measurable expectation of success.  If you want to activate innovation in an organization, you need to:

> Know where you want to go — *Vision*
>
> Know where the rest of the world is going — *Foresight*
>
> Have ambition — *Stretch goals*

Have freedom to achieve your goals — *Empowerment*

Draw from and work with others — *Communication, Networking*

Be rewarded for your efforts — *Recognition*

Passion and courage, however difficult they are to measure, are also essential in new product development. I can tell you from my experience in championing Post-It Notes that we had to have passion and courage. We were told several times by management to kill the program. I know that if we had had some of the processes like the ones described in this book, we could have had that product in the market two years earlier than we did.

Companies of any size must hire innovative people to join their team. These people should be creative, have broad interests, be capable problem solvers, be self motivated, have a strong work ethic, and be resourceful.

And so in your passionate and courageous effort to get new products successfully into the market by using the tools in this book, always keep in mind the six phases a program is likely to go through:

1. Enthusiasm

2. Disillusionment

3. Panic

4. Search for the guilty

5. Punishment of the innocent

6. Praise and honors for the non-participant

A final message: Enjoy the book, innovate for the customer, network with your colleagues, and have fun. But most of all, I wish you success with your new products.

— Dr. Geoffrey C. Nicholson, Retired 3M Vice President

# Introduction

· · · · · · · · · · · · · · · · · · · · · · · · · · · · · · · · · · · · · · · · · · · · · · · · · · · · · · · ·

**D**o you watch the Super Bowl on a high-definition flat-screen television? Does your microwave heat up leftovers in the blink of an eye? If so, thank a new product developer. Are you confident that the package you sent today will reach its destination by tomorrow morning? Have you found a retirement package that meets all your needs? If so, thank a new product developer.

Are you hoping that someone will solve the planet's energy problems and find cures for the diseases that plague the world? A new product developer is already on the case.

The people who develop new products look for problems they can solve, gaps they can fill, and ways they can make consumers' lives better, easier, and more exciting. They take on these tasks because they're curious, creative, and ambitious. They also want to make money — for themselves and for their companies. Unlike visionaries who like to invent for the sake of invention, new product developers commit to getting new products into markets where people can benefit from them, and for good returns on their investments. If you're looking to grow your business, sustain it for the long haul, and become a hero to your customers, jump right into *New Product Development For Dummies.* You can thank us later!

## About This Book

We wrote this book for people who develop new products. Don't let the title of this book mislead you into thinking that developing new products is a walk in the park. Developing new products is not only the most rewarding thing you can do in business but also about the most challenging. It calls for both creativity and discipline, and it requires a willingness to make mistakes and then learn from them.

We first met at product conferences, where companies from around the world came together to trade stories of their successes and share the reasons for their failures. We were anxious to collaborate with others. Fifteen years or so ago, though, none of us really knew how to make new product development pay off on a consistent basis. We'd look at each other and say, "Do you suppose it would help if we had cross-functional new product teams?" Or, "I wonder if we ought to get management to review this project before we bet the farm on it." Many of us were willing to make the kinds of stupid mistakes people make when they have no obvious answers.

Today, we *do* know what's important to achieve success in developing new products. We don't mean that only we, Robin and Beebe, know. We mean that many professionals know, and plenty of people in small and large companies around the world use the practices that we describe here.

In this book, we give you tons of tips, examples, and pointers that illustrate what successful new product developers do, and we help you to implement the practices that separate "the best from the rest." We had a blast writing this book, and we hope that you have a blast reading it and applying it to your work. After all, what's more exciting than creating something that didn't exist before? You do very important and very hard work. Our biggest motivation as we wrote this book was to make sure that everything we put on paper is accurate, helpful, and clear and represents the respect we have for you and for the work you're doing.

# Conventions Used in This Book

To guide you through this book, we include the following conventions:

- ✔ *Italics* point out defined terms and emphasize certain words.
- ✔ **Boldface** text indicates key words in bulleted lists and actions to take in numbered lists.
- ✔ `Monofont` highlights Web addresses.

Here are two important definitions:

- ✔ People who develop new products don't develop only things; they develop things *and* services *and* improvements to things and services that already exist. When we use the term "new product," we're referring to all the new products and services that solve customers' problems and make their lives better.
- ✔ When we use the term *develop,* we're referring to all the activities that occur between the time when a company sees an opportunity for a new product and when it introduces the product to the market.

# What You're Not to Read

We really didn't include anything that we don't think is important, but if you're in a hurry (and if you're a product developer, we bet you are), here are some suggestions:

- ✔ Look at the Table of Contents to figure out exactly which chapter deals with the problem that's bugging you right now. You can skip all the rest, until another problem or question rears its head.

- ✔ You can skip all the sidebars or save them for a rainy day. These shaded boxes mostly give examples and pointers from real-world experience. If you don't read them, you won't lose the thread.

- ✔ You can skip the text marked with a Technical Stuff icon. We put some things in those paragraphs that seemed a bit, well, technical — it isn't the kind of stuff product developers talk about on a daily basis.

# Foolish Assumptions

One of the cardinal rules in new product development is "Know thy customer." For us, that customer is you. We had to make some assumptions about you in writing this book, and some of them may be foolish or just plain wrong. Anyway, here they are:

- ✔ We assume that you're interested in developing new products or in supporting people who develop new products.

- ✔ We assume that you have some business background. We use terms like "return on investment" and "business case" throughout the text — terms that we assume you learned in school and/or use in your everyday work.

- ✔ We assume that you work in any industry imaginable and that you play just about any conceivable role in your industry. Your company may be large or small, old or just starting out. Also, we assume that you may be changing roles or industries.

Product developers often create character sketches of people for whom they develop their products. Here are some sketches that helped us picture our readers:

> I'm the VP of R&D at a small company that builds homes for first-time homeowners. I'm sure we could do a better job of designing, constructing, and marketing our homes if we treated them like new products. After all, we go through a pretty complex design/development process each time we introduce a new model. I need some kind of primer, an entry-level guide to help me understand what product developers do.

> I'm the CEO and founder of a small company that manufactures "environmentally friendly" air-conditioners. Dave, the head of R&D, is always suggesting ways to make our air-conditioners better, but Mike, the head of manufacturing, usually manages to squelch Dave's efforts. It's probably just as well, because I'm not sure that Dave's bells and whistles would be useful to our customers. I think we need to look into how some of the leading companies develop their new products.

*I'm the process owner for new product development in our company. We're successful at developing new products and services, but I know we could do more. Where I could get the most bang for my buck would be to bring all my processes — front-end, development, lifecycle — up to speed. I'm going to take a look at* New Product Development For Dummies. *Who knows, it may give us the baseline we need across all our divisions and all our processes.*

*My partner and I have a great idea for a new product. We're a long way from getting it to the market, though. We need to understand what all the steps are on the way. How do you get started? What are the necessary resources? And if we want to hook up with an established company, how would we go about it?*

*My boss, who's the head of marketing at our company, wants me to go to a Product Development and Management Association (PDMA) conference. He thinks that we could improve our product-change and product-introduction processes. I think I'll learn some useful things there, but I want to find a basic book that introduces me to the field before I go to the conference and make a fool of myself!*

*I'm about to graduate from college, and I think that new product development looks like an exciting career field. However, I didn't learn much about the field at school. I need something that will help me understand the field so that I have an idea of where to begin.*

*I work in Purchasing. My company, a mid-size furniture business, has been extending the amount of outsourcing we do in designing and developing new products. I'm feeling increasing pressure to become more of a thought leader and less of a responder in new product development. I wonder, would* New Product Development For Dummies *help me understand the processes better and teach me to be more of a contributor?*

*I'm the Chief Technology Officer for a process chemical company. People in my industry don't really think about developing new products or services. My company has been doing what we do for years now and continues to get decent margins. But I think we have a huge opportunity to extend what we're doing into new areas. I need to learn more. I could hire a consultant, but then I'd get only his or her approach. I want to find a book that gives me the skinny so I know how to take the next step.*

*I'm the process owner for a mid-size company's NPD division. We produce consumer goods. We're extremely successful in new product development; in fact, I'm traveling today to give a presentation on our voice of the customer process at a professional conference. But I've found a book called* New Product Development For Dummies. *One thing's for sure in NPD, the finish line is always moving. You know, I may learn something from this book. If not, I can always leave it in a seat pocket on the plane so that no one will know I was reading it.*

# How This Book Is Organized

To be successful at new product development, you have to know how and why new products are important to your company; you have to develop a way to continuously explore new opportunities; and you have to manage a disciplined process that will bring the most promising opportunities to market. The first three parts of this book address these important topics. In the final parts of the book, you discover some of the new challenges that product developers are facing, and you find some tips that help you navigate issues that are important to product development.

## Part 1: The Basics of New Product Development

Exactly what are "new products," and how do they contribute to your company? Until you can answer those questions, your company's efforts at new product development are likely to be helter-skelter. Your success will be hit-or-miss, with "miss" usually coming out on top. In Chapter 1, you discover what it takes to develop great new products, and you find out what role you and others must play in NPD activities. In Chapter 2, you take a look at the many different outputs we call "new products." You get a handle on which ones are important for your company, and you see how to integrate new product development with your company's overall strategies. Chapter 3 takes you into the world of product portfolios, product lifecycles, product platforms, and profit models — topics that help you come up with a clear NPD strategy.

## Part II: Charting the Ocean of Opportunity for New Products

The most successful new product developers stay on the lookout for opportunities. The point isn't to build a better mousetrap, unless you've really researched what will prompt the mice to run to your door. In this part of the book, you go through the best practices of visiting customers (Chapter 4), you find out how to turn your company into an "idea factory" (Chapter 5), and you discover how to survey technology both inside and outside your company (Chapter 7). You also discover how to identify the most promising ideas within the ocean of opportunity (Chapter 6), and you read about the disciplines that help your teams focus their efforts on those potentially winning ideas (Chapter 8).

## Part III: Navigating the River of Product Development

Developing and launching a new product requires discipline, hard work, and risk management. To help you through this part of the product development landscape, the five chapters in Part III give you the scoop on the "river of development," which starts when management charters a team to develop the business case for a new product idea or concept and runs all the way to the market. Chapter 9 lays out the standard new product development process from idea to launch. Chapter 10 gives information on how to assemble and run a cross-functional NPD team.

Chapter 11 is the gearbox of the whole book: It shows how you can join the strategies, the opportunities, and the products that your company already has in the market with the ongoing work of the product development teams. Chapter 12 discusses reviews and business cases and their roles in assessing the progress of new product projects. Finally, Chapter 13 gives you advice for making a successful transition from development to the market.

## Part IV: New Challenges in Product Development

Being best-in-class in product development is a moving target you'll continually aim to hit. You'll face many challenges, and your company will have to branch out to new areas of the product development tree. In this part, you get to see some of the changes that are making the old dogs of NPD learn new tricks.

In Chapter 14, we discuss the digitization of information. In Chapter 15, you find out how companies are going global to create new products. And in Chapter 16, you discover the increasing importance of partnering in product development. All three trends impact product development, and as they interact with each other, their impact becomes even greater.

## Part V: The Part of Tens

Testing and measuring are important throughout the product development process. We gathered some handy information that product developers use to accomplish these important activities and put the info in the Part of Tens. Chapter 17 tells you about the role of testing in NPD, and Chapter 18 presents some ways you can measure NPD success.

# Icons Used in This Book

Whether you want to flip through this book to look for tidbits or study each section as if we're about to give you a final exam, you should pay attention to the icons; they'll lead you to pocketable and useable take-aways.

Here's a rundown of the icons you'll see in this book:

 We use this icon to flag bits of text that we think are very important to remember. This icon may present some new, breakthrough advice, or it may recall something that we present in another chapter that also applies to what you're reading now.

 Once in a while, we want to go a bit deeper into some specialized stuff. We tip you off to that type of information by using this icon. You can skip over these icons and be just fine, but the info they contain will add to your understanding of new product development.

 This icon flags actions or strategies you can use to set yourself up for success.

 This icon flags the pitfalls and landmines that can derail your company's new product development train. We've tried to identify the most important traps so you can concentrate on the positives and avoid the negatives.

# Where to Go from Here

You don't have to start reading this book at the beginning and continue straight through to the end. In new product development, you really can't define a beginning or end anyway. Wherever you start, you're always in the middle of things — your existing products, your customers, your technology, your business goals . . . the list goes on.

We advise you to take a look at the Cheat Sheet at the front of the book and locate yourself and your NPD job on the map. You may be an executive whose key responsibilities lie in strategy. If so, you may want to start with Part I. Perhaps you're a functional head who's in charge of a business unit or an NPD process owner; if so, you may want to start with Part II to get a handle on what feeds the NPD pipeline. If you're a member of a cross-functional new product team or of a function that supports new product development, you may want to read Part III first.

No matter where you start, though, we have one strong belief: Chapter 11 should be required reading for everyone — especially for executives. Get to it when you can, but make sure you get to it.

When developing new products, you must keep your eyes on many balls at once. You need the cooperation and collaboration of many people within and outside your organization. We wrote this book so that you could see all the pieces in one place. If you understand all the things that need to go right in order to succeed in new product development, you'll be able to work with others — and to teach, coach, and influence others — so that all the balls stay in play.

# Part I

# The Basics of New Product Development

The 5th Wave                    By Rich Tennant

"Take it easy. It's a nice idea—not a fourth 'M.'"

# In this part . . .

If product developers behave like the blind men with the elephant, they won't get too far. You'll find the engineer at the trunk exclaiming over the functional elegance, the marketer at the tail stressing how easy it will be to sell, the manufacturer tapping on the legs and complaining that his current infrastructure won't accept them, and so on.

Developing new products takes a whole company (and sometimes even more than one). When companies take the new product development challenge seriously, they become learning organizations. They take off their functional blindfolds and discover how to communicate across internal boundaries. Employees work together to understand and share the work that they have to complete. They set clear goals and objectives for their new product development initiatives. They create common languages in which to articulate their strategies.

To optimize your company's ability to succeed at new product development (NPD), you have to come to terms with the organizational challenges that NPD presents. Part I provides an overview of how NPD impacts a company, and how the company can respond to that impact.

# Chapter 1

# It Takes a Company . . .

*D*eveloping new products that will succeed in the marketplace goes way beyond simply coming up with a great new idea, a great new invention, or a great new design. Developing successful new products is a complex job that comes with many tasks and many responsibilities. And how many different people, with how many different skills, do you need to accomplish the tasks? How about inventors, scientists, designers, and engineers? And manufacturers, marketers, and salespeople? How about heads of businesses and functions and people with finance and legal expertise? Maybe we should also include suppliers and partners, and what about customers, and . . . well, you get the idea. Instead of a village, "it takes a company to develop new products . . ."

Oh my! It's no wonder that so many companies find it hard to be successful at developing new products. In this chapter, we give you the general requirements for new product development (NPD) success, and we look at a map of the processes that you can take on your NPD journey. We identify the players in your company who have important roles in the NPD drama. Finally, we review what role you, our faithful reader, play in your company and what that means for your NPD participation.

We hope that by the time you finish this chapter, you're ready to order copies of this book for everyone you work with so that they'll know how to play their parts. NPD is one game you can't play by yourself!

# The Requirements of NPD Success

Over the years, product developers have come up with a pretty good list of what new products need to do to succeed at NPD. They need to

- **Meet the needs of potential customers (see Chapter 4).** This is probably the most important item on the list. If you haven't identified your potential customers, and if you don't understand their needs, the rest of this list won't do you much good.

- **Use technology that your company has access to or can develop (see Chapters 7 and 16).** Peter Carcia at Polaroid used to warn his teams not to design products that required "transparent aluminum." Don't limit yourself to your existing resources. Have an aggressive program of technology development and technology outsourcing and/or acquisition. But don't fool yourself into thinking that you can develop products that require miracles in the course of development (even minor ones!).

- **Attract customers by being different from competitors' products.** What's worse than spending six months or two years working on a product only to find that it's a me-too? Be sure you know who your competitors are and what they're up to, and be sure that you understand your customers well enough to produce a product that will delight them more than your competitors' products do.

- **Be designed so that you can manufacture, package, ship, and/or service them.** Long ago — not any more, we hope — engineers used to consistently design products that manufacturers couldn't build. Successful product developers "design for X" by including manufacturers, distributors, and so on in the early conversations and the ongoing work of product design and development. See Chapter 9 for more on how to "design for X."

- **Enhance or be consistent with your company's brand image.** The best product with the wrong brand is the wrong product. Your products reflect on your brand, and your brand reflects on your products, and if they don't enhance each other they may play takeaway. If you've got a great product that doesn't square with your brand, maybe your company needs a second — or fourth or fifth — brand. See Chapter 3 for a bit more on lining new products up with your brand.

- **Be promoted by a good marketing campaign (see Chapter 13, as well as *Marketing For Dummies,* 2nd Edition, by Alexander Hiam [Wiley]).** Don't make the marketing campaign an afterthought.

> ✔ **Provide a good return on your company's investment.** This is where the rubber hits the road in terms of judging the success of a product. Product development teams and business leaders can make this outcome far more likely by taking the new product's business case very seriously (see Chapter 12) and doing what's needed to make sure the product hits its goals.

Having a successful new product from time to time isn't enough. New product development is a core competency of the company that takes resources and generates revenue. To build its competence at NPD, your company must

> ✔ Develop employees who can make sure your new products meet all the requirements in the previous list, and a little more.
>
> ✔ Assign its scarce resources to projects that are most likely to succeed.
>
> ✔ Ensure that new product projects and business functions within the company support each other as much as possible.

# Moving from Product Possibility to Market Reality

Although it's true that every new product starts with an idea, not every idea ends up in the market. The most successful companies start by exploring many different opportunities and coming up with many different options. You want to make sure that among these options are ideas for products that will appeal to customers, sell in large markets, and take advantage of the latest technologies.

When we go through the product development map in the sections that follow, we say "start here" and "go there" as if we were playing a board game. In this game, though, you can start anywhere and go anywhere. If you just picked up this book and you're in the middle of a new product development project, you can skip to the part that addresses what you're doing. When you have time, read the other parts, too. Often, you can trace what goes wrong or right in one part of the development process to good or bad work in the other parts.

In the sections that follow, we take a quick look at the three major territories of the NPD landscape.

## Discovering opportunities

In the NPD process (refer to the Cheat Sheet for a handy illustration of the process), we call the place where you find product opportunities the "ocean." The ocean of new product opportunity is nearly limitless because constant change opens up new vistas. Think of the changes you've seen just in the past ten years. New technologies, new markets, and new products have enabled people to dive deeper and voyage wider into the resourcefulness and creativity of the human race.

Exploring the ocean of opportunity gives you (and your new product team) the information you need to develop your company's strategy for new product development. By identifying market and technology opportunities, you can focus your development efforts on the most promising ideas and avoid the traps and dead ends. And by reviewing your current product lines, you know whether to direct NPD projects to improve offerings in your existing product lines or develop wholly new products or product lines. (The chapters in Part II describe the ocean of opportunity in more detail.)

## Developing the product

After you've identified a bunch of opportunities, you want to choose the very best ideas that can succeed in your market and that you have the resources to develop. To do this, you use screens that allow only a few ideas to move into and through the development process (also known as the "river of development"). These screens — companies call them *reviews* or *Decision Diamonds* — are places where the company's decision makers review ideas for products against the company's strategic criteria and decide which ideas should use some of the company's scarce resources. Only a small number of opportunities should pass through the initial Idea Screen compared to the vast amount that float around in the ocean of opportunity. After an idea has passed the initial Idea Screen, it becomes the property of the cross-functional development team, which works through the phases and reviews of the product development process (see Chapter 9). At each review, business decision makers do one of the following:

- ✔ Continue funding the project for another phase

- ✔ Stop or hold *(recycle)* the project if the reviewers need more information

- ✔ Redirect, or even cancel, the project if it isn't meeting expectations or if the company's strategic landscape has changed

You can read more about reviews in Chapter 12.

Don't forget that a company's executives need to know that they can get good returns on their new product investments. Therefore, in addition to doing the actual work of developing new products, the product development team has to develop a *business case* for management. You can read more about business cases and how to create them in Chapter 12, and you can find a business case template in the Appendix.

## Launching the product

Your development team has spent months, maybe years, anticipating this moment — the moment when your new product launches from the protected environment of the team atmosphere into the wide world of the marketplace. In some companies, moving a product from development into the market is called "crossing the valley of death." Why? Because many new products fail at this point. To avoid launch failure, you need to plan for the launch throughout the development process instead of waiting for when your product is nearly ready for the market (see Chapter 13 for more on this topic).

# Identifying the Roles of the Functions

The major players in the development of new products are the people on the new product development team. These people have different roles, which may include the team leader, the members of the core team, and members of the extended team. One thing they have in common, though, is that they come from different functions and departments within the company. In this section, we give you an overview of what each function contributes to your new product development efforts, and we explain the particular roles the functions play throughout the process.

Even if your company is too small to have distinct functions, you can recognize the roles that individuals and groups play in your company. This section, as well as the information in Chapter 10, can help you do a better job of making sure the people and groups in your company are collaborating to make your NPD efforts as effective and efficient as possible.

Many new product efforts include partners from outside your company. You need to understand the basics of working with different functions when "outsiders" are part of the development picture. See Chapter 16 for more on partnering in product development.

# Marketing

Success in new product development depends in large measure on how well you understand the market, including the following:

- ✔ The existing markets for your products
- ✔ How your markets are growing or shrinking
- ✔ What new markets you may be able to enter
- ✔ What your competitors are doing in the marketplace

The marketing function in a large company, along with market research, may be responsible for collecting and managing market knowledge. In a small company, one person may be most interested in the market. But here's the thing: Understanding the market isn't the same as being good at selling in it. Your company, big or small, and your new product development team need to develop a deep appreciation for your customers and your markets. And your marketers must be able to communicate their knowledge to others with whom they share the responsibility for developing new products.

# R&D

Research and development is where many of your scientists and engineers live. Members of the R&D department contribute their understanding of technology to the company's product development efforts. Much of what your R&D experts know is pretty arcane (like that word, which means mysterious, deep, esoteric!).

Successful product developers make sure that their scientists and engineers work with others to share their knowledge and to understand how it relates to what the other functions know and do. This type of collaboration and sharing needs to happen in all the parts of the product development landscape.

Technologists can be very perceptive during customer visits (see Chapter 4). They also have the best understanding of existing and emerging technology (see Chapter 7). Members of R&D on an NPD team are likely to offer suggestions about technology innovations or technology tweaks or that may just provide a competitive leap forward as your new products meet their competition.

# Manufacturing

The role of manufacturing in NPD is to make the product concept a reality. Within this role, manufacturing has the following tasks:

✔ Ensuring that the company's manufacturing capabilities and infrastructure are adequate to produce the new product

✔ Deciding what parts of production the company may need to outsource (see Chapters 15 and 16)

✔ Managing the supply chain for the new product

Your manufacturing function must be able to produce as much of the product as you think you can sell, at the expected quality and performance. Therefore, members of this function should be involved in the development process from the very beginning. Include them when you visit customers to understand customer needs (see Chapter 4). Not only are their insights different from the insights of individuals in other functions, but they also have a much better idea of what it takes to put products into production.

# Service

Some of the new "products" that companies create are actually services. Airlines, for example, distinguish themselves on the services they offer. So do hotels, restaurants, and companies that deliver your packages overnight to anywhere in the world. The people in your company who design and market services should take the lead in developing services.

However, when the product a company creates is a product, companies may make the mistake of paying little attention to service. The individuals in your company who are responsible for providing service should be integral parts of the new product effort whenever a product entails aftermarket service.

Integrating service into the NPD process can alert product developers to new opportunities and help them avoid costly mistakes. For example, an NPD team that includes a member from the service function is less likely to design a product that's overly hard to service. Integrating service into development also can help NPD teams think about installation and repairs — whether these are the responsibility of the customer or of your company, and how expensive they should be (the easier and cheaper, the better for everyone).

# Packaging

Packaging impacts your new product's attractiveness on a store shelf, a computer screen, or in any other place customers are likely to find and buy it. Your new product's attractiveness — and often the size and shape of the final package — sometimes impacts a store's willingness to stock it. Here's a bottom-line way to perk up management: How much it costs to ship your new product depends, in part, on its packaging. And the cost of shipping impacts the final price, which impacts everything!

Our point? Involve your packaging function early in the development process. The members of the function can help the team understand the preferences of retailers and wholesalers; they can help influence product design to simplify packaging; and they can participate in consumer preference tests (see Chapter 17). At the end of the process, the packaging of your product often is the first impression your product makes. Use the resources of your packaging department to make it a good one.

# Distribution

The four Ps of marketing include product, pricing, promotion, and *place.* Your new product won't sell unless you distribute it to places where customers can buy it. A company's distribution and channel strategy shapes the choices that are open to the NPD team. Does your company sell through one of the "big box" stores? Do you offer products through catalogues or on the Internet? Is your distribution through dealers or distributors? Which of the existing routes will the NPD team choose to get its product out? Or will it try to carve out a new route? The distribution function should be involved in the product development process to make sure your NPD team understands the distribution options so it can get the new product out in front of an eager audience.

# Information technology

Your information technology (IT) department provides your NPD team (and your whole company, really) with valuable tools for development and business. For instance, through IT, you have the ability to

- **Communicate internally:** Many of us now send e-mails to the person in the office next door instead of getting up and knocking on the door. Most NPD teams are linked together via e-mail and instant messaging, and teams can send and share documents and keep an assortment of others "in the loop."

- **Store data:** Your NPD team can use an Intranet site to post documents and progress reports to facilitate work, communication, and company involvement. Your IT department can help with document formatting, document control, and your ability to access and use data from other parts of the company.

- **Communicate with the outside world:** Many development teams are spread throughout the world (see Chapter 15), and many development efforts require companies to outsource work to other locations (see Chapter 16). IT provides the tools that help these teams communicate, including Intranet sites where project information can be stored and shared. Teams can access documents from a shared site, and team members located in different places can work on projects simultaneously.

Go to Chapter 14 for more on the role of IT in NPD.

# Finance

You can't assemble the data your NPD team needs to represent the value proposition for your new product (which is what management and your customers are interested in) without the expertise of your finance department. Involve members of this function early in the process as you map the ocean of opportunity, and keep them involved as you build your business case (see Chapter 12).

# Human resources

People develop new products. These people need rewards, career paths, and all the other motivators that keep employees happy and productive. Your human resource (HR) department needs to understand the special needs of employees who develop new products. The performance goals and reviews that work for functional employees may not be appropriate for product developers.

Your HR department may be the right function in your company to create a cross-cutting set of practices that enable the functions to support your product developers. HR can look across the functions and design employee reward structures that balance functional and project work. And these structures can help the company in other ways by leveling the playing field among the functions.

NPD teams should also not hesitate to turn to HR for its special expertise in organizational development. For example, HR can help a team leader understand how to lead and motivate her team (see Chapter 10), and help a team identify the diversity that they need to come up with the best ideas (see Chapter 5).

# Regulatory, legal, and standards

New product development can present challenges to legal and standards boundaries. Many companies have to work within clear boundaries — for example, the pharmaceutical and medical device industries. For others, these issues come up when they're developing some products, but not all. Be sure your team has explored the possibility that its work may need to clear regulatory hurdles or that existing standards may limit what the team can do. Involve the legal department if the intellectual property (IP) it's developing needs protecting.

Your regulatory, legal, and standards functions have the responsibility of supporting your new product teams — as well as executives, business leaders, and functional heads — and helping them to understand regulations that may advance or hinder their work. But they can do their jobs only if the new product developers keep them informed of potential issues.

# Playing Your Part in Product Development

Executives, business and functional heads, members of functions and departments, and so on — all these people play a role in developing new products. In this section, we speak directly to you by identifying the roles people play in product development. Find your title and read away, or brush up on all the titles for a more complete understanding.

## Executives

Executives include CEOs, CTOs — can we say "CXOs"? — as well as heads of business units, vice presidents, directors, functional heads, and so on. These managers are responsible for charting the overall direction of the business as a whole, and their top-down support provides the context for product development.

The specific role of the executive depends a lot on the size of the company. In a smaller company, executives may play a very hands-on role; in a larger company, an executive is more likely to act as a context setter. In a company of any size, executives often appoint a process owner to plan and execute the tasks that build the company's new product capabilities, such as strategic planning and process development.

The executive role also varies depending on the role new products play in the company's strategy. In making the company's new product strategy clear, executives set a frame for everyone else. In Chapter 3, you can read more about the different parameters executives must consider in setting NPD strategy.

## Functional heads

A *functional head* is someone who leads one of the company's functional departments, such as R&D or marketing. In this position, you play an important role in building the expertise, the competency, and the capability your company needs to excel in new product development. Your function is one of the sources of NPD resources, in terms of manpower and expertise. You're also a major source of the information and knowledge that your company needs to chart its NPD course (see Chapter 3). Quite simply, without the functions and your leadership, product development wouldn't exist. (Read more about the roles of the functions in Chapters 9 and 11.)

Your responsibilities as a functional head point in two directions:

> ✔ **You have to make sure that, as you build knowledge and expertise for the product development effort, your function is working with the rest of the company.** Technology maps (Chapter 7) that no one outside

of R&D can decipher are useless; market insights that no one else shares do no good; and process advances that don't contribute to the company's product strategy are a waste of time and money.

✔ **You have to make sure that your function is capable of providing the necessary resources for developing new products (and is willing to do so).** Your function needs to resource the exploration that takes place in the ocean of opportunity; you provide employees and infrastructure for new product teams; and you support products in the market. (For more on the politics of product development, see Chapters 9 and 10.)

## Business leaders

Many companies have business units, or *strategic business units* (SBUs), that focus on different business opportunities. These SBUs are headed by business leaders who come up with strategies for the development of new products that advance the goals of the businesses — goals that should align with the work of other businesses in the companies and in other functions. In a smaller company, the top executives are responsible for NPD strategy creation.

As part of your strategy, you need to make sure that the portfolio of new and existing products is well balanced and in line with your objectives (see Chapter 3 for more on product portfolios). Is your business focused on existing markets and existing technologies? Then be sure your portfolio provides adequate attention to all the markets under your care, and don't be so wedded to existing technology that you overlook new technologies that might come with a "low-risk" price tag. Is your business focused on a volatile market or technology? Then make sure that some of your new product projects explore future options, but don't forget to balance the forward-looking portfolio with support of existing product lines and platforms.

## New product development team members

The members of the NPD team have the job of actually carrying the ball, so to speak. You do the development work from front end to back end. You also have to make sure that your company's executives, business leaders, and functional heads are aware of your value and of your resource needs (see Chapter 9 for more on these relationships and for advice on dealing with company politics, and Chapter 10 for more on the NPD team).

Some companies assign "product champions" to oversee important new product development projects. The champion's role is to advise the team members, understand their needs — and the value of their project — and influence the functions and executives in the company to provide the needed support. A champion usually holds an executive position in the company and has good powers of influence.

## Review committee members

Review committee members hold jobs in the executive, directorial, and managerial levels of the company. As a reviewer, your primary job is to decide whether products in the development process should go forward to the next development phase, stay in the current phase for more work, be shelved or sold, or cease to exist altogether.

Executing the job of reviewer means preparing for and attending all scheduled reviews, listening carefully to the product team's presentation, and discussing your thoughts openly and honestly with other reviewers and the team members.

As a reviewer, you need to do your homework before reviews, which includes reading the executive summary and the business case provided by the team. Be sure to talk with team members if you have questions or concerns before the review.

For more on phases and phase reviews, head to Chapter 9. For much more on reviews, executive summaries, business cases, and the role of the reviewers, check out Chapter 12.

## Functional support people

The functional head — of, say, marketing — is responsible for making sure that the product development process has the functional resources it needs (see the earlier section "Functional heads"). The functional employee, however, has a different responsibility: You need to be sure that you understand the product development process (see Chapter 9), and you need to know how you can contribute.

For example, if you work in the service function and a new product team asks you to join — either as a full-fledged member of the core team or as a resource at points during the product development process — your task may be to identify ways in which product design might influence service issues later on. The team will depend on you for a variety of expertise: anticipating the impact of different designs, modeling the financial implications of one service option over another, and so on. The more you understand about the NPD process as a whole, the more effectively you'll bring your experience to bear on the team's issues.

# Chapter 2

# What Are You Developing, and Why?

*T*he term "new product" covers plenty of ground. A new product can be a baseball bat or a toaster, a car or an airplane, a piece of software that includes support and installation, a vacation package, a new type of checking account, an in-home cleaning and babysitting service, and so on. Bank of America, for example, won the Product Development and Management Association's Innovator of the Year Award for its innovative "products," which are actually services, like its "Keep the Change" program which allows customers to round their credit-card payments up to the next dollar and put the difference into savings accounts.

Many companies think of products as *solutions* that include the range of products and services that address a customer's needs. For example, a company might offer everything a customer needs related to computers, from wiring to hardware to Internet connectivity to software to ongoing support — all bundled into one product package and priced accordingly. Some "new" products are actually the result of relatively minor changes to existing products. Other new products are so radical — often called *breakthrough* products — that no one has ever seen or thought of them before.

No matter what form new products take, you can make money from them in many different ways:

- ✔ You can simply charge customers when they buy them (think clothing).

- ✔ You can rent or lease them (think cars and copy machines).

- ✔ You can practically give them away and charge for supporting services and supplies (think razors, cameras, and printers).

In this chapter, we show you many different ways of defining and profiting from new products. We help you figure out how you want to grow your company, and we look at whether developing new products is important to your growth. If you decide that it isn't, you can put this book down. But we bet that after reading this chapter, you'll be more convinced than ever that developing new products is critical to the success of your business.

# Growing Your Business: Market Expansion, Acquisition, or Innovation?

A company's ability to grow is essential to its long-term success. Business growth is tied to shareholder equity growth and to the ability of the business to fund new initiatives. Organizations that fail to grow over time usually find themselves slipping behind their competitors and may end up out of business altogether. So, how will you choose to grow your company?

Companies can grow their businesses in three ways: Some put more emphasis on expanding into new markets with existing products, others grow by acquisition, and some focus mainly on developing new products. Here are closer looks at each of these ways of growing:

- ✔ **Expanding into new markets with existing products:** You may have plenty of products in your traditional markets, but have you thought about how to put your products into new markets? For example, a company could extend its products' lifecycles by selling products developed for more sophisticated markets in less sophisticated markets (see Chapter 3 for more on product lifecycles). Last year's computer may not sell well in Tokyo or California, for example, but it may sell very well in Venezuela or Senegal, where consumers will see it as brand new.

- ✔ **Acquiring other businesses:** Other businesses may have technologies, products, markets, customers, or other assets that would complement yours. Companies merge with other organizations or acquire them in order to gain access to new markets and sell more products. Mergers and acquisitions also can significantly expand your company's technology and product development capacities (see Chapter 16).

Nearly everyone complains that the total value of two companies that have merged is almost always less than the value of the two companies before the merger. Be prudent in your decision to merge, and expect that M&As (mergers and acquisitions) may create at least as many problems as they solve.

✔ **Developing new products:** Because you're knee-deep in this book, we assume that you're very interested in this option. No surprise, it's our favorite, too. When your company's growth strategy includes a healthy measure of new product development (NPD), you focus on your internal strengths in NPD and technology, encourage your development teams to understand your customers very well (Chapter 4), and stay on the look-out for markets and acquisitions that can support your NPD efforts. Clateo Castelliani, former CEO of Becton-Dickinson, used to say that of the three growth choices, new product development is the one that spurs the organic growth of a company.

We believe that the best growth recipe is to blend the ingredients from the previous list in ways that allow them to enhance each other in order to meet your growth goals. A new market can often be the key ingredient in a new product's success, and partnering brings in added technology and other capacity. See Chapters 13 and 16 for more on the connections between new markets, new partners, and NPD success.

# Assessing the Importance of New Products in Your Growth Plans

Some companies pay lip service to their dedication to developing new products. Their executives put on their smiles and talk about the importance of innovation and new products. You may even see the word "innovation" in these companies' core values. But when push comes to shove — and it does, more and more, in resource-constrained companies — these companies often put their new product projects on hold.

When investors are screaming for quick, high returns, companies find it hard to provide resources for projects that won't pay off for months or even years, and developing new products doesn't happen overnight. Many companies that face these pressures focus their investments on improving the sales of existing products. Other companies focus on cost reductions or incremental improvements to existing products. Both of these strategies are low risk and have quicker payoffs.

But if you try to survive in the market with aging products, you'll get passed by competitors that are putting out brand-new, shiny products that lure away your customers. Developing new products is an investment that will sustain your company over the long haul. You need to determine the importance of developing new products in your growth plans and then take appropriate actions.

Companies that truly value new product development tend to exhibit the following characteristics:

✔ They set targets and have metrics to predict and measure how many new products they'll develop each year, and they take them seriously (see Chapter 18).

✔ They manage their products as *portfolios* by focusing on the aggregate of products in development and in the market when they assess how well their companies are meeting their strategic goals. For example, they make sure that their portfolios include some radical and risky projects as well as lower risk, incremental projects (see Chapters 6 and 11 for more on product portfolios).

✔ They implement new product development processes and practices, and they have individuals who are accountable for managing and improving these processes and practices (see Chapter 9).

✔ Over the course of several years, they introduce a stream of successful new products that range from incremental to radical (see the later section "Defining the Types of New Products" for more on product types).

Are these traits evident in your company? If so, we hope that you'll use this book to assess the success of your company's development efforts and to see where you can improve when it comes to NPD. If not, or if you're not sure, read on to find out what being successful at developing new products can do for you.

# Identifying the Role of NPD for Your Company

How your company approaches new product development depends on many factors. Your company's unique culture and personality shape your approach to risk, the way you connect to your customers, and so on. The industry you're in also impacts how your company plays the NPD game. The oil industry does NPD differently from the medical device industry. If you're in food or fashion, the board on which you play the NPD game is different from the one for trucking or hi-tech.

## Putting your hands into all their pockets

Many businesses gain revenue from hybrid profit models. GE Medical, for example, loans other companies money to purchase equipment (financial product), sells other companies the equipment (product), sells supplies for the companies to use with the equipment (after-market product), and sells services to customers (service). Xerox almost didn't survive its early years when it was trying to make a profit by selling its copy machines. Only when it learned to rent equipment and charge for supplies and services did the company take off.

Whatever industry you're in, take a look at other industries to see what they're doing. Can you learn from the way Harley-Davidson implements Lean development, or the way P&G manages its product lines? Many of the improvements in NPD over the past decades have come from cross-company and cross-industry learning.

Take a look at some of the ways in which industries differ:

- ✔ If you work in the food industry, you probably come out with "new-and-improved" versions frequently but radical innovations relatively rarely.

- ✔ The pharmaceutical industry tends to have long lead times (it often takes ten or more years to develop a new product), but competition and advancing science and technology apply consistent pressure to innovate.

- ✔ Financial companies always are looking to differentiate through new product development.

- ✔ Many of the large commodity businesses (including oil companies and waste management companies) are beginning to use their vast wealth to innovate and develop new products.

- ✔ In fad and fashion industries, you measure product development cycles in months, not years. How different is NPD in these companies than it is in the pharmaceutical industry, for example?

Other business elements that impact NPD are more company-specific. Here are five elements to consider:

- ✔ **Where does your company fit in the "value chain"?** The *value chain* describes the process for turning raw materials into end products. Are you on the front end of the value chain, where you sell raw materials to others? Do you process raw materials to make them more useful to others? Do you make parts and pieces for final products? Or do you produce products that are sold to end-users?

You can find room for innovation and product development at every point on the value chain. For example, TetraPak launched a revolution in packaged food when it created the aseptic cartons that are now widely used for packaging for juices and soups. (Take a look at Chapter 4 for more information on the value chain.)

✔ **Who are your customers?** The answer depends on your company type:

- For some companies, the customer is the consumer or end-user; these are the B-to-C (business-to-consumer) companies. B-to-C companies have to be very focused on their customers. They need to design, develop, and sell products that will fly off the shelves. These companies have to understand the rest of the value chain as well. How can they get parts and materials that will support quality and keep the cost low? What are the requirements of retailers and wholesalers, without whom the product will have no shelf to fly off of?

- For many companies, other businesses are their customers; these are the B-to-B (business-to-business) companies. B-to-B organizations have to understand their customers *and* their customers' customers. TetraPak, for example, had to understand not only the food producers to whom it would sell the cartons, but also the distributors, the supermarkets, and the end-users who would have to learn to buy soups and juices in cartons rather than in cans or other forms of packaging.

✔ **What's your industry's "clockspeed"?** If rapid innovation and quick turnover are characteristic of your industry, your company needs to move fast, too. The market for hand-held personal devices has no room for a manufacturer whose products take years to develop and commercialize. On the other hand, if your industry is a slow mover — for example, the chemical industry, where typical products last five or more years — your company should implement product development processes that are appropriate to this slower cycle. Knowing your company's clockspeed and the clockspeeds of the suppliers and customers you work with is critical to understanding the right pace for product development and innovation in your company.

✔ **What's your source of profits/revenues?** Some companies make profits from selling products. Others profit from selling services, from leasing, or from services and/or products that customers will need after they purchase the original product (known as *after-market sales*). Many companies bring in profits from a hybrid business model, which gets revenue from many different sources (see the nearby sidebar). (You can read more about this topic in Chapter 3.) Recognizing where your profits come from is critical to the product's business case (see Chapter 12). It also helps product developers understand where they need to focus their efforts.

↙ **How long does it take to go from idea to product?** Companies that are implementing a Lean or Six Sigma product development process talk about the cycle time that a process is "entitled to." That rather odd way of speaking is how they communicate that there's a certain amount of time that it "ought" to take to develop a particular product. In the real world, it often takes longer, but the notion of entitlement implies that there's some low number that you can't do better than. Cycle times tend to be characteristic of industries: The automotive industry has longer cycle times, the clothing industry has shorter cycle times, and so on. *Note:* Radical changes can and do alter the expected cycle time in an industry. For example, the introduction of high throughput screening changed the basic cycle times in the pharmaceutical industry.

It's a good idea to do some research to find out how much time your product developers are entitled to by comparing your cycle times with others who make similar products.

# Defining the Types of New Products

What do we mean when we say "new product"? The term covers more ground than you may think. Sometimes a new product is just that: the cars that hit the dealers' showrooms every year around Presidents' Day, or the new drug that does a better job of lowering your blood pressure. Some new products introduce new lines of products and are often based on new technologies or processes. These *platforms* may include a new line of furnaces, a new kind of hotel, and so on. Still other new products are radical departures from existing products — think cellphones or online banking — while others are just tweaks or slight alterations on existing products.

## How mature is your company?

Usually the companies that make the mistake of placing all their bets on radically new innovations and products are young and headstrong. Many of them don't survive. The ones that make the mistake of betting solely on yesterday's successes are usually on the older side. Some of these sink into oblivion, some are acquired for their existing competencies, and some wander off into a complacent old age. The right new product strategy can help you survive to maturity and stay there, healthy and vibrant, for a long time.

# Breaking through the eye of the tiger (team)

Some companies separate breakthrough product development projects from their ongoing NPD work. Often, the teams for these projects are called *tiger teams,* or *heavyweight teams.* Members of management make sure the tiger teams get the resources they need and protect them from overt political battles with their individual functions.

Advocates of separating such projects from the daily grind feel that teams are more likely to develop really radical ideas if they're not in daily contact with the existing culture of the companies. It can be good to get away from the legacy of "how it's done around here." For more on the tiger team approach, head to Chapter 10.

Most companies that succeed in NPD create products in all three of the following major categories:

- Breakthrough products (sometimes referred to as *radical products*)
- Platform products
- Derivative and support products (also called *line extensions* or *incremental products*)

Understanding the differences among these types of products helps you focus your company's new product strategy on some projects that will provide short-term revenues and on others that will provide growth and revenue in the future.

## Breakthrough products

*Breakthrough products* bring new technologies to the marketplace and often enable or require customers to do things in new ways. For example, in the late 1940s Edwin Land invented a film that developed as soon as it was exposed. This technology breakthrough changed people's expectations about photography. Although its image quality never matched that of 35 mm film, the instant camera allowed amateurs to snap photos and share the results on the spot. The technology also provided the movie industry with a way to document sets (a process that people in the industry still call "polaroiding," even though the technology is now digital), vastly simplified the process of making picture IDs, and won contracts from industries and governments all over the world.

Corning, the same company that makes the nearly unbreakable cookware that can go straight from your refrigerator to the oven, devoted huge resources to develop the catalytic converter in the 1970s. It was a huge success and every car and truck has one. However, a few decades later, Corning put a similar effort toward developing photonics technology. The company ended up wasting significant resources as the world went wireless.

Breakthrough products sometimes allow companies to change the game. The really good ones can send your competitors onto the rocks as you sail off to new markets and new profits. But breakthrough ventures also entail risk:

**Technology risk:** Because we're talking about a breakthrough — a radical departure from what's been done before — no one can guarantee that the product will really end up working. Many pharmaceutical products are breakthroughs — the first of their kind to introduce a whole new class of drugs or a whole new approach to a disease into the market. Automobile manufacturers are working on breakthrough engine designs, from electric to hybrid to hydrogen fuel cell.

**Market risk:** Because radical new products often require new customer behaviors and literally create new needs in the market, there's always a chance — sometimes a big chance — that customers won't adopt the new product. Many radical market entries fail to "cross the chasm" from the small percent of the market that's intrigued by the latest gadget to the market majority who have to buy the gadget before it becomes a money maker.

What the company is risking is opportunity — the opportunity to devote time and resources to other, surer bets. The risk entailed in developing breakthrough products includes the following:

- ✔ **They usually take a long time to develop.** Typically, radical or break-through products start as a vision of what the company could do in a particular technology or market area. Unlike improvements to products that already exist, the company must place its bets on a possibility that requires research — maybe not basic scientific research, but research into the technology feasibility and the potential market acceptance of its new idea.

- ✔ **At some point, developing a breakthrough product usually requires a lot of resources.** The company must invest significant amounts in R&D, in infrastructure (such as manufacturing), and in market research and development.

When Japanese car companies decided to develop and market the hybrid auto, they had to invest significant manpower over significant periods of time, and they were taking a market risk that none of the major U.S. companies were willing to take. In retrospect, as other automakers scramble to keep up, it's clear that the Japanese automakers' decision was a smart one. But when they took the step, they were taking a chance that very few of their peers were willing to take.

To be successful at developing breakthrough products, a company needs strong management support for the necessary risk taking and innovation. It also helps to have a robust "bottom-up" culture where people regularly work on projects that fall outside the normal routine.

A product champion — a person in the organization who works with the NPD team and is committed to the project — can make the difference between "flash-in-the-pan" status and success for breakthrough projects (see Chapter 1 for more on product champions).

## *Platform products*

Many companies develop *platform products* in order to make major changes in existing product lines and to come up with new product lines. A *platform* is a product that forms the base for a whole set of products. For example, a blender manufacturer will design the basics of a new blender line — the motor, the container, the base, the cover, and so on — and use that as the fundamental architecture or framework for a whole line of blenders. It's an easy job to add or subtract dials, to add a fancy cover, and to use other tweaks to differentiate the top of the line from the bottom. This can be a very cost-effective way to develop a whole range of new products. (For more on platforms, take a look at Chapters 3 and 11.)

It's too expensive to incur infrastructure costs or to make radical changes/innovations every time a team comes up with a good idea. Therefore, many companies wait until they have a handful of prospective changes and bundle them together to design a new platform.

Companies in the automobile industry use a product development strategy based on a clear, timed sequence of product platforms. Every five years or so, automakers come out with new vehicle models. The models have differences, such as the engines, the styles, the interiors, the brakes, and so on. The new autos that you see in between these platforms are based on relatively simple changes that don't require new manufacturing capacities or changes to the vehicle platform.

When new safety regulations hit the power-tool industry, many companies responded by making their power tools larger and more unwieldy. At Black & Decker, product developers — led by platform guru Al Lehnerd — pondered over what to do and came up with a brilliant solution: Instead of simply adding more stuff to the company's existing products in order to comply with the regulations, why not redesign the whole platform?

The team developed a modularized motor that could be stacked to provide different amounts of power for different tools. Using this and other "platform" approaches, Black & Decker met the new regulations with tools that performed even better than its previous models, and it nearly put the competition out of business.

The two previous examples — from the power-tool industry and the auto industry — suggest two different ways of thinking about product platforms. When you change one of your product lines, be sure you review the whole product at the same time and create efficiencies of design, architecture, and infrastructure. Even more important, try to bring platform thinking to the way you develop new products. Instead of viewing every new product as an opportunity for your product developers to be "creative," try to regularize and standardize how you develop products. Seek common architectures, increase the modularity of your designs, and reward your engineers for how much existing design they reuse. Be sure, however, that the specifications you design for meet a wide range of clearly identified customer needs (see Chapter 4).

Platform thinking requires management oversight, support, and encouragement. Platform projects require more resources in the beginning for payoffs later in the process. To succeed at platform design, NPD teams need to have a very good understanding of customer requirements (see Chapter 4) and of the state and future of technology (see Chapter 7). Bottom line: You shouldn't leap into platform development without planning and support.

Developing a platform takes a larger investment than developing a single product — both in time and in people and other resources. The business case for a platform project isn't the same as the case for a single one. The NPD team that creates the business case should show financials over a spread of projects that the platform will spawn. (See Chapter 12 for more on writing business cases.)

## Derivative and support products

*Derivative and support products* include line extensions (for example, adding a new faucet to an existing faucet line), incremental improvements (adding a spray feature to a faucet that's already in the market), cost reductions, and other changes to products that a company already has in the market. Derivative product changes are very important. They enable your company to refresh existing product lines and to maintain its investment in those lines.

### Customer needs cross platforms

Becton-Dickinson (BD) builds its blood analyzers to serve two markets: the research market and the clinical market. BD used to design different machines to sell to its two different sets of customers. The company realized that platform thinking could help them become more efficient in designing its blood analyzers. They brought co-author Beebe in to work with a team that visited customers in both markets and developed sets of requirements for them (see Chapter 4 for more on customer visits). When the team compared the two sets of requirements, it discovered that the company could design one basic analyzer and differentiate it for the two markets, which was much more efficient than its old approach of developing two totally different machines.

The food industry is famous for its line extensions and product improvements — you can't walk through the supermarket aisles without "new and improved" flashing from boxes of crackers or cans of soup. And no software company ever hesitated to advertise the newest version of a game or word processing program.

Planning for derivative and support products is part of the planning you do when you design and launch a product platform (see the previous section). For example, you may launch a platform into the market as a mid-priced product aimed at familiar customers. The platform project includes plans to create next-on, or derivative, products aimed at other markets and/or other price points.

Good product line management requires that you stay abreast of changing customer needs and technologies (see Chapters 4 and 7) so that your derivative products will attract new customers, retain the old ones, and take advantage of technology advances. Well-managed product lines can bring in handsome returns, over time, on your company's investments.

## Balancing your product portfolio

You want to distinguish between the types of new products so that you can assess how well your company's new product portfolio is balanced. Do your projects address both the long range and the short term? Are you taking the kinds of risks that "breakthrough" implies? Do you pay enough attention to your existing product lines and refresh them appropriately?

You have many other questions to answer about the balance of your product portfolio. For instance, are you focusing on a strategic range of markets? Are you distributing your resources across product lines? We talk about these product portfolio questions in Chapter 11.

# Making the Most of Products, Services, Solutions, and Experiences

Some companies develop and market products, and some companies develop and market services. In today's business world, though, more and more companies look first at the needs and wants of their customers and then they develop solutions and experiences that combine products and services to meet all those needs and wants. You shouldn't limit your thinking about products to just products, or your thinking about services to just services. Expanding your horizons can expand your customer base, your profits, and the lifecycles of your products.

## Connecting inside-out and outside-in

From the viewpoint of a company, the product or service that it develops and sells to the customer is what truly matters. This describes the *inside-out* view. From the customers' point of view, the experiences they have with the product or service and how well it solves their problems are the most important factors. This describes the *outside-in* view.

We're sure that the broadband Internet features that allow us to watch thousands of movies, live sporting events, late-breaking news, and even live cop chases (if that's your thing) required amazing technology to develop. We certainly admire the very intelligent people who made it possible. But co-author Beebe Nelson wants to get this off her chest: It routinely takes her and her husband 15 minutes or more to figure out how to get the broadband to work. She won't settle for the conclusion that she and her husband are just dumb, and even if they are, they represent a big percent of the market. They'd gladly switch to whoever can solve their problem!

Customers don't really care how smart product developers are, how elegant their technologies are, or how well they stick to their cost and schedule targets. Customers care about the products they buy solving their problems, improving their processes, or making their lives a bit brighter and happier.

The following list presents some examples of "products" featuring extras that customers pay for; some of the examples are more like "services that come with extras":

- ✔ **The product includes the experience.** When you buy your coffee at a high-end coffee shop, you pay much more per cup of coffee than you would if you bought the beans and made the coffee yourself at home. You're paying for what product developers call the *experience*. Maybe you like calling the person behind the counter a "barista" and listening to the soft jazz that permeates the establishment. The same experience logic is at work when you pay big money for a birthday cake that comes with a party or for food at a fancy restaurant.

- ✔ **The solution includes specialized knowledge.** Product developers know a lot about their industries, their technologies, and their products. When product developers visit their customers (see Chapter 4), they often find that their knowledge, as much as their products, can fill customers' needs. For example, a company that provides a chemical ingredient to small businesses discovered that its customers needed consulting services to help them optimize their manufacturing processes and their use of the chemical. Combining the commodity ingredient with the knowledge of how to use it meant the company could attract more customers and charge a higher price.

✔ **The product developer takes over some of your work.** Johnson Controls, for example, doesn't sell air-handling equipment. They come to your building, ask you lots of questions, look around, and figure out the best system for you. The company then delivers the system, manages it for you, and keeps your air at the temperature and humidity that you want. Because Johnson Controls does its job well, the process doesn't cost as much as it would if you did it yourself, so part of what the company makes money on is those savings.

✔ **Other great things support the product or service.** Automakers and dealerships are waking up to the fact that part of what can make cars attractive includes providing excellent service. Toyota, for example, makes sure that its customers are aware that after they fall in love with a new Lexus, they have the chance to fall in love with the company's luxurious service offerings. Airlines used to add give-away products (dinners and such) to complement their services. Today, airlines try to substitute funny flight attendants and the latest in peanuts or pretzels. The airline industry is an example of a cash-strapped industry that, for now, is competing pretty much only on price.

✔ **You get the service plus more.** Enterprise offers nice rental vehicles at okay prices. But the company wins a customer's heart by picking her up at home so she doesn't have to pay for a cab or get a ride from a friend, and adds little benefits like remembering to give her a bottle of water before she drives away.

✔ **The brand/cause influences the purchase.** Sometimes, a customer just wants to be able to identify himself as the cool person on the block. Young women buy Coach handbags and middle-aged guys buy Harley motorcycles, for example. Today, brands often try to associate with causes in an effort to attract new customers. For example, many companies are "going green" by becoming more environmentally sensitive in their manufacturing and packaging processes. Other companies contribute portions of their profits to AIDS research or hunger relief.

This list gives you a sampling of how products and services endear themselves to customers by being wrapped up with extra features. It certainly isn't an exhaustive list; product developers add to the list every day. Always be on the lookout for what could make your camera (photography lessons?), your adhesive tape (graffiti?), or your dry-cleaning service (a home delivery service or environmentally friendly fluids?) more attractive to customers.

# Chapter 3

# Defining Your Product Strategy

· · · · · · · · · · · · · · · · · · · · · · · · · · · · · · · · · · · · · · · · · · · · · · · · · · · · · · · · · · · · · ·

· · · · · · · · · · · · · · · · · · · · · · · · · · · · · · · · · · · · · · · · · · · · · · · · · · · · · · · · · · · · · ·

*A* company's product strategy guides its decisions and actions with respect to developing new products, entering new markets, improving or retiring existing products or product lines, taking risks, and so on. A product strategy also defines how a company's products will make money — in other words, its business model or profit model. All companies have product strategies, but some have never taken the time and trouble to make their strategies explicit.

Your company's product strategy must consider your markets and your brand. Your organization will have great contacts and good customer relations in some markets; in some, you may not be so well thought of; and in other markets, no one has even heard of you. Your company is part of an industry in which you play a role: a supplier to some and a manufacturer to others. Your brand shapes your approach to products as well, opening some doors and closing others.

As you can see, you have many things to consider when defining your product strategy. In this chapter, we lead you through the thorny underbrush of your company's existing landscape. We show you when you should "go with the flow" with how you relate to customers, products, markets, and your brand. We also show you how to map your opportunities and the risks and benefits of pursuing the conservative and the adventurous options.

# Understanding the Market

The best new product idea in the world won't succeed without a market in which to find customers. Duh! So, why do we mention this? You want the market for your product to be accessible, full of potential customers, and devoid of competition. Okay, even we can't tell you how to get that situation. But in the sections that follow, we tell you what to look for in real-world markets so you can improve your chances of selling your new products.

## Assessing markets

The most successful companies focus their new product strategies on portfolios of markets where their products — existing and new — have the best chance to succeed. Your marketing executives often have the responsibility of assessing markets, but your cross-functional NPD team should carry out the process we describe here to make sure that you include relevant information from plenty of differing viewpoints.

Your organization should answer the following three questions to help you decide which markets to enter, which to stay in, and which to leave:

✔ **How attractive is the market?** Look at the size of the market, your company's existing share of the market, and your ability to get to customers in that market:

- **How many customers do you have in that market, and how many could you have?** These numbers show the potential of the market. If your company already has a large market share, you can't count on that market for a lot of growth. It may provide you with good revenues, but it may not be a good candidate for new products. The exception is a market where your company could lose customers because your tried-and-true products won't continue to please customers in the future.

- **Can you get to customers in the market?** Maybe you have channels of distribution that work really well to get products to customers in this market. On the other hand, maybe you don't know how to get your product to the customer. If you don't already have good distribution in a market, don't despair; a good channel partner may solve your problems.

  *Channel partners* can get your products to customers who will buy them. For example, a medical device company might pair up with a company that sells a variety of medical equipment, and companies that manufacture pens might choose distributors of stationery supplies. For many products, a big-box store such as Home Depot or

Wal-Mart can make or break the deal. And don't forget the Internet! Many products reach customers through a variety of Web sites.

- **Can the customers in the market afford your product(s)?** You have to be sure that customers in your targeted markets want your product, that you can get it to them, and that they can pay for it. U.S. pharmaceutical companies, for example, continue to struggle with the dilemma of how to get drugs to the customers and markets that really need them but can't afford to pay for them. In these markets, distribution is usually a problem as well.

✔ **Where is the market headed?** If the market doesn't have room to grow, it may not be an attractive option for your new products. Look for a growing market where the kinds of products you want to introduce may be just taking off. What are the "aging boomers" going to want in a couple of years, for example? What opportunities will awareness of healthy foods open up? In a growing market, your product sales have a chance to meet your expectations and goals.

When you identify growth rates and trends, you're predicting the future, which means you can't be certain of your conclusions. Examine the market, gather data, review it, and check your assumptions to see whether they're accurate. Just because you can't be certain of your conclusions doesn't mean you can't make educated guesses.

✔ **Who are your competitors in the market, and what threats do they pose to you and your product(s)?** You need to understand who your competitors are, how many of them exist in the market, and exactly how they'll compete with you and your product. You should assess their offerings, determine the pricing structure for these offerings, and identify which customers the competitors appeal to. Also, take a look at the technical capabilities (see Chapter 7) and the launch strategies (see Chapter 13) of your competitors. You may be able to compete with them on those parameters and win away some of the market.

Don't forget that some competitors can help you — think of how fast-food joints often turn up on the same corners, or how automobile dealers tend to herd to one strip of road in what we've started to call "AutoMiles."

## *Comparing markets with a market portfolio*

Your company's decision makers can use the market information you gather when researching existing and potential markets (see the previous section) to build a picture of how potential markets compare. This picture is called a *market portfolio.* A market portfolio also enables your company to update market information so that you can build a corporate knowledge base that improves your company's decision-making process over time.

The market portfolio in Figure 3-1 shows how potential markets stack up against the criteria of market attractiveness and competitive threat. This portfolio view also includes several other variables that are important to strategic decision-making.

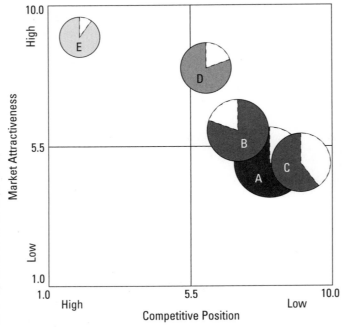

**Figure 3-1:** A market portfolio view allows decision makers to compare different markets at a glance.

In Figure 3-1, each circle represents a potential market. The white portion of each circle shows the company's share of that market. The shading shows the overall growth rate of the market, from fast (light) to shrinking (dark).

The following list explains some of the things you can figure out by looking at the portfolio in Figure 3-1:

- ✔ **Markets A and B are the largest.** In A, the company has a large share of the market, which is shrinking. Not a good bet for new product introductions!

- ✔ **Markets B and C are holding steady.** A company could still gain sizeable market share, so it should take a look to see whether a new introduction could take share from competitors.

Be aware that taking share in an established market often is harder than gaining share in a growing market.

> ✔ **Market D is experiencing moderate growth, and the company's share is relatively small (less than 25 percent).** In this market, the competition will greatly affect the company's probability of success. Are the other companies large and aggressive, with good channel and technology assets? If so, Market D may be a tough market for new products. However, if the competition is more fragmented, Market D may be a good bet for new product introductions.

> ✔ **Market E seems almost too good to be true.** The market appears to be highly attractive, and the company's competitive position is strong. The company has only a small share of this rapidly growing market. Research your assumptions; if they check out, you may want to put several of your chips on this space.Identifying

# Opportunities in Existing Product Lines

The new products that a company develops and commercializes arrive in the market alongside existing products and product lines. Many "new" products are tweaks to products that already exist in a market — incremental improvements or even cost reductions, for example. Some companies introduce major changes and improvements to products that consumers are familiar with — for example, automobile companies make major changes to their car lines every four to five years. The cars still have the same names, such as Camry or Wrangler, but the companies have updated them, restyled them, made them more efficient, and so on.

Some new products launch whole new product lines — sometimes called *product platforms* or *product families.* New product lines can take a company into a new business, or they may offer additional products within an existing business. For example, a pharmaceutical company could reformulate the drugs it developed for humans and offer them in the veterinary market. Or, a company may find that the process it developed to form glass for test tubes and other lab equipment also works for producing specialty glass products.

Sometimes, a company develops a radical, or *breakthrough,* technology or product. A company may find itself entering a market so new that it has to figure out new ways to bring its product to market. Even at this stage, though, a company has to take into account its existing products and existing brand. The fit may be as neat as an iPod into an Apple. Sometimes, a breakthrough cannibalizes an existing product and shifts a company's brand image — like when Harley-Davidson decided to introduce the much racier Buell motorcycle.

In this section, you find out how to chart your products and the lifecycles of your existing product lines so that you can go after opportunities strategically. (Check out Chapter 11 for more about how companies diversify their new products across portfolios of incremental, new, and breakthrough projects, and head to the final section of this chapter for more on introducing new products to your brand.)

## *Mapping product lines*

A *product line map* shows your products and product lines against a timeline so you can see what your company has in the market, what you're developing, and what you're planning. But, hey, your company is in the thick of it. You don't have enough time or resources to do everything you want to do. Everyone is busy. You're developing products that meet your customers' needs. Wall Street and your investors seem pretty happy. What will making a map of your product lines do for you?

Companies that work from inside the "thick of it" run into trouble in several ways:

- ✔ **They tend to focus their efforts on "me too," incremental products.** Companies without explicit product strategies tend to choose the safe and familiar over the risky and unfamiliar. They stop being innovative and find their competitive edge slipping away.

- ✔ **They focus almost exclusively on the needs of their most important customers.** "What's wrong with that?" you ask. This is why it's a problem. When companies focus too much on the needs of only a few of their larger customers, they forget that one of their most important responsibilities isn't to say "how high" when customers say "jump." Companies need to innovate: to understand future trends, to develop resources to meet those trends, and to coordinate their capabilities so that products they develop for one customer help satisfy the needs of another. Innovation is what keeps companies competitive.

- ✔ **Their product development efforts have no rationale or strategy.** The work they do isn't leveraged. They don't plan for the future. And they operate in an opportunistic or responsive mode. Every new opportunity seems to require a "back to the drawing board" development effort. If the companies get lucky, things work out; if not, their development efforts fail. For sure, they don't sit in the driver's seat.

To find your way through the "thick of it," you literally need a map. The following sections show you how to make the map you need.

### Making a template to map your product lines

The first step in mapping your product lines is setting up a mapping template. Figure 3-2 shows a straightforward template for your mapping tasks. You can tailor this template to fit the needs of your company and your product lines. We recommend that you add dates to the map to show, for example, when your company plans to introduce or retire different products.

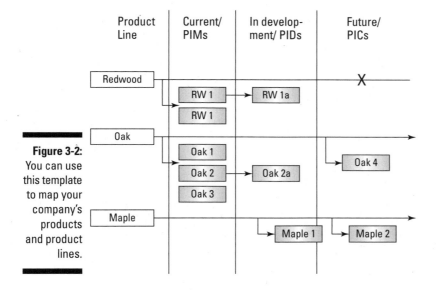

**Figure 3-2:** You can use this template to map your company's products and product lines.

You can use the following labels for easy identification:

- **PIMs:** For "products in the market"
- **PIDs:** For "products in development"
- **PICs:** For "product innovation charters"

PICs are projects that are in the ocean of opportunity; PIDs are in the river of development; and PIMs are in the market, earning money. Take a look at the Cheat Sheet in the front of the book for more on these stages.

"Redwood," "Oak," and "Maple" are the names of the three major product lines for the fictitious business shown in Figure 3-2. Redwood has two products in the market; Oak has three. Each of the product lines has one PID. Maple's PID will launch that product line. The company also has two product innovation charters.

When you come up with an acceptable template, keep using the same format over and over. This way, you can compare the information you map between different product lines and periods of time. Also, when you use the same template, people involved in product development efforts can concentrate on the information instead of being confused by the format.

### Starting the mapping process

The process of mapping your company's product lines is a business level strategic process. The people who do the mapping are the planners and decision-makers at the corporate or business unit level. Like all strategic initiatives, you won't map your product lines in a sitting. In the list that follows, we sketch the basic do's and don'ts for getting the process right:

1. **Assign someone to be the process owner.** The mapping process needs a shepherd — preferably someone with a strategic mindset and good facilitation skills. The process owner should report directly to the business unit executives.

2. **Decide on the scope of your product line map.** Corporations, like chickens, have joints. Sometimes, the right way to "divide" the chicken is to serve it whole. You can include all the company's or business unit's product lines in a single map if your company is fairly small or if your product lines are similar (based on the same technology and/or focused on the same markets).

   If your company is divided into business units, you may want to carry out a mapping process for each business unit. If your company is large and diverse — think 3M, GE, or J&J — you may implement several mapping processes within a single business unit.

3. **Gather the business's key planners and decision makers to discuss the process.** Mapping product lines is an iterative process. Often, the best ways to map product lines emerge after several discussions.

4. **Set up a series of meetings to kick off the process.** For instance, you can set up four 2-hour meetings — one each week for a month.

5. **Hold the first meeting.** At this meeting, you identify the company's or the business unit's product lines. What are the product lines? How many are there? How will you divide the products in a useful and rational manner?

Make sure that what's said at the meeting is documented — preferably on large wall charts so that everyone can follow the conversations. We find that it works to use sticky notes to post ideas; this way, everyone can nominate candidates, and you can easily move and change the nominations.

Don't expect to come up with easy answers to the question "What are our product lines?" The reason you hold several meetings to kick off the mapping process is because you can't finish right away. The first meeting gets everyone's ideas out on the table (or up on the wall). Instead of continuing to slog it out, you call a break so people can come back several days later with a fresh outlook.

6. **Do work between meetings.** At the end of the first meeting, the group should agree on assignments for group members to finish between meetings. Two pieces of work, in particular, need to be completed:

   • **Document the discussion at the first meeting.** It's best to distribute the documentation soon after the meeting, so the person handling this task should save some time that afternoon or the next morning for documentation.

   • **Answer questions that come up during the meeting.** These questions may include: When did that product line first enter the market? What are the financials/P&L for that product line? Which markets do these products currently serve? The process owner should assign people to bring these answers to the next meeting.

7. **Hold the next meetings.** As people in the group think more about the product lines and gather more information, they'll start to make decisions about how they want to map the products and product lines.

8. **The facilitator or process owner should pick a format for drawing the map.** The example we provide in Figure 3-2 is a good beginning. Be sure to include a timeline, and keep in mind that timelines vary from industry to industry. Take a look at the technology maps in Chapter 7 for examples of some maps that include specific timelines.

We recommend that the facilitator draw the first draft of the map on a large wall chart so that everyone can contribute. After the meeting the facilitator can create an electronic version. PowerPoint works, but a more updatable medium like Microsoft Excel or Visio works better.

Many companies now make software that can produce, update, and share product line maps. You may want to look into what's available. Just be sure that the software helps you do what you want to do; some software packages can lead you down an endless path of process redesign.

9. **At the last meeting, if not before, set up the process by which you'll use the map to guide your strategic decision making.** Maps don't do you any good unless you use them! You need to think of the following things:

   • Who should you include in the reviews?

   • How often will you update the information, and who will you allow to add or change information?

   • How will you share the information, and who will have access to it?

   • How will you communicate decisions?

   • How will this process relate to the product development process, the technology development process, and so on?

# Defining product lines

What defines your product lines? Is it the razor or the razor blade? The camera or the film? The software or the service? The motorcycle or the owners' groups? You need to spend some time puzzling over this question because the answer isn't always crystal clear. You want to consider such things as the following:

✔ What generates your profits?

✔ How do your customers identify you?

✔ What's your base technology, and how does it relate to your products?

In one photography company, for example, film drove profits, technology, and even customer perceptions. Its cameras were important, no doubt, but their importance was to support media sales and media use. The company mapped its film product lines and integrated everything else around that.

## *Making strategic decisions based on your maps*

Now comes the point where your decision makers get to use the information from your product line map to identify the good, the bad, and the ugly in your existing and planned product lines.

Consider the example from Figure 3-2 once again in order to see this process in action. The organization's map shows the following characteristics:

> It currently has two product lines and a total of five products in the market.
>
> It has two upgrades (Rw1a and Oak2a) in the development pipeline.
>
> Redwood's timeline ends with an "X," indicating that the company will phase it out in the near future.
>
> The company is planning a new product line, Maple; the first product is in development, and the second is in the planning stage.

So, what do you think? With this scant amount of information, how would you judge the company's product line, and what changes would you make?

Here's our take on it. For the company's small number of existing products (from which we assume we're looking at a small company or business unit), it seems to have good balance. We believe the company has made good decisions about how to use its resources to generate a steady stream of new products that complement its existing product lines. Why do we believe this?

✔ The organization devotes some resources to upgrading existing products.

✔ It plans to add an entirely new product to one of the lines (Oak).

✔ It made the decision to phase out one product family and replace it with a new line.

✔ It plans to grow by adding a whole new product line.

If the product map you create looks this good, congratulations! If not, you now have the tools to conduct the discussions, gather the information, make the decisions, and take the actions to rationalize your product line map.

The fictitious company in the product line map based some of its decisions on the lifecycles of its products and product lines. Take a look at the next section to find out how understanding the product lifecycle helps you make product decisions. And take a look at Chapter 7 to see how to connect product line maps with technology maps andfor more on understanding the role of maps in product planning.

## *Understanding the product lifecycle*

Most products have fairly predictable lifecycles:

1. They enter the market and their sales grow (hopefully!).

2. If all goes well, they plateau into a period of healthy maturity. If not, they may fall off early and generate disappointing returns. On the other hand, some products seem to go on forever.

3. Toward the end of their maturity, the products either die off or continue in a kind of limbo existence.

Innovative companies track and manage their products' lifecycles. They find ways to improve their products and extend their lives, and they retire products with dignity when they've served their purposes. However, too many companies aren't very savvy when it comes to understanding product lifecycles. (We're very much indebted to Steven Haines and Sequent Learning Networks for gathering information on how some successful companies manage their product lifecycles. Without Steven's work, we'd still be in the dark!)

When you draft the business case for a new product (see Chapter 12), you should plan on the product taking some time to achieve maturity (how long it takes depends largely on the industry). You often can figure on robust profits and margins for several years. Again, how many depends on the industry; typically, the lifecycle is longer for drugs and trucks and shorter for software and services, for example. Too many companies make the bad assumption that after they launch their products, they can go on enjoying profits forever.

See Figure 3-3 for a picture of a "normal" lifecycle curve. We say "normal" because the different products you develop and market may have variations on normal, so you need to check their progress by looking at key indicators, which include the following:

- ✔ Sales
- ✔ Customer acceptance
- ✔ Market penetration
- ✔ Key financial metrics

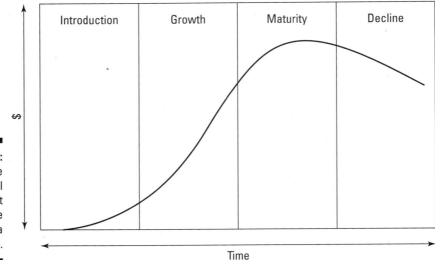

**Figure 3-3:** You can use this typical product lifecycle curve as a baseline.

Always be aware that you can influence the shape of the lifecycle curve by the market tactics you employ and by the timing of new product introductions.

In the following sections, we introduce the stages of the product lifecycle. We also include some information on the lifecycles of product platforms, which are somewhat different from the lifecycles of products. Understanding the difference will help you manage your existing platforms. (For more on managing product lifecycles, we recommend that you read "Overview and Context for Life-Cycle Management," by Bill Ausura, Bob Gill, and Steven Haines. You can find it in *The PDMA Handbook for New Product Development*, 2nd Edition, by Kenneth Kahn [Wiley].)

Many companies appoint product managers to be the mini-business owners for products and product lines in the market. Their job is to work with the product development teams — they often lead these teams — to make sure that the products are successful in the market.

## Introduction

In the introduction phase of a product's lifecycle, you can expect relatively small sales and low initial revenue. The most important tasks in the first part of the lifecycle are to promote the product and build awareness in the marketplace.

Many newly introduced products have to "cross the chasm" during the first stage of the lifecycle. When a product hits the market, it often starts by appealing to a small group of customers who don't represent the larger target market. You want to promote and distribute your product so you'll get to not only the early enthusiasts, but also the much larger market you must reach to make your product successful.

## Growth

The second phase of the product lifecycle — the growth phase — is vital to the product's success. In Figure 3-3, you can see that profits are directly linked to how fast and how high the curve rises during this early phase.

The most important tasks in the growth stage include the following:

- Promote the product.
- Make sure the product is available by managing the channels and the supply chain.
- Keep close to the market and your customers.

What do your customers adore about the product? What doesn't please them? And what can you do to improve the product? You can use the answers to all these questions to support your product in its growth phase.

When your product is in its growth phase, you need to start thinking ahead to new products and product improvements:

- You begin to plan improvements and cost reductions.
- You try to identify opportunities for enhanced margins through product add-ons or services.
- Your understanding of customers provides insight about what new product you may want to develop next.

For example, you may find that your product sells well to your more sophisticated customers. However, a defeatured, easier-to-use, and perhaps less-expensive product may work well for another niche. You can use your work in managing the growth phase to build your product lines and pursue an effective and comprehensive product strategy. See previous sections in this chapter for more on product lines.

### Maturity

As your product moves into the maturity stage of the lifecycle, you should expect to see competitors moving in to take some of your market share. This competition is likely to drive down margins. In addition, the technology or innovation on which your product is based may be beginning to mature.

At this point in the lifecycle, your job is to optimize your product "mix" by exploring one of the following options:

- **Prune your offerings to provide better focus.** If your dealers are having trouble selling five different furnace options, for example, you may want to cut back to the most popular two.

- **Add "new and improved" products to attract new customers.** This trick works especially well with many consumer products. Cracker companies, for example, keep us coming back for the next new flavor, size, texture, package size, shape, and so on.

- **Fill in your product line to extend the offerings.** If your standard product has done well, maybe you'll want to add features. For example, make a cell phone that can take pictures or a blender that can whip up exotic drinks.

The maturity phase is a good time to rethink your pricing, explore new markets, and perhaps investigate options like private labeling — allowing a distributor like Wal-Mart or Target to put its brand on your product and sell it as if it were its own — to extend the viability of your product.

### Decline and retirement

In the decline phase, product revenues slow down. Customers wander off to greener pastures and newer products. You need to be willing to recognize the signs and make plans that are appropriate to the decline. Don't make the mistake of blindly supporting a product that has pretty much outlived its useful life. Be sure to take good care of your remaining customers; keep your focus on any revenues or gains you can make by selling the product you have; and only produce what you need to keep going during this phase.

Before you make the decision that your mature product is on a decline, take another look. Some products and product lines can maintain excellent sales, consumer loyalty, and good to great margins for a very long time. Coke Classic is an example of this. Coca-Cola's near-fatal error to try to improve Coke Classic is a good warning to leave good enough alone — as long as that good enough is building brand loyalty and bringing in the profits.

Some of the things you should do when a product or product line hits decline include the following:

✔ Cut back on inventory.

✔ Cut back on advertising, or even stop advertising altogether.

✔ Consider selling intellectual property if you won't reuse it in another product (see Chapter 15 for more on IP).

When one product or product line is in decline, it may be the perfect time to introduce a whole new product line. If you go this route, see whether you can lure existing customers to your new products, perhaps by offering them an incentive such as a percent price reduction.

During the decline phase of the lifecycle, you also need to make plans for product retirement. Your decision makers should specify the conditions under which your product will exit the market. For instance, you may cut ties when existing inventory runs out or when a new product is introduced.

## A platform on platforms . . .

Different companies have different definitions for the term "platform." Some use it to describe a technology that can produce many different products or parts of products. For example, think of the braking system that GM puts into all its cars. Others use it to describe a basic product that can be varied so that one product development effort can produce many products. Most customers don't notice or care that the products they buy are built from the same base.

An example is the ink jet printer. You can buy one with plenty of bells and whistles, no bells and whistles, or just a few. The printer's developer saves a ton of time and money by not having to invent many different products. Some low-cost and low-function products even contain the added functionality of the high-priced products; consumers just can't access the additional features. If they want them, they need to pay the higher price.

---

## Whirlpool's global refrigerator platform

A series of product introductions leverages the investment you make when you develop a platform. Several years ago, Whirlpool introduced a refrigerator to markets in Asia, India, and Africa. The customer needs in these places were different from Whirlpool's usual markets and from each other. Whirlpool designed a refrigerator platform around the product core (the refrigeration unit, the insulation, and so on) and tailored products for the different markets by differentiating features like the size of the freezer compartments.

---

### Platforms

You know that products and product lines have lifecycles. What you may not know is that the engines that support those products and product lines — product and technology platforms — also go through lifecycles (see Chapter 2 for more information about what product platforms are and how product developers use them).

When companies develop platforms, they look across a spectrum of customer needs and technologies to see how they can best leverage their new product development investments. Platforms are like the soup stock you made from last year's Thanksgiving turkey. You don't put the turkey stock on the table; you use it as a base for sauces, soups, stews, and so on. In the same way, you don't sell a platform to a customer; you use it and reuse it to build many attractive and competitive products.

When a platform approaches the end of its lifecycle, you should consider developing a new platform. Here are two situations in which developing a new platform would be a good idea:

> ✔ **You have an idea for a new product or service that you don't currently offer.** The project will require technology, design, and development in order to make it to market. All this development will cost quite a bit — maybe so much that the business case for a single product doesn't make sense. However, if you can plan a sequence of products, the business case may look a whole lot better (see Figure 3-4).

When you write the business case for the product platform, remember that the first product may not look like a financial winner. You have to base your business case on the platform or product family, not on a single introduction (see Chapter 12 and the Appendix for more on writing a business case).

⌐ **You've been making minor changes to improve a product line, but recently the changes have been less minor.** Every few months, it seems like you have to fix something just to keep up with quality issues and competitor pressures. You also may see that new technology opportunities are hitting the market or that customer requirements are changing (see Chapter 4). You need to sell that car and get a new one! Wait a minute, that's not what we meant to say! You need to launch a whole new platform effort to bring your product lines up to snuff. There, that's better.

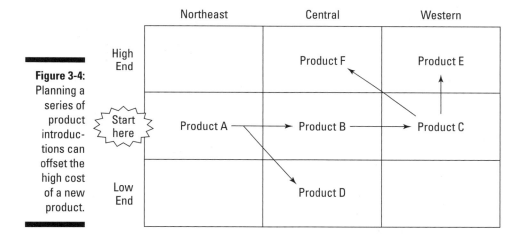

**Figure 3-4:**
Planning a series of product introductions can offset the high cost of a new product.

# Constructing Your Profit Model

Your product strategy has to include how your new products will make money. Your newest new products — the ones you may call "radical" or "breakthrough" — often have to make a profit in new, perhaps unusual ways. These products also often ask customers to behave differently, and they may require different channels of distribution. For example, with technologies like the Internet or digital film, companies within the music industry, the photography industry, the newspaper industry, and many others must figure out how to use their ability to create value for customers in ways that create profits for them.

But it isn't only radical products and technology changes that require new ways of making money. A shift in a profit model can make all the difference to many kinds of product introductions. For example, think of what a difference it made to the copier industry when companies decided to lease copiers to customers and charge for supplies.

Many organizations are overly committed to their existing business/profit models. Their ways have been successful in the past, and the business leaders can't imagine any other way of making money. When companies remain stuck on past models, they can overlook ways of making money; worse, they can get locked into ways that used to work but don't work anymore. In his book *Open Innovation* (Harvard Business School Press), Henry Chesbrough makes the point that serious innovations often demand innovative business models. How and where your products make a return on your company's investments are crucial parts of your new product strategy. In this section, you get the lowdown on some important profit model issues. What aspects of your product are customers willing to pay for? And which part of your industry can you earn profits from?

## Deciding what your customers will pay for

Of course, as a business, you have to cover your costs and make a profit when you develop new products (those shareholders are very demanding!). This sets the lowest threshold for what your customers have to pay. But you can charge your customers for the value they get from your products, and fortunately the value your customers receive often is considerably more than the costs you must cover. When you take advantage of that, you're using a technique called *value pricing*. (See Chapter 13 to read more about pricing new products.)

Many companies have a pricing strategy that informs the way they design, develop, and market their products. You can use the following list to determine how you'll charge your customers for the value you give them.

New product pricing strategy isn't the same as pricing tactics, which may vary over the lifecycle of a product and respond to situational variations: opportunities for discounting, seasonal demand, and so on.

- **Single-product pricing:** In single-product (or service) pricing, a company doesn't expect additional sales or revenues that may accrue from the sale of its product. With this pricing, you hope that your satisfied customers will buy from you again and spread the word about how much value you provide. However, your profit model doesn't count on these things happening. Most of the products consumers buy every day are single-product priced: clothing, food, books, and so on.

- **Product-plus pricing:** This pricing strategy includes the expectation that a customer's initial purchase will generate further spending. This spending can include warrantees, extended service contracts, and ongoing product/service repair (when you buy a car from a dealer that also provides service options, for example). The bigger the uptick from additional spending, and the more certain you are that these sales will come your way, the further you can lower the cost of your product to attract the initial purchase.

✔ **Product plus-plus pricing (also known as "razor/razor blade"):** You can "sell" some products more as carriers of media than as products in their own right. Polaroid, for example, sold cameras for close to cost in order to maintain the flow of film media, on which it made enormous margins. Gillette invented this pricing model with its cheap razors and expensive razor blades. The list goes on. Printers, fax machines, and copiers — have you noticed that companies practically give them away only to catch you later when you go back to buy ink? Do you think that American car manufacturers are in cahoots with the oil companies? Why, maybe they sell those SUVs just so Exxon can sell more gas!

✔ **Percent pricing:** Companies price some products — usually services and software — in relation to what they'll save the customers. For example, Johnson Controls manages air quality (heating, cooling, and so on) for business-to-business customers. The customers don't buy an actual product from the company. Johnson Controls manages the customers' air quality, saves them money, and makes a tidy profit based on their savings. (This pricing model is similar to renting and leasing.)

✔ **Renting and leasing:** Another way to realize profits from a new product is to lease or rent it to customers instead of selling it. When Xerox (way back when it was known as Haloid) changed its profit model from selling copiers to leasing them, its sales and profits took off. (You can read more about this in the book *Open Innovation* by Henry Chesbrough [Harvard Business School Press].)

## Making yourself at home in your industry value chain

Few companies in today's business market span the whole value chain from raw materials to finished product. Even a neighborhood roadside stand that sells organic vegetables during the summer probably gets material from a supplier: mulch, seeds, or perhaps organic fertilizer. Even if the farmer produces everything herself, she's almost certainly connected to electricity and other energy sources and buys tools from the local hardware store.

Most companies have far more complex value chains. Some buy much of what goes into the finished products that they sell to end-users. Others provide materials, parts, or services to other companies that produce products for end-user markets (see Chapters 15 and 16 for more on supplier/partner relationships).

Understanding your organization's place in the value chain is critical to making good strategic decisions. Sometimes, that understanding can help you capture more of the value in your value chain. Here's how to get a good view of the value chain and your place in it:

1. **Make a map of your value chain.** Draw a horizontal line, and put raw materials at the left end and the customer (the end-user) at the right end. Fill in the spaces. Who turns the raw materials into the pieces and parts used by the product developer? Who actually builds the product? Who distributes and sells it? (For a sample value chain map, take a look at the motorcycle market example in Chapter 4.)

2. **Locate your company in the value chain.** Most companies fill one of the spaces, but some companies play a role in several. For example, oil companies explore for oil, pump it, refine it, and then sell it through retail outlets.

3. **Estimate the total value of the value chain and how much of that value is gained in each of the spaces.** Typically, the raw materials have much less of the total value, and the final product has the most.

4. **Look to see if you can capture more of the value in the value chain.** The most likely places are in the steps adjacent to your current place. Although much of its R&D centered in raw materials and formulation, Hercules Chemical, for example, discovered plenty of opportunities in the next step of the value chain: manufacturing.

The companies in your value chain are your suppliers and your customers, so if you change your role, you have to worry about disrupting your existing relationships. For example, when 3M decided to capture value further down the value chain by installing the graphics it manufactures, the company had to take care of its former customers — the companies that used to do the installation!

# Fitting Your New Product Lines with Your Brand

Every new product you introduce has an impact on your organization's brand — what identifies, and what customers expect from, your company's products and services. If the product is consistent with your brand, it will give your customers a comfortable feeling — that is, if they like your brand. If it's inconsistent with your brand, it may give your customers the impression that your organization is daring and forward-thinking, and they may like you even more. Or, they may feel that you're drifting away from their comfort zone. In the sections that follow, you discover some of the ways in which brand influences product strategy.

## *Every brand has an image — what's yours?*

How do your customers relate to your brand? In other words, how do they view the products and product lines you've introduced in the past? Are you a youth-oriented, counter-culture brand, like Apple? Do you appeal to the successful professional, like BMW? Are you what co-author Beebe's kids used to call "earthy-crunchy," like Trader Joe's?

If you aren't sure how consumers tag your brand, do some market research to find out. Following the customer visit process we introduce in Chapter 4 will give you a chance to understand, at very basic levels, what you mean to your customers.

## *Do your product concepts build your brand?*

When you have a good sense of how your customers view your brand, you can assess your new product offerings to make sure they'll contribute to your customers' appreciation of and loyalty to your brand. If your brand just shouts "quality and value," for example, don't succumb to the temptation of introducing a low-quality product to make some fast profits. If your brand says "cheap — I can afford it," don't bother with a fancy product that belongs in a high-end store.

The fastest growing segment in the U.S. motorcycle market is women who buy and ride their own motorcycles. This segment posed a challenge for motorcycle giant Harley-Davidson. The company didn't want to ignore the market, but executives were having a hard time figuring out how to serve the new market with the company's tough-guy brand image. "Whaddya want us to do? Paint 'em pink?" one Harley executive asked co-author Beebe when she inquired about the segment.

In the end, Harley solved its problem and preserved its brand. In fact, the problem turned out to be not such a big deal as the company discovered more and more about the women who were buying and riding Harleys. They didn't want pink, and they didn't want girly. They wanted what Harley has to offer. As Beebe's product development class concluded after interviewing many women riders, the Harley woman rider's slogan is, "I am woman, hear me roar!"

Harley hit the nail on the head with a subsequent advertisement. In the ad, a guy is bragging to a girl about a motorcycle parked on the street. He acts macho and claims the bike is his, saying that he's really into Harleys. A few minutes into the conversation, just as the girl's eyes start to widen with admiration, another woman walks up, jumps on the bike, and rides away, leaving the macho man embarrassed.

## Can you connect your brand and your new product strategy?

Your brand opens some development doors and closes others. The following list presents some advice on how to leverage your brand and how to know when the time has come to modify it:

- ✓ **Find out what your brand means to your customers.** When you know what effect your brand has on customers, you can direct your product strategy to take advantage of that. During a customer visit process (see Chapter 4), invite your customers to share what your brand means to them. A brand means more than the sum of its parts. Brands include myths and stories. Brands respond to our values and to how we want to live. (For more fascinating stuff on how customers perceive brands, look at Gerald Zaltman's book *How Customers Think* [Harvard Business School Press].)

- ✓ **Assess the strength of your brand.** Does your brand help sell products? Or does your brand tend to turn customers off? If your brand is strong, be sure your product strategy takes advantage of its strength. If it isn't, plan to devote some of your resources to brand improvement (check out *Branding For Dummies,* by Bill Chiaravalle and Barbara Findlay Schenck [Wiley]).

- ✓ **Get clear about where your brand is leading you and what paths it's closing off.** Direct your product strategy to build on a strong brand, but don't let your brand close doors. When Toyota wanted to come out with a car that could compete with the Beamers, it didn't call the car a Toyota. The company created a brand-new brand called Lexus.

# Part II
# Charting the Ocean of Opportunity for New Products

The 5th Wave                    By Rich Tennant

"According to our survey, most end users would like more 'bee bee goo goo,' and less 'kah kah tee tee.'"

# In this part . . .

Companies can get stuck on their own views of the world and on their opinions about what's good and exciting. Putting customers first, and really understanding them, gives companies a "higher power" that can shake them loose of their stuck-in-the-mud ways. When "customer intimacy" fuels a company, the organization won't have any trouble coming up with plenty of ideas for new products. The problem becomes choosing the best ideas. For that, a company needs discipline and focus.

The chapters in Part II take you into your customers' wide world and introduce proven ways of using the knowledge of your customers to create great solutions for them. The chapters in this part also help your company focus its efforts, both in developing products and in developing or acquiring the necessary technology. Finally, we show you how to put everyone on the same page to work together for NPD success.

## Chapter 4

# What Do Your Customers Really Want?

*Y*ou don't have to be a dummy to fail at new product development. In fact, around 50 percent of new products fail in the marketplace. And the biggest reason for failure is that the products don't fill the needs of customers.

In this chapter, we walk you through the *customer visit process.* This process gets you right into your customers' worlds — past, present, and future. We begin with preparing for the visits, move on to how you'll gather customer information, and end with the all-important topic of how you can use the information to jump-start and sustain your product development efforts.

Through the customer visit process, new product development teams acquire a gut-level understanding of customers that enables them to come up with great and often unexpected solutions to customers' problems. It is this understanding that can put distance between you and your competitors.

## Dissecting the Customer Visit Process

The customer visit process is a qualitative market research program that companies have used to develop thousands of products and services in every industry imaginable — from blood analyzers to insurances policies; from software products to custom homes; from air conditioners to semi-conductor chips to chocolate-chip cookies. The following list presents the customer visit process in a nutshell:

1. **Focus the development team on an opportunity.**

   Select a good market or technology opportunity to research, assemble a customer visit team, and choose and schedule your customer visits.

2. **Prepare for the customer visits.**

   Before you set off to visit your customers, you need to take the time to write a visit guide and practice your interview skills.

3. **Execute the process.**

   Now it's time for the teams to get in cars or on planes to go visit the customers. You should travel in teams of two and bring back loads of information — notes, tape recordings, photos, videos, and memories!

4. **Distill the results.**

   What do you do with all your notes, tapes, and photos? We'll show you a disciplined way to map the essential elements of your customers' worlds and to figure out their requirements.

5. **Quantify the results.**

   Before you develop that great new product, check with a wider sample of customers to make sure what you've identified are the factors your customers consider the most important.

After your customer visit team completes these steps, you'll be ready to generate ideas for products that address the customer needs you've identified (see Chapter 5 for more on coming up with winning ideas).

# Building the Foundation for the Customer Visit Program

You're about to take a dip in the "ocean of opportunity" (see the Cheat Sheet in the front of this book). The ocean of opportunity is vast; it includes everything you might do to please your customers, all the technologies you could use, and all the information you could gather about markets and competitors. One of the most important things you can learn as you swim about in the ocean is what your customers really want.

In this first step of the customer visit process, we walk you through how to choose an opportunity, how to assemble a visit team, and how to select a small group of customers to visit.

# Identifying an opportunity

A customer visit program allows your company to explore NPD opportunities and come up with plenty of ideas for new and different products or services. Before launching a customer visit project, however, you need to identify a valid and important opportunity on which to focus. The following list presents some different opportunities to look for, along with examples that show how several different companies chose a focus for their projects:

- **Technology opportunity:** Successful customer visit programs are often based on technology opportunities. Changes in technology can be large (the digital revolution and nanotechnology, for instance) or small. Can your new product pump gas faster? Can you reduce the amount of packaging needed for your cookies? Can you increase the amount of memory on a hard drive? Can your fertilizer work for every plant in your customers' gardens?

  If you can do something new and different, you need to go out to customers to see just how this ability may affect their lives. If cookies need less packaging, how might that affect the cookie manufacturer? The distributor? The customer who wants to put cookies in his kids' lunchboxes?

  Be on the lookout for changes in your industry or your company that may lead to changes in your customers' behavior, needs, expectations, and so forth. These kinds of changes can provide good focus for customer visits. For example, say a small manufacturer of respiratory devices is planning to acquire a new oxygen-delivery system. The company commissions a team to interview doctors and therapists and to visit hospitals. Along the way, the team discovers that the company's new system could make a radical change in patient care.

- **Market opportunity:** Changes in the market also can provide direction for a customer visit project. Try to identify new behaviors from customers in your existing markets. Be on the lookout for trends that influence customers' preference — for example, the impact of a diet fad on what kinds of foods customers want, or the impact of heightened environmental awareness on customers' buying choices.

  Also take a look at potential new markets. Your company may be quite comfortable selling its products to existing customers, but you may have great market potential in areas you haven't yet focused on. For example, around the time of this writing, the motorcycle industry woke up to the fact that more and more women were entering the market as buyers and riders. That type of demographic change is fertile ground for a customer visit program.

- **Regulation change opportunity:** Regulations — which can be local, state, or federal government regulations; legal statutes; or industry codes and agreements — have a huge impact on customer needs and provide interesting opportunities for new products or services. Be on the lookout for regulatory changes that affect your industry, and figure out a way to turn them to your organization's advantage.

Many companies simply try to comply with regulations. However, the smart ones take the time to discover how the regulations impact their customers. For example, an educational publishing company might commission an NPD team to research how new federal regulations on educational testing impact teachers' needs and preferences in textbooks. The team might visit teachers, administrators, and students around the country in order to help the company redesign its textbooks so that teachers can do a better job of complying with the regulations.

## Assembling your customer visit team

In order to get a project off the ground, you need to have a customer visit team. The team should consist of 8 to 12 members from different business functions. (We talk more about why you need functional diversity on your teams in Chapter 10.) The team needs a sponsor and a team leader. If your company has carried out customer visits before, it's a good idea for the team leader, and also several of the team members, to have experience working on customer visit projects.

The team's responsibility is to gather customer information and to shape it so that the members or others can use it to generate new product ideas (see Chapter 5), to develop new products, and to make improvements to existing ones. (See Chapter 9 for more on how understanding customers helps focus the product development process.)

### First things first: Getting a sponsor and charter

Customer visit programs take time and money, and customer visit teams require resources, which fall under the control of many different people: the head of R&D, the head of marketing, the head of manufacturing, and so on. Every customer visit project should have a sponsor who can negotiate with the different department heads to acquire the needed resources. The sponsor might be a director, an executive, or the head of a business unit or functional department.

Whoever the sponsor is, make sure she or he has enough political capital to secure the resources you need.

At the beginning of the customer visit project, you should draw up a project charter that acts as a contract between the visit team and management. We emphasize this because customer visits are often "out of the ordinary" projects. Unless members of management have signed on the dotted line, they may think that it's okay to cancel or under-resource the projects. In addition, a project charter helps to spell out, for the team members, exactly what they're responsible for.

The project charter should include the following information:

- ✔ **The number of customers the team plans to visit:** Research and experience establish that between 10 and 20 customers is a good number.

  If your team can visit customers in a place that offers opportunities for several visits, by all means take advantage of that. You've made the trip, so absorb as much information as you can.

- ✔ **The opportunity the team is exploring:** For example, the opportunity may be to discover what draws women to motorcycle riding so that a motorcycle company can design products for them.

- ✔ **The planned project outcomes and time frame:** A project should take between three and six months, depending on the amount of travel involved, the number of team members available, and the number of customers the team plans to visit.

Formal chartering assures that a customer visit team will have adequate support and resources, clear goals, and defined deliverables.

### Deciding who should make up the team

A customer visit team should have 8 to 12 members who come from different business functions. The team sponsor and the team leader should select team members with an eye to experience and diversity; however, the final say about who will make up the team is usually up to the functional heads.

It's important to include people with different experiences and perspectives. For example, a marketing member and a manufacturing member will each come away from a customer visit with very different experiences and observations, and they'll interpret the information the team gathers differently. Different perspectives are essential to creating a 360-degree view of the customer's world.

A customer visit team should have a strong team leader who can help the team align on the goals and the tasks and make sure that the project sponsor stays informed and on board with the program. Ideally, the team leader has led or participated in such a program before. If not, choose someone with experience in leading teams and projects — someone who, if possible, has led projects that may go in unpredictable directions. The sponsor, working with the business and functional leaders, should make the decision about who will lead the team.

# *Creating and choosing from a customer pool*

You can't visit all your customers for a customer visit project, and you certainly don't need to. In the following sections, we help you create a list of the customers you may want to visit and construct a matrix to narrow down your choices.

You may meet with and interview several customers on a single visit. For example, on a visit to a hospital, you could meet with a doctor, a nurse, a therapist, a patient, and a purchasing agent. That's five interviews, which could count as one-third of your whole program. You don't want to limit your customer sample to just three hospitals, however. A good compromise may be to visit five hospitals, for a total of 25 interviews.

### *Tagging the most desirable customers*

The following steps show you how to identify the many different customers who may be relevant to your opportunity (the section after this one shows you how to narrow the field to a manageable number):

1. **Brainstorm a list of the people and organizations that together would provide the product, service, or solution that the end-user would buy.**

   For example, if your company produces motorcycles, your list should include the manufacturer, the dealer or distributor, and the places that service motorcycles. You can include organizations and businesses that make cycling attractive to consumers, like owners groups and apparel shops. You also can list infrastructures that support or get in the way of people who ride: highways, traffic laws, insurance agencies, and so on.

   One graduate student group explored the market opportunity of women who ride motorcycles. In Figure 4-1, you can see a value chain diagram that shows how the students represented their list; the bubbles show some of the other stakeholders the students included.

   Using a value-chain diagram for your list of stakeholders can help your team remember all the parties you want to include.

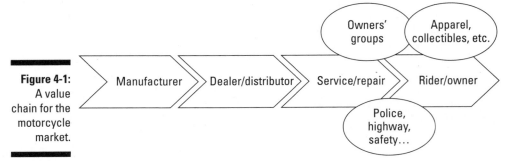

**Figure 4-1:**
A value
chain for the
motorcycle
market.

Owners' groups

Apparel, collectibles, etc.

Manufacturer > Dealer/distributor > Service/repair > Rider/owner

Police, highway, safety...

2. **List any other segments of the customer population that you may consider important.**

   Include the typical demographics that marketers use: age, gender, geography, socioeconomic grouping, and so on. In the motorcycle example, the students focused on women, but they divided the population by age, from the 20s to the 60s. If you're focused on a business-to-business opportunity, where the customer is another business, the demographics could include large and small businesses, urban/rural/suburban businesses, and so on.

   We recommend that you list these segments or demographics on sticky notes so that the team can move them around when you're selecting the most important segments.

Now your team has two lists: stakeholders (or the value chain) and customer segments. In order to keep your whole team focused, write up these lists on big flip chart pages, and tape the pages to a conference room wall. If the team has written segments on sticky notes, paste the notes to the wall chart. (We find that putting the lists into digital format too quickly tends to limit discussions.)

## Creating a customer visit matrix to focus your efforts

But wait! Your team now has lists that highlight everyone you can think of who may relate to your development opportunity, and we say earlier you should visit 10 to 20 customers. Exactly right. Your team must now decide where to focus its efforts. This can be kind of like making sausage: a messy process. One expert calls it "part art, part science."

### Setting up the matrix

You start by making a *customer visit matrix* by drawing rows and columns on a large sheet of paper. The headings for the columns should list the stakeholders you've brainstormed, and the headings for the rows should list the important customer segments you've identified.

Where the rows and the columns cross is where you find the intersection of the stakeholders and the segments. Within the matrix, the team will identify some intersections as more important than others. For example, the opportunity you're researching may be more relevant for older customers who live in cities (imagine a new product for coloring gray hair) or for large hospitals located in urban areas (imagine big, expensive medical testing equipment). Your team should highlight the intersections in the matrix that you identify as the most important for your project — the groups you'll select customers from to visit.

You should do your best to keep the customer visit matrix simple — in other words, limit it to two or three dimensions. Human beings can't think in four or five dimensions very well! However, your team may want to include other customers that aren't part of the two-dimensional matrix. We suggest that you list groups of customers whose needs may be different from the needs of the customers and segments you've selected. Teaching hospitals, for example, have different needs than other hospitals. As you select your customers to visit, you can make sure you've included some of these different groups, but make them your second or third priority.

### Selecting your customers

Each box you highlight on the matrix includes many customers — possibly even hundreds. For example, your team could locate hundreds of motorcycle dealers, repair shops, and owners groups. You also could contact thousands of riders. With the matrix, you've decided which categories are most important to your project; now you have to identify one or several customers in each box that you'll actually visit. The following list presents a way to go about selecting who you'll visit from your many options:

1. **Decide which geographic areas you want to visit.** If your list includes different parts of the United States, for example, each visit team can choose one location for all its visits. This saves on travel costs and wear and tear on your team.

2. **Within each geographic area, identify which kinds of customers each team will visit.** In the motorcycle example, each team could visit riders, dealers, owners' groups, and so on in each designated area. In order to spread the visits among the customer segments, the team that goes to Indianapolis, for example, may decide to visit customers in their 20s, and the team that goes to Massachusetts may visit customers in their 40s.

3. **Identify customers in each area who represent the segments each team will visit.** Cold-calling, searching the Internet, and perusing phone books can help you identify customers and schedule visits (see the following section). Your sales and marketing folks can also help.

Here's where a list of other "dimensions" can come in handy. If the Massachusetts team sets up a visit with a 40-year-old woman who uses her motorcycle for transportation, the team that goes to Indianapolis could visit a 20-year-old woman who rides as part of a couple or group.

If your customers are business customers, you probably won't have as many customers to choose from, and someone on your team may personally know customers the team should visit. When visiting business customers, be sure to set up visits with different functions within the businesses. Customer needs differ widely depending on whether an employee uses the product, pays for it, or oversees the function in which it's used.

If your team can't pinpoint appropriate customers from the multitude of options, you should call in resources from sales, market research, or other functions that may be willing and able to help.

See Figure 4-2 for an example of a completed matrix for a customer visit project. You can adapt this matrix to your own project and write the actual customer names in the boxes.

|  | Manufacturers | Distributors and dealers | Service/ repair | End-users/ consumers | Gov't regulatory | Society/ community |
|---|---|---|---|---|---|---|
| Geo. Region | *Conduct visits in northeast, southeast.* | | | | | |
| Urban/rural | | *Yes (2 each)* | | *Yes (4 each)* | | *Yes (1 each)* |
| Large/small | *Yes (1 each)* | | | | | |
| Old/young | | | | *Yes (4 each)* | | |

**Figure 4-2:**
A completed
customer
visit matrix.

Your lists and matrix show your team exactly what you did when targeting customers — and, just as important, exactly what you didn't do. You won't make the mistake of thinking that the information you collected for customers in North America automatically applies to customers in Japan, or that what you learned about small rural hospitals applies to large urban hospitals. And later on, if you want to find out more about other segments, you'll be able to focus your efforts and streamline your process.

## Scheduling the customer visits

As soon as you decide which customers to visit (see the previous section), you should start scheduling the visits. We recommend that you visit customers in pairs (you can read more about the roles team members play in the section "Setting up a practice interview"). Your team members may know some customers or know someone who does, which makes contacting them much easier. If you don't have many connections, consider doing some *cold-calling* — calling current customers and potential customers you find on the Internet or in the phone book — to set up some of the visits.

No matter which contact method you use, we recommend that you schedule the visits as early in the project as you can. Your project can stall if a customer you want to visit is unexpectedly unavailable. If you schedule early, you can make alternate plans.

The following list presents some tips to keep in mind when you begin scheduling customer visits:

- ✔ **Schedule a 1.5 to 2.0 hour interview with each customer.** It can be interesting to meet with several customers, perhaps over lunch, in addition to your "two-on-one" interview. Ordinarily, however, you get the best information from a single customer reflecting on his or her experiences.

- ✔ **Don't schedule more than two visits in one day.** If a team is traveling, you want to take advantage of their time on the road and pack in a couple visits. But don't overload them. The visit team should be able to conduct one or more interviews, observe the work that people at the organization do, perhaps visit with one or two other people in the organization, and still have time to debrief together afterward. If the visit is local, and travel time isn't an issue, one visit in a day is quite enough. (See the following sections of this chapter for more on the interview and review processes.)

- ✔ **Don't underestimate the difficulty of getting visits scheduled.** In our experience, customers usually are glad to talk with you if you can clearly explain the purpose of the visits. However, you have to reach them at good times, the customers have to find time on their calendars, and the proposed times have to fit the times your team has available.

- ✔ **After you schedule a visit, send a letter thanking the customer and briefly explaining the purpose of the upcoming visit.** If you asked for a tour or other opportunity to observe the customer's site during your visit, confirm this. Also, you should offer an honorarium for an end-user customer or a token gift for a business customer to express your appreciation. If one of your products makes a nice gift, use that.

When scheduling your visits, make sure you include your company's current customers as well as customers your company may have lost. You can learn plenty by talking with someone who decided not to use your products anymore! Also include people or businesses who are your competitors' customers. Who knows, maybe what you discover will entice them to become your customers in the future.

# Dipping Your Toes into the Visiting Process

Before your teams of two actually go out to visit your customers, you need to do some preparatory work. You don't go into a job interview without a résumé and some prepared answers, do you? For starters, your team should prepare a visit guide. When you have the guide drafted, you can start practice interviewing. For most people, really listening and asking good questions are new skills. You also practice collecting information. With all this prep work under your teams' belts, you can unleash them into the world of interviewing — allowing a bit of time to make necessary adjustments along the way.

The following sections address these topics and start you down the road to successful customer interviews.

## Preparing a visit guide

A *visit guide* includes a list of themes and topics that each visit pair should cover with each customer. Although each customer visit has a flavor and a character all its own, you want your teams to cover the important points with every customer. A visit guide ensures that this happens.

Your team should follow these steps to create a useful visit guide:

1. **Brainstorm a list of all the information you want to gather during the customer visit.**

   Maybe you want to know what your customers' typical work processes are, what frustrations they encounter, and how they ideally like to get their work done. If you're researching a consumer product, you may want to know about typical situations customers encounter when they use the product and what their frustrations are.

   You should write the items you come up with on sticky notes so you can post them on big wall charts.

 A real treasure that comes from customer visits is discovering "what you didn't know you didn't know." During this process, you may come up with a whole new set of questions that allow you to understand your customers better. Be open to the unexpected, and be willing to alter your visit guide to include research into new insights.

2. **Group the items into categories, and give each category a title.**

   If the team members have written their learning objectives on sticky notes, they can paste the notes on a large wall chart and begin to sort them into categories. Each category will be a *theme* in your visit guide. Categories might include different situations in which customers could use the product — for example, at children's parties, Super Bowl parties, and so on. Categories also can include the customer's work processes that may involve your product: drilling, refining, processing, shipping, and so on.

3. **Choose the most important categories.**

   You don't want to have more than six or eight categories. Usually, when each team member puts check marks on the categories she feels are important, using a simple voting method, you end up with the right number. If you still have too many, we recommend that you discuss the project focus with the team, because maybe your focus is too large. In that case, now's the time to narrow the focus.

If the customer visit team changes the focus, that change will influence the project charter. Be sure that the people who are providing the resources for the project are on board with the changes. Don't force functional leaders to cancel the project because you don't meet their pet objective (see the earlier section "First things first: Getting a sponsor and charter").

4. **Use the items in each selected category to develop probe questions.**

   Within each theme (category), the team needs to develop *probe questions* that will encourage the customers to elaborate. For example, if the theme is taking pictures at children's parties, probe questions could include the following:

   - "Could you describe a time when taking pictures went really well?"

   - "What was it about that time that made you really happy?"

   - "What else can you imagine that you'd like to be able to do when taking pictures at children's parties?"

   Consider the motorcycle team example introduced in earlier sections. The team thought of a number of probe questions that would help its customers discuss their experiences. Some of the questions the members asked included the following:

   - "Do you go on trips with others?"

   - "Could you describe a recent trip? Where did you go? What did you do?"

   - "Describe any clubs or groups you ride with. (If they don't ride with groups, ask, "Do you wish you did? Why?")

5. **Put the important categories (themes) and the probe questions into a logical flow on a visit guide (see Figure 4-3).**

   Putting the categories in a logical flow helps the interviewers and the customer to feel more comfortable with the interview's progress. The categories could go in order of time — for example, "How patients contact their doctors" followed by "Visiting the doctor." They could go in order of importance — for example, "Visiting the doctor for routine check-ups" followed by "Visiting the doctor for serious illnesses."

Another "logical" order for an interview is when you can start by asking a customer to describe a typical day, a typical process, or a typical event. You can discover plenty by listening to what really happens in your customer's world. Next, you may want to ask about the really great and really bad experiences the customer has had. You also can ask what would improve the customer's life and work. Customers often have great suggestions, and even if they don't, you can find out what's bothering them and what they want changed.

**Customer Visit Guide:**
**Understanding How Customers Live in Their Homes**

| Theme | Observations and Probes |
|---|---|
| **Living in/Using Your Home** Would you to tell us a bit about how you use your home? You might describe a typical day... | Where do you spend most of your time when you're home? [If they have kids] How does the house work for kids? (Ask for example of good/bad...) What is your favorite room? Why? |
| **Living in the Community** How does the community you live in affect you? Can you describe a time when you particularly valued your community? A time when you wished there wasn't one? | Are you involved in the Homeowners' Association? Do you value it? How do you use the greenspace or other amenities? |
| **Your Investment** How do you feel about your home as an investment? | How important is it to your overall financial picture? Are you making sacrifices to own your own home? Describe... |

**Figure 4-3:** Preparing a visit guide prepares your customer visit teams.

# Conducting practice interviews

An interview with a customer isn't just an ordinary conversation. In fact, it may be quite unlike any conversation you've had before. The visit team has a complex task to perform. The pair has to

- Make the customer feel comfortable and encourage her to talk frankly about her work, her life, her experiences, and so on.

- Follow the outline of the visit guide (see the previous section) so that they cover the points your team has agreed on.

- Listen for what's important to the project in what the customer says, and ask questions or give responses that encourage her to say more about the important things.

- Document the interview by using a tape recorder, hand-written notes, and perhaps photographs.

Learning to juggle this many balls takes practice. In this section, we provide guidelines you can use to practice before your teams go out into the field.

### Setting up a practice interview

For the practice sessions, we recommend that you divide your team into groups of three. In each practice group, you have the following members:

- ✔ **A lead interviewer:** This member of the practice team is responsible for initiating the different themes or topics of the interview and for doing most of the follow-up or "probe" questioning.

- ✔ **A notetaker/observer:** This member is primarily responsible for collecting information. The notetaker may get the chance to ask an insightful probe question or to steer the interview in an interesting direction, but he or she should never cause the customer to wonder if there's any conflict over who's running the show. When in doubt, the notetaker should keep his or her mouth firmly shut. (See the upcoming section "Practicing your information collection" for more advice on notetaking.)

- ✔ **The customer:** This member should "introduce" him- or herself as the customer — "I'm a respiratory therapist in a large urban teaching hospital," for example.

Make the roles in the interview very clear before you start. Set a time — five minutes works well — for the "interview." Advise your team members to pretend that the session is real, to listen, and to be fascinated by what the customer is saying. Chances are your team members will choose customer roles that they're somewhat familiar with, so everyone can learn something.

Three rounds of interview practice gives everyone on the team a chance to play all three roles and a much better sense of how the interview process works. Start each round of interviews in a different place in the visit guide to give the team a sense of how a longer interview would flow.

### Interviewing the "customer"

Your lead interviewer can start the practice interview with an overarching question. For example, the lead interviewer might ask, "Could you describe a typical day in your job? Maybe start with what happens when you first arrive . . ." Now comes the tricky part: The interviewers have to *listen*. Their body language should signal that they're interested — leaning a bit forward, nodding, and not looking around the room or at their notes. The lead interviewer can use verbal cues, such as "hmmm" and "ahhh." Remind your interviewers to ask questions or say things that show their interest: "Tell me more!" "How exactly did you do that?" And so on.

A good interviewer recognizes the moment for a "probe." He or she knows when to ask, "Can you tell me more about that?" Or, "Can you describe a time when that happened?" Another kind of probe is a simple reflection back to the customer of what the interviewer is discovering. The interviewer might say, for example, "So, I take it that this step is very important to you." An interviewer wants to lead his or her customer from generalities and abstractions to specifics and from solutions to needs ("If you had that, what would it do for you?"). The practice interview is a great place to practice providing an atmosphere in which a customer can talk, reflect, and explain how things are from his or her point of view.

The group of three should spend about five minutes conducting the practice interview, with each group member playing his or her role.

### Debriefing the interview

After the practice interview, the three-person practice team should take another five minutes to debrief the interview:

1. **Assess the lead interviewer's performance.**

   Did the customer feel comfortable, and was she able to talk? Were the questions open-ended? What improvements can the lead interviewer make?

2. **Debrief the visit guide.**

   Was the guide helpful? Were the probe questions open-ended? How could you change them? The team won't have time to get through the whole guide, but they can learn enough about how it works to know whether it needs to be revised.

3. **Debrief the notetaker role and assess what the interview pair learned.**

   How well did the notetaker record the customer's words? Did the notetaker record images? What other images or insights can the team reconstruct?

To help your pairs draw out the customer's unspoken needs, you should ask your visit teams to focus on images. The images your teams bring back help them share their understanding of customers with others. Images also spur the whole team to think creatively about solutions to your customers' problems. Right after an interview is a good time to look back over the notes and record images that you may forget after a day or two. (See the section "Organizing the image information" later in this chapter.)

### Sharing insights with the whole team

When all the three-person teams have completed their practice interviews, the team leader should call the whole group together so the teams can talk about what they've learned. Hearing the strong and weak points of other interviewers can help everyone improve. During these sharing sessions, the team builds a common understanding of what makes for a successful interview.

Be sure to share critiques and strong points you've identified with respect to the visit guide. A team member should take the responsibility of revising the guide if necessary and making sure the whole team gets to review the revisions.

Write the insights and ideas shared at the meeting on a flip chart to help the participants focus during the meeting. You can type up the list afterwards so team members can refer to the learning later in the process.

## Practicing your information collection

The notetaker of the visit pair has the job of collecting information during the customer visit. When you first hear about "notetaking," you may think of being back in school and trying to transcribe an entire lecture in a notebook. Taking interview notes that way is unbelievably frustrating, and it makes your hand hurt.

However, the actual, verbatim words of the customer are invaluable sources of insight for the team. We human beings tend to listen in generalities. We hear "I liked using that device" rather than "When I used that device, I was able to provide much better patient care." When the interviewer follows the latter statement with a probe question and discovers that "When my hands are free, I'm able to adjust dials much more accurately," the team has information to begin to design a product around.

Therefore, we recommend that your notetaker bring a good tape recorder to the interview. One of the important resources a customer visit team can have is a skilled typist who can transcribe interview tapes verbatim and include them in the team's store of information.

Some teams videotape their visits. For example, a Kodak team videotaped customers dealing with hard-copy photos to help the team design solutions for digital photo archiving. The videotapes provided both images and interview text. Videotaping presents a challenge because the team gets so much information, but it provides team members and others in the company with what amounts to a real re-creation of the visit.

Even if the notetaker has a tape recorder, though, we recommend that he or she take some verbatim notes during the interview. Here's why:

- **The tape recorder may malfunction.** You want to have as full a record as possible after your team travels many miles to visit a customer.

- **People tend to listen in generalities.** Taking notes verbatim actually gets the notetaker in the habit of listening to what others are saying rather than filtering words through his or her own ideas and opinions.

So, how does the notetaker take verbatim notes? Glad you asked. Here are some tips:

- ✔ Have a large pad with plenty of paper, your favorite pen, and a spare.

- ✔ Even though you can't write down *everything* the customer says, be sure to write down *what* the customer says.

- ✔ If you get behind, don't paraphrase; draw a line and start again. You'll eventually get the hang of leaving out the "um's," the "ah's," and the "well, I think it was's." When you sit down to review the notes after the visit with your visit partner, you can fill in many of the gaps.

If you bring a tape- or videorecorder to a visit, be sure to ask the customer's permission to record the interview. Your team needs to build relationships with the customers, and if you come across as sneaky, you risk these relationships! Leave the recorder in plain sight; most customers forget all about it after a few seconds.

In all transcripts and notes, identify the customers and the companies with coded letters and numbers. Using a code — Company A, Interview 1, and so on — helps protect customers' confidentiality when the team shares information (with the executives, for instance).

## Baby steps: The first visit

The first time team members actually go out to visit customers is a big step. They're going from inside the safety of the company to outside into the big wide world. Although the marketing members of the team may be perfectly comfortable visiting customers, engineers and manufacturers usually find the whole idea rather strange.

This section introduces two ways of conducting the first visit. The first is fine for most visit teams; we introduce the second in case any of your teams need some extra help.

### Going on your first visit

The first visit for each two-person team should serve as a smooth transition from the practice interviews. The first real visit should be

- ✔ Local, to save on travel costs.

- ✔ With a "friendly customer" who knows the company.

- ✔ With a customer your team can easily contact in case the interviewers miss something or have further questions.

Nothing is really different about this visit compared to subsequent visits, except that it's the first one. The first time is always the hardest! During the first visit, your team will

- ✔ Confirm the visit details.
- ✔ Briefly explain the purpose of the visit.
- ✔ Have a tape recorder and ask permission to use it (see the previous section).
- ✔ Conduct the interview, following the themes and probes on the visit guide (see the section "Preparing a visit guide").

A customer may wander all over the place and make it hard for the interviewer to follow the visit guide. Here's how your interviewers can deal with that: They shouldn't feel that they have to follow the themes in any particular order, but they should listen for how they can bring the customer back to the themes of the visit guide. With practice, the guide will become a background for a normal conversation that "just happens" to cover all the points (because of the interviewer's skill and familiarity with the guide).

- ✔ Thank the customer and confirm that they can call later if needed to clarify points.

Customers typically want to know how your NPD team will use the information you gather during the visits. Always reassure them that you won't connect anything they say to their names or their companies and that only people inside your company who develop products will have access to the information (and then make sure this is true!).

After the first visit, your visit team will

- ✔ Debrief the visit with each other.

    They can add things they noticed and talk about any confusions. Try to hold the debrief meeting the same day as the visit — maybe over dinner at the end of the day.
- ✔ Write down any images you identified during the visit.

    Include what you observed in the customer's environment *and* what the customer said.
- ✔ Have the interview transcribed.
- ✔ Send the customer a follow-up thank you letter, along with any fees or gifts you promised.

### *Holding interview practice for real beginners*

If customer visit team members are very inexperienced or are unnerved by the thought of conducting visits, you may want to include special practice sessions — sessions that are just like "real" interviews but with much lower stakes. Co-author Beebe Nelson once used this approach with a very nervous scientist who couldn't imagine visiting customers unless he was the expert. By the end of the project, he was thinking of going into the customer visit business himself!

Here are a few suggestions for setting up a low-stakes practice interview:

- ✔ If you have a team member who has experience in the market segment that you're researching, ask him or her to be the "customer" for a full hour interview. Follow the whole process (see the previous section), including taping the interview.

- ✔ Find an employee in your company who may be an "internal customer" for the opportunity you're exploring — a researcher or a salesperson, or someone in purchasing or manufacturing, for example. Again, follow the whole interview process. Make it as real as you can.

- ✔ Set up a practice interview with a customer in your area whom you know well. Explain that you want your team to gain some experience. Ask if the team can come back another time if they need to clarify some points.

- ✔ Interview a friend or colleague who has experience in the area the team is researching.

## Working out the kinks: The mid-course debrief

After all your team's visit pairs complete and transcribe their first real visits, your whole team should gather to work out the kinks. This meeting, called a *mid-course debrief,* gives your team a chance to approve what's working and fix what isn't.

Don't forget your charter! We recommend posting it on a wall in the meeting room so that the team can refer to it when they have questions about the scope or purpose of the project (see the earlier section "First things first: Getting a sponsor and charter").

One of the most important questions to ask is, "Are we getting images of our customers' environments?" (See the section "Organizing the image information" later in this chapter for more on images.) So, start the meeting by having a facilitator or a team member ask the team members to report images from the visits. You can write the images on the wall charts.

Next, ask team members what they've learned about interviewing and conducting visits, including the problems they had. Write headlines on the wall charts, and give the team members time to describe their issues. The team discussion of these points usually clarifies any problems.

Use the last part of the meeting to discuss any logistical issues — problems with the interview guide, scheduling issues, problems with transcription, and so on. Take the time to solve these issues or make plans to solve them. Be sure that the team leader or facilitator gets back to the team later to let them know how any issues have been resolved.

By sharing this information, the whole team can learn from one another. You can read all the books you want, or listen to all the experts, but personal experiences and the shared experiences of colleagues make all the difference.

# The Final Push

You've prepped and practiced. You've worked out any kinks with your recording and transcription process. Your team is seeing and hearing images everywhere. You've scheduled all the remaining interviews. You're ready to execute your full customer visit program.

## Tackling the rest of the visits

A program of customer visits can take way too long if you don't complete the visits promptly. The whole project, including preparation time, usually runs from three to six months. If it goes much longer, the team and your executives may begin to lose energy and enthusiasm. Therefore, it's critical that your team keeps to the proposed schedule. If, as can happen, a customer postpones or cancels a visit, you should reschedule or replace the visit with another customer as soon as you can.

Be prepared to take advantage of unexpected opportunities during your customer visits. A customer may ask, "Want to see where we do the assembly?" Or, "One of our customers is here on-site; would you like to meet with her?" As long as you allocate 1½ to 2 hours for an interview with the customer, you should take advantage of any chance opportunities that will give you more insight into the environment the customer works or lives in. Unexpected opportunities are often great ways to collect real live images. One of our favorites is from a tool company visitor who saw "one of our tools lying rusting on the shop room floor."

## Assembling the visit data

The program of customer visits is a knowledge-building project. The information the team gathers is important for the team and the company. It often contributes to other teams and projects long after the current project is complete.

Your team needs to put all the information you gather into a format that you can store easily, that your team members can access without issue, and that can provide a permanent and accessible record for other teams (these days, that pretty much shouts out "Internet!").

The following list inventories the pieces of information you should update after the visits are complete:

- **The customer selection matrix,** which records the customers and segments the team planned to visit and those they didn't (see the section "Creating a customer visit matrix to focus your efforts")

- **A list of the customers** that the team actually visited, including their contact information

- **The visit guide**, which provides an overview of the learning objectives of the project (see the section "Preparing a visit guide")

- **The transcript of the interviews,** plus interviewers' notes, which will include the images they logged right after the visit (see the section "Practicing your information collection")

- **Photos or videotapes** the team shot

- **Images of the customer environment,** including the final map of the images the team found most important (see the upcoming section "Organizing the image information")

- **Customer requirements** the team generated (see the section "Writing product requirements: What does your customer want?")

## Staying in touch with customers

During your team's customer visits, you form important relationships with the customers who give you valuable information you can use to develop successful new products. They're useful to you in many ways during the visits; what you may not know is how useful they can be in the future. You have several reasons why your team members may want to contact these customers in the future:

- You may have questions about something you heard or failed to ask during the visit. At the end of the visit, a member of the team should ask the customer if you can call, e-mail, or write if you have additional questions.

- You may want customers to participate with you in future idea-generation sessions (see Chapter 5) or in another aspect of product development.

- Some customers could make perfect candidates for product or prototype testing later in the development process (see Chapter 17).

- Customers might participate in advertising or promotional campaigns.

The first thing you should do to maintain your relationships for the long term is to send thank-you's! Draft a letter that your team can use. Each pair of interviewers should personalize the letter with a few of their visit details. Be sure your teams send their letters within a few days of their visits.

# Distilling the Results: Images and Requirements

Visiting customers to gather product information is like drinking from a fire hose. No, really! Each visit may produce 20 or more pages of transcribed notes and observations, complete with photos, insights, and images. What's your team supposed to do with all this information?

Lucky for you, in the sections that follow, we show you how to organize the information and shape it into a form that your team can use and share. We concentrate on two kinds of information: images of the customers' environments and what your customers want or need — the "customer requirements."

## Organizing the image information

What to do with all the gathered images from the customer visits? In a list, all by themselves, they don't make much sense. At best, they're contradictory — they show the confusion and richness of the real world.

The following sections explain how your team can assemble the images and then shape them so that the team members, and others, can use the images to deepen their understanding of customers.

### Writing and assembling the images

The first step in organizing and shaping visit information is to generate a simple list of the images. By listing the images, you give the team members and others access to a rich repository of customer information. The best time for the visit team to identify and select images is right after each visit.

When the visits are complete and you have a pool of information (see the section "Assembling the visit data"), your whole team should meet to compile a complete image list and to select some of the most powerful images. These selected images — which members can write on sticky notes — will help the team to identify customer needs.

The following list presents some examples of images from customer visits:

"A doctor climbing on a filing cabinet to get a picture." Quote from a camera manufacturer on a visit to a doctor's office to find out how dental surgeons document operations.

"I make a complete mess pipetting solution into the receptacles." Quote from a customer of a manufacturer of blood analyzers.

"I'm spending too much time learning new applications — I'm frustrated!" Quote from a customer of a software manufacturer.

At the simplest level, these images are pictures. When you read or hear about an image, you can picture the situation. The image often involves action — "climbing on the filing cabinet," for example. Notice that in some of the images in the previous list, emotion is clearly involved — "I'm frustrated." In others, the images imply emotion — "I make a complete mess." You can think of an image as the scene a video camera would capture — a little slice of the customer's life.

A customer's words (verbatim quotes) can make good images. Just be sure that the emotional overtones are there before you label the situation as an image. Sometimes, for example, the emotion is clear but unspoken — "I make a complete mess when . . ." Go ahead and throw in the label in these cases.

The visit team members should select images that they feel are important in your customers' environments. As much as possible, select images that cover what was learned during the visits. For example, the doctor's office image in the previous list showed the team many things, including how badly the doctor wanted to get the picture, and how poor the available process was.

Some interviews will be overflowing with compelling images. Some will be less vivid. The team should include the compelling images, of course, but also include some images that represent the depth and breadth of what they learned about the customer environments — even if some of the images are weaker or less interesting.

### Grouping and mapping the images

After the visit team has identified the important images from the customer visits and written them on sticky notes, the next step is to group the images so that team members can begin to see some patterns.

Call a team meeting and follow these steps to bring some order to your images:

1. **Sort and group the images.**

   You can follow this process:

   a. **Post the sticky notes on a blank wall, on wall charts, or on dry-erase boards.** Make sure the sticky sides of the notes are on top!

      b. **Weed out duplications.** We prefer to put duplications in a stack instead of tossing them out so that we don't lose wording that may come in handy later.

      c. **Group the images.** At this point, it's okay to group them logically.

These three steps get the team members familiar with all the images and allow them to sort the images into manageable categories.

2. **Reduce the number of images.**

Each team member puts a check on all the images she or he wants to include in the final count. When that round is done, eliminate all the images with no checks, and repeat the process. Take off all the images with one check, and do a third round. Your goal is to identify 25 to 30 images. Keep the earlier round losers in your team documentation.

3. **Start grouping the selected 25 to 30 images.**

"WAIT! Not that way!" Most people will want to group the images by obvious properties or characteristics — which ones talk about paint and which ones talk about wallpaper, or which ones happened to old patients and which to younger ones, for instance. That's how our little logical minds usually work.

Try this instead: Try having group members work silently, looking to gather the images on the sticky notes into groups that represent some other image — an image at a higher level of abstraction, perhaps. For example, a team that visited hospitals grouped these three images:

- Therapist having to explain to a patient's family member that a needed supply is in backorder

- Therapist fumbling to find the right connection

- Therapist custom designing an oxygen-delivery system for each patient

The team came up with this higher level abstraction: "We never have exactly what we need."

The grouping process shouldn't take too long. If you're still grouping after half an hour, call a halt to the exercise. Have a brief discussion about what you're doing and what's not working. Then have the team come to a workable consensus on the groups. It helps to say "Be sure the grouping is 60 percent okay with you."

4. **Label each group — with images that give the flavors of the images in each group, if possible.**

The team that visited the hospitals imagined something a therapist might say that depicted frustration and covered all the lower-level images.

5. **Repeat Steps 3 and 4, if necessary, until you have five to seven groups.**

You group the initial groups and give them titles, and then you group again and give the second-level groups titles, and so on. For example, when the hospital visit team did a second-level grouping, they put the title "We never have exactly what we need" together with "Changing to products that work differently is annoying" and then labeled both with "Listen to us before you come up with solutions."

6. **Paste all the groups formed by sticky notes on flip chart pages to form a map, and decorate your map with real images.**

You can use pictures, drawings, or whatever helps you to convey your customer's environment.

# *Writing product requirements: What does your customer want?*

Now that your customer visit teams have completed the visits, gathered information, and mapped the images, your team is ready to identify clear customer requirements. Things your customers desire in a product. Things that make the difference in your customers' buying decisions. Things you want to concentrate on providing.

## The taming of the screw

Most product development teams are interested in product requirements. They tend to think that what customers want and what team members think would make a better product are one and the same. But not so fast!

Co-author Beebe Nelson once worked with a manufacturer of tools and equipment for the automotive and aerospace industries. The firm wanted to improve its handtool line. Everyone the firm's development people talked to — from sales people to the tooling engineer at one of the company's largest clients — told them that the company's mechanized screwdriver needed more torque. The manufacturer ordinarily would've followed this advice and increased the speed at which its screwdriver could set a screw — from, say, 5 seconds to 2.5 seconds. But this time, before starting, the company's development team decided to do a series of customer visits. The members of the team visited tooling engineers,

purchasing people, and designers. They also wanted to visit the operators who actually used the tool. "Why do you want to do that?" a tooling engineer asked. "They use the tools the way I tell them to."

This statement sparked the team's interest. Fortunately, the team got access to the floor where the operators assembled parts. This is what they saw: The assembly line would stop for about two minutes in front of an operator. The operator would use the screwdriver to tap screws into position and then to drive in the screws. The issue wasn't the screwdriver's torque; and it wasn't how long it took an operator to drive in a screw. The issue was how long it took an operator to line up a screw so that the screwdriver could do its work. The team now had an entirely different set of issues to work with in order to solve its customers' problem.

One of the keys to succeeding at new product development is understanding what the customers want — what will satisfy, please, or delight them. By visiting your customers, hearing what they have to say, and mapping the images of their environments, you begin the process of understanding the customer. The information in this section enables your team to come up with clear and precise requirements. The advantage of identifying clear requirements is that when product developers have to make hard and sometimes unexpected choices during the development process, they can be absolutely sure that their choices will meet the customer requirements identified during the customer visit program.

The following list conveys what the visit team should do to create customer requirements from the information they've gathered:

1. **Go through each transcript from the visits and pull out any requirements you find.**

   Customers often know exactly what they need, and these insights are valuable sources of product ideas. For example, a customer may have said, "I need a way of measuring the salinity before I start the process."

   Start with the transcript your team thinks is the "richest" in terms of requirements. You should find plenty of requirements in this first visits, and probably fewer from the next ones.

2. **Use the image map (see the previous section) to shed light on other statements — complaints, suggestions, and so forth — that may yield requirements.**

   For example, a customer may say, "That's way too slow. You should make it faster." Product developers could jump to the conclusion that the customer needs a faster process, but if you've created an image map, you may be able to see the customer's complaint in the light of an image. The image "I'm spending too much time learning new applications" may lead the team to think of other ways of dealing with the complaint.

3. **Write clear requirements — one per sticky note.**

   Here are some guidelines for writing customer requirements:

   - **Each requirement should start with "I can."** For example, "I can complete the process quickly." If you start with "I can . . . ," you're sure to think about the customer, not about the product.

   - **The requirement shouldn't contain or imply a solution.** For example, a requirement shouldn't state, "I can use a thinner mixture to complete the process quickly." Maybe the development team will end up with exactly that solution, but if the statement doesn't contain a solution, it gives product developers more freedom to invent solutions when the time comes.

- **The requirement should be as specific and clear as possible.** "I can do the process better" gives the team no clue about what has to be improved.

- **The requirement should be positive.** For example, instead of writing "I can keep from getting wet in the rain," say "I can stay dry in the rain." Positive statements help your creative team come up with more and better solutions.

**4. Group, select, and organize the requirements.**

Thirty or so is a good number of requirements to work with. You can use the same process we describe in the previous section for grouping and selecting images. Each initial group should have three to five sticky notes. Use the "I can . . ." style for the group labels as well so the labels are also requirements.

Figure 4-4 shows a sample "I can . . ." diagram produced by students in one of co-author Beebe's classes.

| | | |
|---|---|---|
| I can relax and control my TV anytime without pressing buttons | I can relax and be in control of my TV at any time | I can rest peacefully and not worry about where the remote is |
| | | I can forget about finding the remote |
| | | I can control my TV around any obstacle |
| | I can operate my TV without pressing buttons (remote/TV) | I can control my TV without assistance |
| | | I can change the channel without new batteries |
| | | I can control my TV even if my remote breaks |

**Figure 4-4:** You can group your requirements with a tree diagram.

When you're ready to brainstorm for product ideas and concepts (see Chapter 5), and later when you're developing your product, the "I can . . ." tree will help you and your team stay on track. You'll be able to think of ideas that will help your customers do what they want to do, and when you make changes during the development process, you'll be able to refer to the important customer requirements that you want to fulfill.

# Quantifying the Results of the Customer Visit Program

Before your product development team depends too heavily on the research you've done with customers — known as *qualitative research* — you should do *quantitative* checks. You want to make sure that a sufficiently large number of customers value the customer requirements you've identified to make it worthwhile to design products to accomplish them. You also want to know which of the identified requirements are most important to your customers.

Your company's marketing or market research department should be able to help your visit team conduct research that's statistically valid. Here are a couple approaches we've used:

- **Assessing the relative importance of requirements:** Your team can do a quick sanity check by asking customers how important a particular requirement is to them. One way to quantify this is by asking, "If you had $100 (or $1,000 or $10,000, depending on the product), how much of that money would you spend for . . .?"

- **Assessing whether a requirement is a "must have," a "pleaser," or a "delighter":** Noriaki Kano, a Japanese quality expert, found that requirements fall into three categories:

  - **Things a product must have:** The wheels on a car, for example

  - **Things that make a product more attractive:** Better gas mileage, for example

  - **Things that make a product delightful but that aren't expected:** Built-in televisions in the back seat, for example

Checking with customers to make sure which requirements fit which category can really help focus the development team's efforts. Take a look at Chapter 17 for more information on product testing.

# Chapter 5

# Turning Your Company into an Idea Factory

*W*e want your company to be an "idea factory" — a place where ideas for new products pop up all over the place. Ideas are the starting point for new product development success. Without creativity — without the ability to see what could be rather than only what is — a company can't come up with new products of any kind.

Coming up with ideas for new products isn't a random occurrence. It doesn't happen just because you, by chance, hired very creative people. Becoming an idea factory requires the creation of an environment and a process that enable your company to continually generate new ideas in abundance.

Why in abundance, you may ask? Because for every good idea that gets puts into development, your company may shelve or discard hundreds of "not so good" ideas. You may even identify hundreds of "good" ideas that unfortunately don't fit with your new product strategies. To ensure success, you need plenty of ideas, good and bad, to choose from.

In this chapter, you find out what some of the leading product developers do to turn their companies into idea factories. You discover how to bring together the right mix of people who will spur each other on to more and better ideas. You find out how to provide the structure that enables people to be creative and how to incorporate an understanding of customer needs and wants to provide a foundation for idea building. You see how ideas can provide solutions for customers. Also, the best product developers aren't shy about bringing in outside experts to provide the sauce, and sometimes even the main course, for idea-generation sessions. Therefore, we describe how to involve experts to give you a leg up.

# Drafting Your Creative Teams

Some companies rely on individual contributors to come up with great ideas, and others have processes in place for soliciting new ideas from employees. Both of these strategies can be effective, but in this section we focus on the most powerful and predictable way of generating new ideas: selecting and using a creative team.

The teams that develop new products — cross-functional teams (see Chapter 10) — should be included on your creative teams, but you shouldn't limit yourself to the functional experts who know how to do what it takes to develop new products. Reach out beyond the experts to bring in the kooky, the uninhibited, the scientific, and the curious — in other words, the folks in your company *and* outside your company who will bring spice and fire to your proceedings.

Often, companies run customer visit projects (see Chapter 4) and creative sessions before they have any product concepts or new product teams. Members of the creative teams you assemble may end up on the new product development teams for the concepts that they helped bring to life, or they may go on to generate more concepts and leave the hard work of development (see Chapter 9) to others.

Who's responsible for drafting the creative team? In some companies, the person responsible is the NPD process owner. In others, the task may fall to the heads of the business units. Ultimately, it's managers and executives who need to make sure that their company's idea factory is providing plenty of inventory for the NPD pipeline.

To make sure that they assemble a team that is indeed creative, managers need to pay attention to the mix of people they include. You want people who can work well together, spur each other on, and make the most of each other's creativity. Usually, this means you need people who don't often see eye to eye with each other; in other words, you need people from different backgrounds and with different worldviews. We recommend that you gather people from different functions, and sometimes from outside the company as well, including suppliers, partners, and customers.

# Identifying creativity styles

Creativity style differences are real. You may even say they're hardwired in everyone. People process information differently and relate to people and tasks differently. For example, some people respond to problems by coming up with ideas that improve the existing system; others tend to generate more radical ideas — ones that call for drastic changes. As you put together your creative team, you need to be aware of these differences. When you have different creativity styles working together, you get the best of all worlds.

Another big difference is between extraverts and introverts. You may think that you'd prefer to have all extraverts on your creative team. These are the people who will jump into a session, call out their ideas, and never be at a loss for words. But if you manage creativity sessions well, you can design ways for the introverts to participate, too, and you'll get the added benefit of their thinking, which can be more carefully considered than the extraverts'.

If you have a qualified person to administer them, you can use surveys to assess your employees' creativity styles. Some of the most widely used assessments include the Myers-Briggs, the Herman Brain Dominance, the I-Opt, and the KAI (the Kirton Adaptive/Innovative Scale). You can find out more about these assessments on the Internet.

Knowing the styles of your prospective participants will help you to build a diverse creative team. But even if you can't effectively assess creativity styles by using surveys, you can observe to get a sense of how people relate to the world — how radical or conservative they tend to be, how talkative or silent they appear, how thoughtful or off-the-cuff they seem, and so on. Use your instincts to make sure that you include people who fall on all sides of these spectrums.

# Uniting the styles and functions

When forming a team that will stock your company's inventory of new product ideas, you must remember that diversity is essential. You need people with different types of creativity styles (see the previous section). Furthermore, you should add people with different skills, experiences, and roles in the company, because they'll see processes and ideas from different points of view and will approach the task of being creative differently. Marketers will come up with different ideas than engineers or software experts; together, they'll come up with ideas that none of them would've thought of alone. You should also include people of differing age, gender, and cultural or ethnic background whenever possible.

## What's missing here?

Co-author Beebe Nelson walked into a meeting held by a team that wanted to improve sanitary products for women. Every participant was an engineer, and they were all men. All they could think of to improve the products was to find ways to prevent leakage.

Co-author Robin Karol once worked with a creative team at a consumer products company. The team was charged with generating ideas for a new deodorant made especially for teens. No participant on the team had teenage children.

In the first example, it would've been easy for the team to ask female employees to participate in the creative session. In the second, the team could've found employees with children and asked whether their children could participate. Don't overlook the useful resources in your own company — the people whose experiences might make them perfect members of creative teams. And don't fall into the trap of thinking that one type of knowledge or experience — for instance, marketing savvy or scientific know-how — is all you need to come up with ideas for products that will please your customers.

In addition to the team members, each creativity team should include a facilitator who can guide the team through the creative process. The facilitator also helps team members to "get along" despite their diverse perspectives and styles.

People who play different roles in a company, and who have different skill sets and experiences, often find it difficult to work together. Perhaps you've heard old stories about marketing and R&D members trying to talk to each other. Engineers from China and the United States tend to be more like each other than engineers and marketers from the same country and culture. However, these business differences, blended in the task and spirit of a creative team, are necessary. They provide impetus and incentive for many more ideas, from process changes to product concepts, than you'd get from one business function on its own. (See the later section "Breaking the ice" for tips on creating a friendly environment.)

## *Enticing customers to participate*

If you've carried out a customer visit program — and, ideally, you should do this before the creativity sessions — you should have plenty of information from customers on what they dislike in the marketplace and on what they desire and need from prospective products (flip to Chapter 4 if you want to get going on customer visits). In addition to sharing information from customer visits with the creative team, it can be very useful to include customers as members of the creative team.

### Finding customers

One of the easiest ways to involve customers on a creative team is to invite employees from your own company who are members of the target customer group. Co-author Robin, for example, was once part of a group of scientists who held a technical creative session to generate new ideas for hair-coloring products. She asked the session manager how many people in the group actually used hair coloring. The answer was zero. Robin suggested that they invite the administrative assistants in the department who used hair-coloring products to join the scientists. The scientists would've been reluctant to put outsiders in the room because the session would reveal information about proprietary technology; however, the administrative assistants were employees, so the scientists agreed.

The "customers" on the team provided outstanding insight into how people used the products and what improvements they would want. The result of the session was very positive, and the session was extremely motivating for the administrative assistants. They found the day exciting and stimulating, and they got an inside look at what their company was up to.

If your development team has been visiting customers — and we hope they have — you probably have contacts outside the company whom you could invite to participate in a creative session. If not, your sales department should be able to introduce you to some appropriate customers. Always be aware that you're looking for diversity. Even as you invite customers, think about creativity styles, company role, age, gender, and cultural diversity.

Customers aren't always easy to manage! Co-author Beebe once invited a therapist to participate in a creative session for a product he used in the hospital. He had very strong ideas. So strong that instead of an idea generation session, the meeting turned into a lecture on the best way to design the product. The creative team did learn something from the customer, but it didn't accomplish the goals of the session. If you invite customers from the outside, you have to realize that they have their own agendas. Make the details and goals of the session and process very clear to the customers.

Many outside customers expect to be paid to participate in idea generation sessions, which is perfectly appropriate. You should also follow up with a thank you and a gift if it seems appropriate. Some companies build groups of loyal customers whom they can count on to participate in sessions regularly. Treat them well — they are your customers!

### Scheduling a session with customers in mind

You should always allocate at least two days for a creative session (see the following section for more on setting up sessions) — especially when you're working with customers. You can invite the customers to participate on the first day and then spend the second day fleshing out the customer input in an employees-only session.

You don't have to reveal proprietary knowledge when you run idea generation sessions. However, to build on ideas, you need to understand what your company can do. Customers can generate plenty of ideas without knowing the technology; on the second day of the session, the internal team can elaborate on the ideas with knowledge of the company's resources.

You may want to schedule a half-day session that includes only customers before you put them in with the creative team. The rest of the team can listen in or observe the session through a one-way mirror; you can even tape the session (be sure the customers have agreed to being watched or taped!). This meeting allows the creative team to understand what the customers are thinking before the actual session, and it gives the facilitator a chance to teach the customers how to be most productive in the creative setting.

# Setting Up and Opening the Creative Session

Creativity may seem like a random or lucky experience; it can be, but more often it's the result of careful planning. An idea generation session needs structure. The people who attend the session — the creative team — need to place all their attention and energies on coming up with ideas. The environment of the meeting should make this easy for them. Why aren't people creative all the time? Probably because their attention is pulled to other, more practical matters. People have things to do, others to meet, reports to write, research to do, and so on. While the team members are working together, they should have as few of these distractions as possible, because your creative team should experience the luxury of being able to focus all their attention on coming up with good ideas.

Every creative session needs someone who's responsible for providing structure, the person we call a *session manager*. Better yet is a small group of people who have that responsibility. If you go this route, the group should include a skilled facilitator, someone to whom the results are important (a team leader or senior manager, for example), and someone who has the time, skills, and contacts to pull off the session design (such as a project manager).

The session manager(s) is responsible for confirming the participants, attending to meeting details, providing an agenda, and getting the session going. The following sections detail these duties.

# Informing the participants

The session manager's first duty is to communicate with the meeting attendees to give them the details of the session. Be very clear about the timing — the date of the meeting and the meeting times — and the logistics. Most creative sessions are two-day affairs, so be sure to let them know whether a dinner will be served for the group. Make sure that everyone has directions to the meeting location and that they know how to get in. If they need to ask for a contact person when they arrive, let them know about that.

If you plan the session well in advance, we recommend that you reconfirm people's plans to attend a few days before the session.

# Providing a conducive environment: The devil's in the details

You have all kinds of details to consider when you're setting up a creative session. You'll want to provide the following for session participants:

- ✔ **Comfortable seating in a comfortable room:** For a creative session, you want a room with plenty of space and plenty of empty walls. Creativity includes walking around, meeting in small groups, and hanging the results of everyone's thinking on the walls.

- ✔ **Snacks, drinks, and meals as appropriate:** Be sure to keep people well fed and snacked while the session is in progress. It's nice also to bring the group together for a relaxed dinner if your session will last more than one day. Such informal settings often get participants thinking in different ways, which may help to produce even more ideas.

- ✔ **Pre-work displayed for all to see:** This includes the results of any prior customer visits — images, requirements, and so on (see Chapter 4). You may also need space and tables for building rough models and prototypes (see the later section "Building a rough concept model").

You also need the right materials to support the creative session. At a minimum, you need an ample supply of the following:

- ✔ Flip chart paper
- ✔ Markers
- ✔ Sticky notes
- ✔ Felt-tip pens
- ✔ Tape

Be sure that everyone supporting the structure of the meeting — for instance, the people setting up the breaks — is clear about the meeting's schedule and the session manager's needs.

We can't overstate the importance of this: Have the name of the contact person who can help you keep the room comfortable and functioning. A/V equipment and room temperature are two areas where you may need outside help!

## Breaking the ice

The creative session participants will be spending quite a bit of time together. The more comfortable they are with each other, the more they'll open up and share their thoughts. Start the creative session with informal introductions. Even if the participants already know each other, they may know each other only as colleagues, bosses, and so on in the everyday world of work. An ice-breaker establishes the possibility of another kind of relationship — one in which the participants are free to say what they think, make mistakes, be outrageous, and have fun.

Here are a few icebreakers that work well:

- ✔ Ask participants to draw pictures of themselves to show to the group. When they introduce themselves, ask them to describe how the pictures reveal something about them.

- ✔ Ask them to share personal facts that no one in the room is aware of.

- ✔ Ask them to share what excites them about the project and what they hope won't happen.

- ✔ Ask them to tell the group about where they were born, using little-known facts. One of co-author Beebe Nelson's colleagues, who lives in Quincy, Massachusetts, introduced himself as coming from the "city of dead presidents."

Almost anything that isn't the typical "My name is X, and I work in Y department" will do the trick.

## Presenting the problem and the ground rules

After the participants of the creative session get acquainted, the facilitator or session leader needs to present a clear statement of the problem that the session is intended to solve. This statement must be much more specific than a broad question like, "What new products can we come up with for our company?" The group members should have a general idea of why they've been invited to participate in the session, but they'll be able to focus their work much better if they have a statement or question that has the following characteristics:

- ✔ Is clear and concise
- ✔ Addresses the true issue/problem
- ✔ Includes any necessary boundary conditions

Here are a few examples of good problem statements:

- ✔ "Our job is to come up with solutions for farmers who own small farms and often must repair their own farm equipment. We should focus our solutions on all different kinds of equipment, from large motorized machines to small handtools, and metalwork."

  The boundary conditions are "own small farms" and "all different kinds of equipment."

- ✔ "We want to come up with financial products that will attract customers to our mortgage services. We can include all sizes of mortgages, from first-time small-home buyers to jumbo loans, and from first to second mortgages and all other kinds of home-equity lending."

  The boundary conditions here are "all sizes of mortgages" and different types of mortgages.

- ✔ "What could we do to make our toothpaste fun, effective, and easy to use? What would totally change tooth-cleaning habits? Do you really need to use a brush? Do you have to brush twice a day? On the 'improvement' side, how can we improve how people brush their teeth now — can we make our product taste better and prevent bad breath?"

The final example really makes room for both product improvement and radical breakthrough products.

 A great icebreaker is to have the participants build a "vision" of the solution by using bits and pieces of materials. You divide the group into subgroups of three or four and give them instructions (for example, you can say "Build a model of your vision of the perfect solution for this problem"). We often ask groups to do the task without talking. After the groups have completed the task, have each group discuss what it has done and then show its "vision" to the whole group. (See "Building a rough concept model" later in this chapter for more instructions on using materials in your sessions.)

In addition to clear problem statements, creative teams need explicit ground rules to focus their work and help the session run smoothly. We find that it works best to generate ground rules in a discussion and to write them up on a flip chart, which should remain posted throughout the session. See Figure 5-1 for an example of a session's ground rules.

Always wait until after the participants have gotten to know each other and have looked at the session purpose before asking them to generate a list of ground rules. The less somber they are, the better — generating ground rules can be a creative act.

---

**Sample Ground Rules for a Creative Session**

- Go for quantity, not quality
- Don't filter your own ideas
- Don't criticize others' ideas
- Don't be afraid to mention <u>anything</u>
- Crazy ideas can lead to other things
- There's no such thing as a "bad idea"
- Cheat!!! Piggy-back on each others' ideas
- >>> push yourself
- Each and every idea is valuable
- Have fun!!!!

**Figure 5-1:**
Ground rules help the creative session run more smoothly.

---

# Getting Creative by Thinking Outside the Box

You hear the phrase "Think outside the box" all the time, but what does it really mean, and where did it originate? It comes from a puzzle that asks you to connect nine dots in straight lines without raising your pencil. To complete the task, you have to go, literally, outside the box.

Thinking outside the box is shorthand for open-ended, divergent thinking. Creative thinking doesn't judge the results. It seeks novelty in whatever occurs during the thinking process. It builds on whatever anyone has said. It asks "How?" in a spirit of curiosity. It doesn't say "Yes, but," it says "Yes, and . . ."

In this section, we show you some ways to help your creative team think outside the box during your idea-generation sessions. But first, we talk about how to "empty the box."

## The bear that climbed out of the box

Once upon a time, a group of people were trying to solve the problem of ice damage to high-tension wires in cold climates. One group member suggested that they could have bears climb up the poles, which would shake the wires and cause the ice to fall off. Another member replied, "Great, and how will we get the bears to climb the poles?" The first group member answered, "We could hang pots of honey at the tops of the poles, and the bears would smell the honey and climb up to get it." "Okay, and how will we get the honey up the poles?" "We could fly helicopters over the poles and drop the honey pots down." A secretary, who attended the session to take notes, exclaimed, "When I was a medical aide in Vietnam, I rode in a lot of helicopters. The downdraft from the blades makes a really strong wind. It blew everything all over the place. I'm sure it would knock the ice off the wires!"

The participants looked at each other in amazement. They had just come up with a viable, inexpensive way of solving the problem. The discussion started with a silly idea and ended with the insight of someone who just planned on taking notes.

# *First things first: Emptying the box*

We like to start creative sessions by *emptying the box*. What does this mean? Well, when you're presented with a problem to solve, you immediately put it in the context of what you already know. Therefore, the first ideas that come to mind usually are familiar, already understood, and easy to think about. These ideas represent the easy solutions. They may work, but they aren't "outside the box." You want to get these ideas out on the table; until you do, the creative team will have trouble moving on to the out-of-the-box ideas.

So, how do you empty the box? If the creative group is small (say, just six to eight people), participants can start by suggesting ideas out loud and capturing them on a flip chart until everyone is "empty." If the creative group is larger, or if it has many introverts who might not participate in an out-loud session, you can give out sticky notes and have everyone write ideas on them. This method is easier on the facilitator or notetaker (she doesn't have to write down the ideas), and it helps the more introverted members who may not be as willing to call out their ideas early on in a group session.

Here's a way to work with the sticky notes:

1. **Each person writes down a minimum of 10 to 15 ideas on individual sticky notes.**

2. **Each person passes her note(s) to the person on her right.**

3. **Each person reviews the note(s) she receives and writes down three new ideas.**

   A participant can come up with a totally new idea, or she can build on an idea or combine two or more ideas into a new concept.

4. **Each person passes the notes to the right again, and the group pairs off.**

5. **The pairs review and discuss the notes in front of them and come up with a minimum of three to five more ideas.**

   Again, these ideas can be new, built on other ideas, or be combinations of earlier ideas.

6. **The pairs paste their ideas on a flip chart page (or two) for everyone to look at and discuss.**

   If, during this discussion, the group comes up with any new ideas, you can add them to the chart.

No idea is a bad idea! Keep these ideas posted during the rest of the creative session. The group may use them to strengthen ideas they come up with later or combine them into a more "out-of-the-box" idea. Sometimes, even though you're just emptying the box and not expecting people to be all that creative, someone comes up with the best idea of the day in the first hour of the session.

## Brainstorming

After the group has "empty brains," the members will find it easier to come up with more creative ideas by brainstorming. The term *brainstorming* refers to the many methods of generating a large number of creative ideas with a group. You can use brainstorming all by yourself when you're trying to find creative ways to solve a problem. And you can use it over and over during the session to capture the ideas that the group comes up with.

The following list presents the basic steps of brainstorming:

1. **Post the brainstorming ground rules.**

   These rules are similar to the ground rules you set for the whole session (see the section "Presenting the problem and the ground rules"), but they include some specific rules for brainstorming. In particular,

   - Don't judge ideas (negatively or positively!).

   - Go for quantity over quality.

   - Cheat (use others' ideas by building on, combining, or altering them).

**2. Set the brainstorming agenda.**

Include a clear time frame. A half-hour works well. If you go longer, people get stormed out; if you go shorter, you'll leave ideas on the table. Review the brainstorming agenda (outlined here in Steps 3 through 8) with the team and post it so participants can remind themselves of the steps they'll go through.

**3. Display the problem statement for the whole creative session, or draft one that focuses on a specific issue you want the team to address.**

**4. Begin the brainstorming by asking people to call out ideas or to write them on sticky notes.**

Ask for full sentences that focus on the problem statement. For example: "We could provide a tool kit that holds a tool for every situation a farmer with a small farm might come across."

If you use sticky notes and put them all up on the wall (hundreds of new ideas, we hope), a useful and productive action at this point is to have the team silently group the notes into common themes. For example, the team may group all the ideas that have to do with storing tools and separate all the ones that have to do with repairing tools. The groupings will sometimes create themes that lead to new ideas.

**5. Write up or post all the grouped ideas, and then have the team members "vote" by placing check marks or dots on the ideas or themes they like.**

Be sure to tell the group members to look for unique ideas and ones that stand out by themselves. You can limit the number of votes — say, by giving each team member three or five — but unlimited also works.

The team is voting in order to narrow down the number of possibilities. But don't let good ideas go down the drain at this point! Here are two ways to avoid this:

- Give every team member the opposite of a U.N. Security Council veto: Any idea that a team member wants to include is in, no matter how many votes the idea gets.

- Keep all the ideas in plain sight throughout the session. Just like the "empty the box" ideas (see the previous section), ideas that get few votes may still be important — by themselves, or when combined with others.

Another fun and useful way to vote on ideas is to give each participant a set of stickers that have values on them, like coins. Each individual should have a fixed amount of "sticker money" to spend on the ideas. After the money is spent, you add the value next to each idea to prioritize and select.

6. **Put the most popular ideas on a clean wall or flip chart page.**

   Make sure you keep the "losing" ideas visible — you may still have a treasure in there!

7. **Pair up the group members and have each pair use the popular ideas to create a new, composite idea.**

   They can write this new idea on an 8½"-x-11" sheet of paper. Instruct the teams to write full sentences to describe their ideas. You can also give them an outline to follow. For example, you may ask them to give a name to an idea, identify what customer needs it will fulfill, and briefly describe it. Encourage each pair to make a sketch of their idea — one picture, no matter how crudely drawn, really is worth a thousand words at this point in the process. (Take a look at Chapter 6 for an Idea Form outline you could use here.)

8. **Post these ideas and have the whole group review, critique, and build on them.**

Each time you complete a brainstorming session, you should have tens or hundreds of ideas, plus the judgment and deliberation of a team in narrowing them down and improving them. The flow of divergent (opening out) and convergent (narrowing down) is typical of creative processes. Brainstorming allows the creative group to be creative (divergent) and also to use their judgment (convergent).

# Mindmapping

*Mindmapping* is becoming increasingly popular for stimulating both individual and group creativity. Mindmapping is a great way to come up with plenty of ideas quickly and to help the creative group find themes or issues it may have overlooked.

To mindmap, you follow these steps:

1. **Pose a question and write it at the center of a large piece of paper, which you hang on the wall.**

   This question provides elaboration on the focus or problem statement for the session (see the section "Presenting the problem and the ground rules"). For example, you may ask, "What kinds of equipment do farmers with small farms use?"

2. **The session manager or facilitator asks for major themes that relate to the question.**

   For instance, if the group is meeting to solve the problem of a farmer who always needs to repair his own farm equipment on his small farm, the themes may include tractors, milking equipment, handtools, power tools, and so on.

3. **The session manager draws lines that jet out from the central question — like the arms of a spider web — and labels each arm with one of the themes.**

4. **The group starts to brainstorm solutions that may serve the different themes.**

   For example, the group may come up with solutions for repairing milking equipment — "Have a spare piece of equipment in the closet" — or for repairing tractors — "Get the tractor manufacturer to redesign how the farmer can get to the engine." Neither of these ideas may lead directly to solutions, but they may spur on others to come up with new thoughts or be useful later on when the team is building concepts (see the section "The solution: Putting together ideas to form concepts").

   If a participant thinks of another theme during the brainstorming, the facilitator can add it to the chart. Solutions that may cut across several themes can appear on several arms of the web.

## Setting sail on a creative excursion

One of the best ways to inspire creativity in your team — and certainly a method that's out of the box — is to go on a creative excursion. Many teams use excursions to set up a brainstorming session. You define the problem — say, for example, "How can we meet our customers' needs for increased safety in using our product?" After you empty the box and brainstorm ideas, your team is struggling to come up with ideas. Give them a break! After some coffee and doughnuts (or fruit and cookies), you can start the excursions.

Ask the participants to consider how they might solve the problem in the jungle. Do a mini-brainstorm with that task in mind, following the brainstorming steps we list in the section "Brainstorming." Ask the group to solve the problem as a plumber might. Ask them to consider how they'd solve the problem if they were at sea in a boat. And so on.

To continue the example from the previous sections, how would our farmer repair his equipment if he lived in the jungle? He might use palm fronds and coconuts to fix broken tools. What if he were a plumber? He'd probably use a plumber's helper to suck liquids out of broken tractor engines. At sea in a boat, he'd use rope to tie the broken parts together. It's the combination of ideas, not any one kooky idea alone, that brings the team to creative and implementable solutions.

A session manager or facilitator should come up with a list of creative excursions that she can pull out of her pocket whenever the energy of the group seems to be lagging. In addition to the previous examples, she could ask the group members what solutions would certainly fail. What would get them fired or would probably lose money for the company? What would break the laws of physics? Don't limit yourself to the obvious. The random and the off-beat can produce the best responses.

# Using Your Knowledge of the Customer to Inspire Solutions

Even if actual customers don't participate in your idea-generation sessions, the session manager(s) or facilitator should make sure to have as much knowledge of the customer as possible in the room to inspire and focus the group. A small group — the session manager(s) and the facilitator, for example — should take time before a session to gather known customer information and put it in a form that will provoke creativity. (See Chapter 4 for tips on customer visits.)

During the idea session, if you have photos of customers or of customer environments, post them. Perhaps you have a map that shows where your target customers are; at times during the idea session, the facilitator may ask the group to focus "just on the customers in Canada," or "just on customers in Japan," or "just on teenaged boys," and so on.

If you've gathered enough information about your customers, try constructing several composite sketches of "typical" customers before the session. These customers should represent all the diversity and contradiction that exist in your customer group. These sketches will influence the creative team, so you don't want to slant their influence in any one direction. Making your customers real inspires your creative team to come up with real solutions for them. Keep the sketches short, and add a picture of someone who might look like your "character." Post the sketches on the wall where everyone can see them. (Take a look at this book's Introduction to see the sketches we drafted to help us picture our customer — YOU!)

## The objective: Enabling the customer to do what he wants

If you've done a customer visit program (see Chapter 4), you already have a list of customer requirements that you can use to come up with ideas and solutions. But even if you haven't followed the customer visit process, you can brainstorm a list of requirements, or customer needs, that your creative team's solutions will address (see the earlier section "Brainstorming"). Your objective in creating new products, after all, is to give your customers what they need and want. Here's how the process should go:

1. **Post and review your customer information.**

   See the introduction to this section for ideas on how to prepare customer information for the team.

2. **Ask the team to brainstorm requirements.**

   Use the sticky-note method or write the requirements on flip chart pages.

   Start each requirement with "I can," which forces your team members to think of what customers want to be able to do. Here are a few "I can" statements that capture the requirements of patients who use medical devices:

   • I can hold onto my device with my arthritic hands.

   • I can carry my device with me inconspicuously.

   • I can clean my device easily.

   If you've made a customer requirements tree by following the instructions in Chapter 4, you can use that.

3. **Narrow down the requirements by voting, and then group them into not more than four or five groups of similar requirements.**

   The team from the medical device session grouped the previous requirements under the following theme: "I can carry out my therapy just the way I am."

4. **Post each group of requirements on the wall of the meeting room, and instruct the team members to wander around the room thinking of solutions for each specific requirement.**

   They can write their ideas on sticky notes — one idea per sticky note — and then stick them to the flip chart pages that list the requirements those ideas relate to.

   As the group members wander around, remind them to focus on each individual requirement rather than the total solution. When a team at Bose was brainstorming ideas for a home-theater system, one of the customer requirements was "I can hide my system so no one notices it." One of the team members drew a picture of speakers cleverly designed as coats in a closet. Another member drew pictures of dog statues — with the big one labeled "woofer" and the little one labeled "tweeter."

## The solution: Putting together ideas to form concepts

When your creative team has produced many ideas and solutions for the individual customer requirements you've identified or brainstormed, take a break! When you regroup, the next step is to gather the solution ideas into concepts (you can use the Idea Form we include in Chapter 6). Each member of the team should wander around the room to collect ideas from the earlier brainstorming to blend into a concept. Let the participants know that they can deviate from, build on, or change the ideas they find on the requirements sheets. They can even come up with totally new solutions that no one thought of before the break!

What's the difference between an idea and a concept? You can't draw a clear line of demarcation, but an idea usually can be expressed in a sentence. "We could hide the speakers inside dog statues!" A concept fills out the idea and provides more information. Often, a concept is based on several ideas. A concept should include a description of the customer needs addressed and a suggestion of "how" — what technology would it use, for instance.

After the team members have created a number of concepts, have each concept author share her concept with the group and post it on a flip chart page or on the wall. All told, you want about eight to ten concepts to work with. If you have more, and you probably will, team members can vote for the ones they feel are strongest and then make those even stronger by cherry-picking from the others.

To improve your team's beginning concepts, you can use a process based on Pugh Concept Selection. We talk about using this process to select concepts in Chapter 6, but we've also gotten great results by utilizing it early in the development process when you want to strengthen concepts rather than select them. Here are the basics:

1. **Create a matrix with the concepts along the top (X-axis) and the requirements down the side (Y-axis).**

2. **Give each concept a name or number at the top of the matrix; leave the concept sheets posted so team members can refer to them.**

3. **Fill in each square of the matrix with a code.**

   For example, a concept that fulfills a requirement well can get a 3 in that box; if the concept fills the requirement just so-so, it can get a 2; and if the concept does a poor job of fulfilling a requirement, it can get a 1.

   The facilitator can get the team through this process by calling out the concept, asking the team members to rank it against each of the requirements, and then filling in the squares.

4. **Strengthen each of the concepts by stealing bits and pieces from other concepts.**

   Because the concepts started from specific customer requirements, they hit that nail on the head. And because you have the chance to combine and strengthen, several of the concepts can end up doing a good job of meeting all or at least most of the requirements.

In Chapter 6, you find out how to select the best product concepts — the ones that will pass through the Idea Screen and into the river of development (see the Cheat Sheet for more on the river).

# Dipping into Your Bag of Tricks to Make Creative Sessions Even More Creative

In this chapter, we've described plenty of activities you can conduct to come up with ideas and concepts for new products. But we couldn't resist adding a few more! After all, this chapter is about being creative, and there's no limit to the things a creative mind can do.

In this section, we explain how you can bring in experts from outside the company to expand the team's appreciation of market and technology issues. We also describe some ways that creative teams can use their artistic propensities in the service of coming up with the next, best ideas.

## Bring in the experts!

Information about technology and market trends — information that can come from experts inside or outside your company — can really help your team think outside the company "box." What new technologies are being developed in industries that impact yours? What are the latest market trends that could affect your customers? For example, has someone developed a new way of delivering oxygen that may impact the medical devices you can develop? Are farmers beginning to use a different line of plowing equipment? How are young professionals dressing these days?

To answer these questions, you can bring in experts in various fields for day-long sessions with your creative team. In this section, we describe how you can collect information that you can bring right into the creative session and post on the wall for teams and experts to work with.

### Creating the session focus statement

For your informational sessions, which should run at least one day (and preferably two), you need clear focus statements to start the days (and to prepare your speakers; see the following section). The problem statement specifies both the customers whom you want to create product ideas for and what issues most interest you. Here are a few examples, each of which might be the focus of a different session:

> "We want to learn about ways people are meeting the needs of parents who want to give their children healthy food. We're particularly interested in the issues of obesity and 'eating on the run.'"

> "Where are the principal markets for healthy foods for kids? Who are the players in these markets? What are the regulatory issues? What are the key cultural factors? How are these factors changing, and what changes/trends should we anticipate?"

> "What are the new process and product technologies that address healthy eating? We're particularly interested in what scientists are learning about trans fats and other ingredients; what the implications are for products in terms of packaging, texture, flavor, and so on; and what new technologies may be on the horizon."

### Inviting the experts

After you've framed your questions, do some research — with people in your company and on the Internet — to identify who the experts are. You want them to visit you to answer your questions — that is, to deliver the wealth of wisdom they have on the topic you're interested in. Often, cold-calls to these experts can secure a visit commitment. If not, use the cold-calls to ask the known experts who they can recommend for an invitation.

It's perfectly appropriate to offer to pay expenses and an honorarium. However, you don't need to pay top price to an expert. If someone is asking for what seems like an outrageously high fee, find a more junior person who may know just as much, will be flattered to be invited, and will likely command a much lower fee.

The agenda for the informational session should include no more than three or four expert speakers and allow plenty of time for questions and discussions. If your speakers can stay for the whole day, they can enrich the discussion with their questions and observations of others' input.

Diversity is important in your selection of experts. You want to hear from people with different points of view. For example, if you want to think of new solutions for customers who drill oil, you want to hear about global warming and the future of energy from someone who's focused on sustainability and renewable energy sources. And you want to hear from someone else who thinks that the solution lies in exploration and production. Try to find out as much as you can about the opinions and points of view that exist in the market.

Bringing in outside experts is great, but don't overlook experts in your own company who can offer a lot of information that the team may be unaware of. There are often "pockets" of expertise in companies — world-class knowledge that rarely gets out to the rest of the folks in the companies.

Having in-house experts at the information session presents two advantages:

- ✔ It helps with confidentiality and the protection of intellectual property (see Chapter 15).
- ✔ Any applicable market knowledge or technology is more easily available if you find later that you want to access it to develop products.

For these reasons, you may think that it's best to invite only internal experts. However, you want to get a broad view of the markets and of emerging technologies — one that isn't limited to what your company already knows. Therefore, be sure to include folks from "away," too, as they put it in the South.

Use the problem statement you drafted for the team (see the section "Creating the session focus statement") to help your invited guests prepare. Ask them to be ready to talk for about a half-hour each, with another half-hour of Q&A. Ask the guests to prepare PDF documents or slides that they're willing to leave with the team for later review.

Here are some additional questions you can present to help the experts prepare:

- ✔ What's the current picture (of the technology or of the market)?
- ✔ What do you see developing or changing in the next six months? Two years? Ten years?
- ✔ What opportunities or threats do you see as a result of current conditions and future changes?

### Organizing the session output

The output of the expert session should be a number insights that relate to the problem area you want to solve for customers. Use the brainstorming process to collect the team's insights and narrow them down. If the team creates storyboards to depict what they've learned, these storyboards can be brought into the room and used as a focus for brainstorming during the creative session. (See the next section for tips on how to create and use storyboards.)

Schedule this session for the next day, which leaves the team free to invite out-of-town speakers to join them for dinner.

Have the team prepare to collect insights as the session goes along by writing their thoughts on sticky notes.

# Enlisting the team's artistic right brain in the creative process

Creative idea generation sessions draw more on a participant's right brain than the left. Your right brain is the more intuitive part that sees things in pictures and that makes nonlinear connections. It leaps to conclusions from scant bits of data; that can be bad in some situations, but when you're being creative, it's all good.

Plan your idea generation session to include some right-brain activities, and have a few in reserve in case you find the energy lagging. A good facilitator can sense when the creative team needs more fuel and will depart from the set agenda to include "playtime."

The tools we describe in this section give your team members a chance to do the right-brained activities usually reserved for artists and kids: drawing, model building, and acting. Each of the activities takes about an hour from start to finish.

Right-brained activities bring a spirit of play into the creative sessions. They can help the team lift its sights to a longer-term vision instead of staying too focused on today. They gather information in a form that can short-circuit the rational, skeptical left brain. But don't worry — the left brain gets to do plenty in new product development. Chapters 6 and 8, in particular, explain how to narrow down, judge, and apply criteria — to look before you leap, in other words.

## Storyboards and skits bring the customer experience home

Storyboards and skits are particularly useful tools to insert the customer experience right into the creative session — and right into the team members' emotional centers. These tools require that your team get creative — artistically creative. We're always surprised and pleased to see how quickly people who've never drawn, painted, or acted get into these activities.

### Storyboards tell a story

We've used storyboarding in creative sessions to help teams understand the customer experience, to represent insights into markets and technologies, and in other ways to condense information and make it readily accessible to the teams. Storyboarding was developed at the Walt Disney Studios in the early 1930s. A filmmaker uses a sequence of storyboards to describe how the film's action will progress. Because each storyboard depicts a specific event, we recommend that you use single storyboards to show what's going on in the lives of customers or in the world of technology and/or the market.

Here's how to construct a storyboard:

1. **Hold an information-gathering session, such as an expert session (see the section "Bring in the experts!") or a program of customer visits (see Chapter 4).**

2. **Identify key themes or insights from the session.**

3. **Pair off your team members, and have each pair choose a theme or insight that they want to work on.**

4. **Have each pair create a poster-sized storyboard that captures the insight in pictures and words.**

   The more the pairs think like Disney cartoonists, the more interesting and useful their storyboards will be.

5. **Halfway through the storyboarding session, bring the groups together to share what they've done so far.**

   Encourage feedback from all the pairs. The team members should let each other know what they see, feel, and understand when they look at the storyboards; they also should ask questions about anything that's unclear and offer suggestions for how to make the storyboards more interesting.

6. **Have the pairs go back to complete their storyboards.**

   Make sure each pair is clear that their storyboard has to stand on its own. If something on the storyboard requires explanation, the team members have to figure out a way to make it self-explanatory to people at the creative session.

If your product is a service, storyboarding can help to bring the steps in the service alive. For example, storyboards might show a customer arriving at the hotel, registering for a room, checking in, and ordering a meal from room service. These storyboards can be constructed before a session to show where the issues are, and/or after a session to show how solutions delight the customers and meet their needs.

Here are the materials you'll need for a storyboarding session:

- ✔ Large sheets of paper that can sit on a flip chart stand or stay taped to the wall. Each pair should have several sheets.

- ✔ A variety of markers in different sizes and colors.

- ✔ Access to the Internet, a printer if possible, and old magazines or other sources of pictures and photographs.

- ✔ Glue, scissors, a ruler, and maybe a compass for drawing circles (remember elementary school?).

The best storyboards combine words with pictures. Team members should use drawings or photographs to illustrate their storyboards. Sometimes, flow charts illustrated with cartoon characters can get ideas across well. And in this digital age, you can easily download a photo or find some clip art online if you don't have the right photo or drawing handy.

### Skits bring customers right into the room

You can turn your creative team members into thespians in order to carry out skits. Seriously, can you picture a group of marketers, engineers, manufacturers, executives, financial experts, and purchasing agents willingly playing roles and acting out scenes in their customers' lives? We couldn't either, but after we tried it a couple of times, we realized that we're all hams under the surface, and we all love stepping into other worlds and acting out.

When people act out a situation, they learn about it. They discover issues they never knew existed. They get "under the skin" to relate to the joys and frustrations of customers. And when they go back to generating ideas, they do so with a considerable increase in empathy and understanding, along with a much fuller appreciation of what product developers call "latent needs."

To do skits as part of or in preparation for a creative session, you need good customer information. You can use the information you gather during customer visits (see Chapter 4). You can use the customer descriptions that you gathered into customer sketches (refer to the section "Using Your Knowledge of the Customer to Inspire Solutions," earlier in the chapter). Perhaps some people from your sales or marketing department could help prepare the scenarios.

The facilitator or small session group that organizes the creativity session needs to plan the skits and activities very carefully. You should allocate time for the skits on the agenda and be clear about the purpose of the skits. For example, the facilitator could say to the creative team: "We're going to do several skits in order to get deeper into the customer experience. After each skit, we'll brainstorm ideas that would be appropriate solutions for the customers in the skit situation."

The facilitator(s) reviews the customer information and chooses several situations and key customers to design the skits around. Plan for a range of topics. For example, for a farmer who needs to repair his own farm equipment, you could present a difficult problem or breakdown, a situation in which the farmer is successful in solving the problem, and a situation that shows a pretty typical event in his life. The characters could be the farmer, the hired hand, the farmer's son, the neighbor, and the repairmen who will be out of a job after you develop all these great solutions!

For each skit, you need to write a plot. This process actually is pretty simple. Each skit needs a beginning, a middle, and an end. You let your actors know what's happening, what issue or crisis happens next, and how they resolve the issue. You don't need to tell the actors everything — part of the fun is how the actors respond to what you prepare for them. However, you can't leave them with blank pieces of paper and give them writer's block, either.

Print the play list (the list of characters) and the plot on a piece of paper. Use at least 14-point font so that team members don't have to scurry for their glasses. As you assign the skits, hand one sheet to each of the groups.

You may want to add a few minutes to a session break, during which your actors can discuss their skits. They should feel free to develop the characters and the situation from their own knowledge of the customers. Instruct them to use any materials in the room to set up their scene, props, and costumes. You may see your room transformed into a ranch, a living room, or the interior of a car dealership or factory.

You can do all the prepared skits at once, or you can space them as energy boosters when needed — for instance, after the team has eaten a bit too much lunch! Each skit should last only about three to five minutes. After each skit, give the actors a hearty round of applause and then hold a brainstorming session so that the team can capture any new ideas inspired by the skit.

We suggest preparing three skits. A group often can't get into just one or two. If you assign more than three, the team may start to get bored. And with three, you usually can give each member a role so that no one feels left out.

### Building a rough concept model

Building a rough model of an idea or concept helps to flesh out the idea and can help the team see new ways to improve it. We're not talking about prototyping here; we're talking about using bits and pieces of "stuff" to create a first rough model of the idea or concept (for information on prototyping, see Chapters 9, 14, and 17). Drawings of ideas are great, too, but the three-dimensionality and the humor in people's models provide both serious and light input to the process.

Chris Miller, the founder of Innovation Focus and a past PDMA president, is one of the "deans" of creative ideation in new product development. He carries cases of pipecleaners with him wherever he goes. Give your team members some pipecleaners and see what they can come up with!

Even better, give your team several tables full of various materials that team members can fashion into different scenes and models. Co-author Beebe collects assortments of "useless stuff." She buys paper cups, pipe cleaners, and toothpicks. She also visits the Children's Museum in Boston to buy recycled "stuff." Craft stores are great sources of "stuff." Pasta makes for a great building material. Beebe once brought dried peat pots to a session, and the teams found plenty of ways to use them. We find that the less the "stuff" resembles anything complete, the more fun teams can have building their models — and doing so creatively.

When collecting your "stuff," be sure to include the following items:

- ✔ Material that can form the base of a completed model — pieces of cardboard, for example
- ✔ Material that will make other objects stick together — glue works, as do toothpicks, paper clips, and tape
- ✔ Scissors

Divide the creative team into groups of three or four, and give each group a set of materials and a space to work in, as well as a set of clear instructions. For example, you can say, "Build your vision of the perfect product for fly-fishing," or "Build a model that shows your vision of how people will get to work in the future." Give the groups about ten minutes to work with the materials.

We suggest that you ask the groups not to talk while they're working on their models, and that they not write much, if anything, on their models. Talking and writing tend to push people to think and judge rather than react and create.

When time is up, give the groups a couple of minutes to talk about what they've done and to prepare to share their creations with the rest of the team. Have all the groups walk around the room to look at each other's creations; the groups should gather at each "station" to hear the creators of that model present their thoughts and motivations behind the model.

After all models have been shared, you can run a brainstorming session to create ideas that the activity may have inspired.

Even if you don't have time in your creative session to do the full model exercise, it's beneficial to have the materials and the models in the room to create an atmosphere of playfullness and fun. People enjoy holding, manipulating, and creating with the materials, even if you don't tell them to do so. Crayons are a particular favorite to bring out the child in adults! And pipe cleaners provide an easy way for people to build 3-D models quietly and without mess.

# Chapter 6

# Picking Winners and Losing Losers

*I*magine a small company that's known for being innovative. It has enough product development resources to work on only one major initiative at a time. The company puts all its energies into developing and launching a single new product.

After the company launches each product, the CEO suggests another project he has in mind, and his employees all go to work on the new initiative. Sometimes his ideas fail, and the company has to return to square one. The CEO starts to get frustrated because his employees aren't helping to come up with new ideas. He decides to send out teams to visit customers (see Chapter 4) and to run idea generation sessions (see Chapter 5). The teams come up with plenty of ideas for products, and the company puts each idea through an Idea Screen. Some of the ideas look like great opportunities, some look so-so, and some appear to be losers.

Take a look at the Cheat Sheet at the front of the book to understand how the strategies implemented by the CEO have changed the company's approach to developing new products. Now it can choose from many different options in the ocean of opportunity. It can balance its product delivery pipeline. At any one time, the company's river of development has large and small projects, risky and safe ones, and projects that address gaps in the company's product lines. The product developers are able to make the best use of the company's resources and maintain a clear vision of what the next big initiative will be.

We hope that as you explore the ocean of opportunities out there, you discover too many ideas for products that you want your company to develop. If you have too many opportunities, you can be picky about what goes into your product development pipeline. If you don't have a good supply of ideas, you may have to put so-so projects into the development funnel just to keep your product developers busy. In this chapter, we show you how to put the ideas you come up with through an Idea Screen so you end up with the best product development options.

The amount of money you spend and the resources required during the screening process are minimal. However, the further an idea travels down the river of development, the more resources it requires. It's important to weed out the weak ideas and to cancel weak projects, or projects that don't fit your company's strategy, before you spend too much on them.

# Screening Your Ideas and Developing New Concepts

We hope you come up with plenty of ideas for products. We also hope that many of your ideas are cockeyed or impossible, or incompatible with your business. No, we're not being sadists. What we're saying is that when you come up with ideas, you should be creative and open-minded. If you try to get it right the first time, you'll get it wrong — that is, you'll stay too close to home and be too conservative. When you brainstorm with an open mind, you give your company a chance to come up with a great idea that changes your industry, your business, or the way your customers do their jobs. (Take a look at Chapter 5 to find out more about being creative and open-minded when brainstorming ideas for new products.)

After you've come up with bunches of ideas, you have to screen all these ideas and pick a small handful to pass on to the executive team, whose job it is to make the decisions about which new projects to fund. You want to make the executives' jobs easier by screening the ideas, turning the best ideas into concepts, and giving the executives the ones that look the most promising. (For more information about how NPD decisions get made, head to the chapters in Part III — Chapters 9, 11, and 12 in particular.)

In the following sections, we explain how to screen your initial ideas, using an Idea Form to help identify the best ones. We then show you how portfolio views of these ideas can help you select a varied group of the most promising ideas to turn into Concept Briefs. The Concept Briefs give decision makers enough information to decide which concepts should be passed into the river of development.

It works best when the team that comes up with the ideas sticks with them through the Idea Screen. The people on the team are familiar with the ideas, so they can do a good job of describing their strengths and weaknesses. Adding a few others to make sure you have diversity of experience and points of view is also a good idea. Also, when the team stays with its own ideas, the ideas are less likely to get lost in the shuffle. Many companies have plenty of ideas floating around with no champions to support them and no processes (or, at best, haphazard ones) for getting them in front of executives.

The more consistent your decision-making format, the better your company's decisions will be. It's a small but important task to develop a "language" for coding information. For example, your company can create similar portfolio maps for every portfolio exercise, and you can use the same forms for logging ideas and concepts. When you're consistent, you don't have to try to figure out how to compare the results of one idea generation session with another. The comparison is obvious because all the teams use the same formats.

## Narrowing the field with an Idea Screen

After each idea-generation session that your company conducts, or whenever you collect a number of ideas for new products, you can hold an idea screening session so that your company can focus on the most important ideas. We often include the screening process we describe here as part of the schedule for generating ideas. That way, a team can review its ideas while they're still fresh in their minds, and its members can be sure that the job won't get pushed aside and left undone.

An *Idea Screen* consists of three steps:

1. **Describe the ideas.**
2. **Select the winning ideas.**
3. **Create an idea portfolio to display the winning ideas.**

After completing these three steps, an NPD team will select several of the ideas and write up Concept Briefs for them. You could call that the fourth step of the Idea Screen.

## Riding through Harley-Davidson's Wall of Fire

Harley-Davidson, the premier U.S. manufacturer of motorcycles, calls the ocean of product development opportunities "The Swirl," and it calls its Idea Screen "The Wall of Fire." You can guess that product ideas don't pass easily into the development pipeline at Harley!

### Step 1: Describe the ideas

For the first step of the process, the team meets to log the ideas and get a rough idea of which ones should be carried forward. Here are the steps:

1. **Divide the ideas among the team members.**
2. **Distribute and fill out one Idea Form per idea.**
3. **Post the completed Idea Forms on the meeting room walls.**
4. **Give each team member a chance to read through all the Idea Forms.**

The completed Idea Form provides a record of the idea that your company can use in making the next decisions about what to do with it. Figure 6-1 shows a completed Idea Form. Team members included enough information so that the people who weren't in on the idea generation and screening sessions could understand the ideas.

The Idea Form should be simple. Don't ask for too much detail at this stage in the development process because, honestly, you don't know very much yet, and you don't want to spend a lot of time and effort researching ideas that may not make it to the next stage. Don't kill off your ideas with too much formality, and don't ask for precision that goes beyond the data you already have or can gather easily.

We recommend that you keep all these forms on file. You may want to go back to an idea that didn't seem so great at one time and rework it into a compelling concept. Maybe your group had an idea that was before its time — the technology wasn't available, or the world wasn't ready yet, for instance.

### Step 2: Select the best ideas

The second step is to ask the team members to "vote" for the ideas they think the company should investigate further. Members vote by placing a check mark or a dot on the Idea Forms they like.

Remind team members to vote for ideas that they think will appeal to customers (even customers who may not yet be part of the company's market) and that are technically feasible. Remind them that it's okay if an idea doesn't fit with the company's existing business as long as they think that someone could develop the idea into a successful product.

You don't want to use rigorous criteria at this point. It's sufficient to get rid of some of the weaker ideas that the team came up with. Wait until you have a chance to review all the ideas together — during the portfolio step — before eliminating too many of them. Some ideas will drop out because no one will vote for them. For example, in a recent session of ours, someone had the idea of sending all the garbage to the moon. No one voted to carry that idea forward! Some ideas, on the other hand, will be obvious "winners" and will get plenty of votes.

## Idea Form

**Code Name:** _____  **Date:** _Feb. 27_____

*Don't Make a Move Without Us!*

**What is the idea?** _Service for people selling their houses/condos to help_ them put the house in the right condition to attract the highest price and sell in the shortest time.

**How would the idea work?** _We would work with individuals and/or real_ estate agents to do all the things we know make houses/condos more attractive to buyers: white walls, spacious rooms, well-placed/bright furniture, and so on. More than a cleaning service, we provide our RE expertise...

**Is there a compelling customer need?** _Sellers don't know what to do,_ and they want to sell at high price quickly. RE agents know what to do, but they don't have the resources.

**Is there a compelling technology story?** _Our company would create a_ partnership with cleaning services in different locations. Need to develop special knowledge of preference in different geographical areas. Fits with company's overall focus on the changing RE industry.

Please use the other side of this sheet to provide more information, including pictures, to tell us more about the idea.

**Figure 6-1:**
The Idea Form collects basic, important information for each new idea.

After voting, the team should discuss the "maybes." This discussion will help clarify the ideas and identify their strengths and weaknesses. After this discussion, the team may decide to drop out some more of the ideas.

We recommend that the team retain any idea that any team member strongly favors. Hunches often turn into the best concepts.

### Step 3: Create an idea portfolio to display the winning ideas

After you review all the available ideas and eliminate the ones that don't look promising, you can create an idea portfolio with your team. An *idea portfolio* shows how the ideas you've selected fit with different criteria that are important to the company.

The collection of new products that the company plans to develop should represent a diversity of size, risk, market focus, product line, and so on. Without the portfolio view, decision makers are likely to settle for a more limited range of projects. For example, they may choose all sure bets or all products that focus on markets with which they're familiar. The idea portfolio shows the decision makers at a glance how the ideas range across several important dimensions.

To create an idea portfolio, follow these steps:

1. **List several portfolio criteria.** Portfolio criteria relate to your company's overall product strategy. Here are some criteria that companies often use:

   • **Market:** New markets versus existing markets

   • **Technology:** New technologies versus existing technologies

   • **Product type:** Incremental improvements versus product platforms versus unique/radical projects

2. **Tape a large sheet of paper on the wall and draw the portfolio dimensions. (See Figure 6-2 for an example.)**

3. **Ask team members to write each idea that passed the Idea Screen (see the previous section) on a sticky note.**

4. **Paste each note onto the appropriate position on the portfolio.**

The ideas also may fall into other categories — for instance, which product lines or businesses they belong to or which markets they serve. Team members might use different color ink or different color sticky notes to represent other categories.

Figure 6-2 shows a sample idea portfolio.

## A Portfolio of New Product Ideas

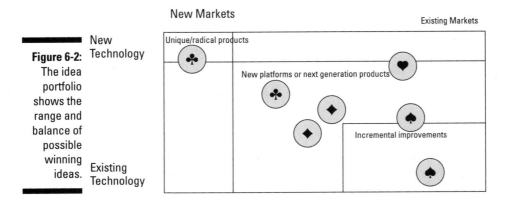

**Figure 6-2:** The idea portfolio shows the range and balance of possible winning ideas.

The team that created this portfolio used market and technology newness to form the dimensions. They indicate product types — improvements, platforms, and so on — by the placement of each idea: The lower-right corner represents product improvements, the middle includes next-generation products and platforms, and the upper-left corner shows unique or radical products.

In this map, the team used different card suits to indicate different product lines the ideas related to. Two of the ideas will improve the "spade" product line; the team has come up with a new technology to serve an existing "heart" market; and they've got two ideas to make some fairly radical extensions to the "diamond" product line. Looks like they've also come up with a whole new line, "clubs," which includes a platform idea and an idea for a radical new technology.

*Note:* A "real" idea portfolio would include many more ideas; Figure 6-2 looks more like the portfolio you might end up with after the team has selected a few of the ideas to turn into concepts (see next section).

## *Turning winning ideas into concepts*

With your team's idea portfolio on hand to refer to, your next job is to select a handful of ideas that the team will turn into concepts for your executives to review. Usually, a team chooses a range of ideas, from incremental to platform to radical. Your team should also take into account any other dimensions that add diversity to the ideas they choose — for example, which market the idea relates to or which product line it would be a part of. A simple process for making these decisions is to ask the team members to vote for ones they want to keep. Usually, a handful are obvious keepers and a handful are obvious losers. The team can debate the others and come to a final tally.

If any one team member feels strongly about keeping an idea, keep it. She may be seeing something the rest of the team just can't see.

Now you're ready to write up Concept Briefs for the winning ideas. A *Concept Brief* has more information than the Idea Forms you use to do the initial screening. It provides estimates and descriptions of many factors, including

- ✔ Market opportunity
- ✔ Technology
- ✔ Financial cost and return

The information in a Concept Brief gives decision makers a way to judge whether a concept is worth spending scarce resources on. Your team should meet to fill out the briefs for the ideas you've chosen. You can complete some of the briefs on the spot, but some may require homework.

See Figure 6-3 and the following list for guidance in creating your own Concept Briefs. The figure gives an example of a Concept Brief in outline form, and the list presents the main topics of the brief.

### Concept Brief

Concept name:                                              Date:

Concept #:

Team Leader:

1. Opportunity Definition and Value Proposition
    1.1    Product or Product Idea
    1.2    Value Proposition

2. Opportunity Assessment
    2.1    Brief Overview of Market Opportunity
    *(Estimated market size and growth)*
    2.2    Competition/Alternative Products

3. Market Overview
    3.1    Target Customers and Users
    3.2    Customer Needs Identified

**Figure 6-3:** 4. Technology Overview
A Concept      4.1    Fit with Available Technology
Brief logs     4.2    Assessment of Technology Hurdles
information     4.3    Assessment of Technology Risk
for "apples
to apples"  5. Strategic Fit
decisions.     5.1    Fit with Company's Strategic Business Objectives
               5.2    Fit with Product Portfolio and with Existing Product Lines
                      *Attach portfolio and product line charts if available.*

✔ **Opportunity Definition and Value Proposition:** Begin by giving a brief description of the concept and explain why it represents an opportunity for the company. You'll go into more detail later on; here, you just want to provide an overview. For example, a team working on wireless communications could say, "To develop a cellphone that meets customer needs for fewer dropped calls. This product would enhance product line X and serve a growing market of XX million cellphone users worldwide." You can also include important *limiting conditions* — for example, "This product must be introduced by Q4 2007 to beat competitor entries into the market."

The *Value Proposition* is a short statement that explains what value the concept will deliver, both to customers and to the company. The proposition answers the following questions:

- "Why would customers find this product attractive enough to purchase it?"

- "How can the company develop, produce, and market this product in a way that aligns with its innovation strategy and provides an attractive return on the investment?"

A clearly written Value Proposition serves as a beacon for the team as it moves into the actual work of developing the product.

✔ **Opportunity Assessment:** You should describe the market opportunity the concept affords. The assessment should include your estimate of the market size, the predicted market growth, and the opportunity to take share or further penetrate the market. You also can indicate the existence of competitive products and assess how the concept will be able to compete against them.

✔ **Market Overview:** Answer the following questions:

- What identified customer needs will this product satisfy (see Chapter 4)?

- Who are the expected customers for this concept?

✔ **Technology Overview:** Answer the following questions:

- Can the concept be developed with currently available technology?

- What's the extent of technology development needed?

- What are the potential technology hurdles and technology risks?

✔ **Strategic Fit:** How will the concept contribute to meeting the company's strategic business objectives (see Chapter 3)? Here, you describe the concept's fit with the following:

- Product lines

- Brand strategy

- Growth objectives

- Any other dimensions of your company's strategic objectives

# Improving Your Concepts with Quality Function Deployment

You have one more trick up your team's sleeve that you can use to improve a concept and narrow the field for the decision makers at your company. The technique is called *Quality Function Deployment,* or QFD. Stuart Pugh came up with the specific process we use here.

QFD is a term that refers to the practice of using a matrix to match customer needs with concept functionality. It comes out of the quality movement, or Total Quality Management (TQM). This may sound confusing, but the process can be quite useful. We'll give you the nuggets from the alphabet soup!

The following list explains how you can use QFD, and Pugh's process in particular, to improve your concepts before submitting them to decision makers:

1. **Set aside a day or more to do this work.**

2. **Set up the meeting room with your teamwork supplies: large wall charts, a ruler for drawing, sticky notes, felt-tip pens, and tape.**

3. **Select groups of concepts that focus on similar customer needs (see Section 3 of the Concept Brief in Figure 6-3).**

4. **Make a two-dimensional matrix and draw in the columns and rows.**

   You'll write the customer requirements along the Y-axis (the vertical line on the left side), assigning one requirement per row, and then put the concepts along the X-axis, assigning one concept per column.

   You can use a catchy name, a cartoon or sketch, or any other moniker to help your team remember which concept you're working with. Just don't use more than ten or so requirements, and focus on fewer than eight concepts.

5. **In the first column of the matrix, enter a concept or product that already exists in the market and does a pretty good job of meeting this set of customer requirements.**

   The product may be yours, or it may be a competitor's. This concept will be your point of reference.

6. **Choose symbols that represent "better," "worse," and "same."**

   The numbers 1, 2, and 3 will do, but you can use more meaningful symbols, such as smiley, frown, and neutral faces. These are more fun and help keep the team interested.

7. **Fill in each of the squares (formed by the rows and columns) with a symbol that shows whether the concept does a better, worse, or similar job as the reference concept with regard to the customer requirement in the row.**

   Hold an open discussion to come up with the team's consensus on each of the judgments. Make note of any disagreements and other potentially useful information that comes up during the discussion.

   Now you have a completed matrix that shows how well, in your team's judgment, each concept meets each of the customer requirements. Now's the time to improve the concepts.

8. **Strengthen each concept by stealing bits and pieces from other concepts.**

   For example, if Concept A meets five requirements well and looks like a winner, can you make it even better by creating a hybrid A/D Concept? Can you blend in a bit of E and G?

9. **Select the best concepts.**

   You'll need to write up new Concept Briefs for the hybrid, improved concepts. Now you have a smaller number of better concepts to pass along to your executives.

We think you'll be very pleased at how much you can improve your concepts with QFD. As a bonus, you also can eliminate some concepts that you thought were okay. With this work, you set up your executives to make even better choices about what will go into your company's product development pipeline.

# Turning Losing Concepts into Assets

Just because an idea for a new product project gets dropped onto the cutting room floor doesn't mean that it has *no* value. A good idea may not work for your company because you don't have the technology capability. Or perhaps the project seems risky, and your organization already has too much invested in risk and not enough in sure bets. In other cases, a good idea may not fit your company's *business model* — the way it goes about making money (see Chapters 3 and 12).

Before you dump an idea, examine it to see whether it deserves some kind of special attention. Smart companies always look for ways to turn their rejected options into valuable assets. The following list presents some options you may explore:

✔ Some companies assign employees to look for ways to create value from technology developments that the organizations won't use. For example, if the company patents its technologies, it can sell or license them, and the company profits from the royalties.

✔ Some ideas are big and bold enough to warrant the creation of new business units if they don't fit existing business models. Questioning and expanding a company's business models is becoming more and more important in this age of open innovation (see Chapter 16).

✔ If your company can't pursue a promising opportunity within your existing business model, you may decide to allow employees to launch a new business with the idea as the focus.

✔ You can offer "losing" concepts on Web sites that allow inventors and companies to search for different patents, ideas, and technologies.

# A tip for entrepreneurs

You may have only two or three great ideas, but you may be able to develop only one or two. You should ask yourself, can I get needed funding by selling or licensing one or more of my good ideas? Larger companies may be anxious to acquire the technologies that they need. The trick is to understand the needs of larger companies (try visiting them — see Chapter 4) and to present your technology in a way that helps them connect your solution with their needs.

However, before you sell or license your ideas and technologies, be sure that you consider which concept could turn out to be valuable to you in the future. Don't be so excited to turn a profit that you give away next year's, or next decade's, blockbuster.

# Chapter 7

# Making the Most of Technology

........................................

## In This Chapter

▶ Learning the benefits of inventorying your technology

▶ Familiarizing yourself with the tools of inventorying

▶ Relating technology to products and markets

▶ Forming a technology agenda

........................................

*T*echnology, broadly defined, is what enables companies to develop products that meet customer needs. The technology in your company includes the output of research and scientific development, as well as the process and manufacturing knowledge that helps you produce products and develop services for your customers. More and more in today's business world, partners and suppliers also provide the technology that product developers need. Technology is important insofar as it helps your organization to be successful in the business you're in.

In this chapter, we show you how to inventory your organization's technology capabilities. With this inventory, you can accomplish a number of things:

✔ You can link technology to products that you want to develop and to the market needs that you've identified (see Chapter 4) so that your technology contributes to your organization's success.

✔ You can identify what technology you'll need for products and markets in the future so that your technology development has a strategic focus.

✔ You can decide what you don't have to develop within your company so that you can take advantage of partners and suppliers (see Chapters 15 and 16).

 Rich Albright and co-author Beebe Nelson developed most of the examples we use in this chapter for their chapter on technology mapping in the *PDMA ToolBook2* (Wiley). Take a look at that chapter if you want to get deeper into this topic.

# Recognizing the Importance of Inventorying Your Technology

"You know what keeps me up at night?" asked the Chief Technical Officer (CTO) of a successful mid-size company. "Wondering if the problem that one guy is working on could be solved by something the guy on the next bench has already done." Even in small companies, it isn't uncommon for executives and managers to be unsure of their organizations' technology capabilities.

If, as an organization, you've never sat down to make a list of your technology capabilities, we're willing to bet that your decision makers and tech specialists don't know the full scope. One person understands how fans work, another in another area of the company is an expert in wiring, and a third has world-class expertise in plastic molding. What might these specialists be able to do if they could talk to each other? You won't know if you separate them with the walls of culture, habit, workload, and functional orientation.

When knowledge of technology capabilities is fragmented, it stays within small groups of people or even in individuals' heads. Your organization can miss opportunities to develop new products. Even worse, the people with the knowledge can walk out the door and into the arms of your competitors.

So, if sharing technology knowledge within a company is so important, why don't all companies inventory their technology capabilities? Here are a couple reasons:

- **It never occurred to them.** When people are doing their jobs and no one sees any obvious breakdowns, companies don't realize that something may be missing.

- **They don't think they need to.** If employees have the know-how, the jobs get done. You have to exert extra effort to get them to share their knowledge, and many people believe they're too busy to do that.

To help you get motivated to inventory your technology, here are several reasons why you should make this activity a priority:

- You may already have a solution you've been searching for — a solution that would allow you to get a great new product to market in half the time you thought it would take.

- You may lose tacit knowledge — knowledge that hasn't been widely shared — when employees retire or leave.

- You may have technology solutions you could turn into unexpected product advantages — for example, ways to make a product lighter or a way to cut packaging or manufacturing costs.

✔ You can plan strategically for technology development and focus your technology resources instead of being at the mercy of ad hoc and arbitrary decisions.

✔ You'll know what to develop inside your company and what you can partner on with outside sources (see Chapters 15 and 16).

Whether you share your technology capabilities with seven others in a start-up company, with several hundred associates, or with people across multiple business units in huge companies (such as 3M or Intel), making your capabilities more explicit will make them more useful. When you inventory your technology, the people in your company will be better able to communicate

✔ Among technical employees.

✔ Among technical employees and marketers.

✔ Among business units, managers, and executives.

✔ With partners and suppliers.

# Surveying Ways to Inventory Your Technology

Before taking inventory of your technology, you probably have more questions than an IRS investigator (which is what brings you to us!). What technology do you have? How does it connect to market and customer needs? How can you use it to develop new products or improve existing ones? How is the technology in your field evolving? What changes will make your technology obsolete or enable radical innovation? These are just some of the questions that you can address with a technology inventory. In this section, we show you two ways to inventory your technology: spider charts and technology roadmaps. Spider charts depict the gap between how good a product could or should be and how good your products and technologies are right now. Roadmaps add the explicit dimension of time. They show what technologies and products you can develop right now and what will be possible in the future.

The good news? Both ways of inventorying technology are simple to understand and implement. Executives, functional managers, and NPD teams can use them to record information, support decision-making, and communicate with each other. They include information from different functions — at a minimum, from both research and development (R&D) and marketing. In the process of building the charts and maps, members of different functions can question each other so that the information is accessible to people with different experiences and knowledge.

You'll use spider charts and technology roadmaps to create a visual record of today's technology inventory and your plans for tomorrow. The fact that the tools are visual — a picture or a map — means that you can see relationships between different elements and that several people can share the information, discuss it, question it, understand it, and use it to make decisions.

## Spider charts

A *spider chart* lets a company compare its product and technology features to its competitors' and to what its customers would like. Companies and teams use spider charts to document how well their technologies meet customer requirements.

Spider charts are also known as *figures of merit* or *radar charts,* but most people call them spider charts because they look like spider webs.

Follow these steps to build a spider chart:

1. **Assemble a group of technical and marketing employees and agree on important customer requirements.**

   Most spider charts depict eight requirements. Our spider chart in Figure 7-1 shows customer requirements for family cars: handling, fuel efficiency, performance, comfort, safety, durability, styling, and interior space.

   If the NPD team has conducted a customer visit project (see Chapter 4), it will know precisely what's important to customers — in the customers' own voice.

2. **Use the customer requirements to create and name the arms of the chart.**

   The dimensions of an arm represent the *figure of merit* — how good the customer requirement could get. The outside circle we've drawn shows the "theoretical limit" of the requirement. For example, the number of miles per gallon (fuel efficiency) could be set at 50 mpg — a quantitative representation. The "softer" requirements, such as comfort, should be defined with qualitative measures.

3. **Put a hash mark on each arm to show how well the industry's current products and technologies deliver on each of the customer requirements.**

   A hash mark placed close to the outside indicates that technology can deliver what the customers want; a hash mark placed closer to the center indicates that companies in the industry still have some way to go. Connect the hash marks — we've used a solid line and labeled it "Industry standard."

**Spider Chart in Automobile Industry:
Industry Standard versus Our New Product**

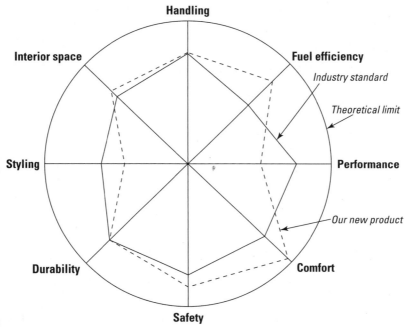

**Figure 7-1:**
A spider
chart
compares
customer
require-
ments and
technology
capability.

4. **Put another hash mark on each arm to show how well your technologies and products deliver against customer requirements, and connect these marks with another line.**

In the example, we use a dashed line to represent how well your company's technologies and products deliver against customer requirements. The gap between the dashed line (your products and technologies) and the solid line (the industry's standard products and technologies) shows what you need to do — and what you've done — to be competitive.

In our example in Figure 7-1, your company is beating industry standards for comfort. You're giving up a bit on performance. Safety and fuel efficiency are both better than the industry. Looks like a great family car!

You also can add hash marks and lines that show how well specific competitors can meet the customer requirements. This helps you to focus your technology efforts. For example, Ford may be much more interested in how well Chrysler is doing than in how well Toyota or BMW is doing.

---

## Watching technology evolve

Sometimes companies use spider charts over years and even decades to show how well they — or even entire industries — meet customer needs. Many years ago, the manufacturers of television sets knew that their customers wanted more brightness and contrast and sharper colors. The industry worked to improve these dimensions. Companies also knew that customers wanted flat screens. Manufacturers made incremental improvements from one year to the next, but it took a technology breakthrough for them to create the flat-screen TV that we know today. Spider charts provided the constant reminder that the industry hadn't yet accomplished all its goals.

---

When a company or industry makes a radical improvement, the dimensions of the spider chart change. For example, in the face of rising oil prices and competition from alternative technologies, automobile manufacturers had to come to the realization that what was acceptable gas mileage in the past no longer satisfied many of their customers. As customer expectations change, technology must try to meet the challenge and deliver what the customers want.

You have multiple formats in which you can create your spider chart. We like to start by drawing the chart on a large sheet of paper taped to a wall or displayed on a flip chart. This setup allows groups to work together as they construct the chart. To preserve the chart and communicate it in digital form, you also can try building it in Microsoft Excel.

## *Technology roadmaps*

*Technology roadmaps* allow your organization to identify the technology it has now and how that technology may evolve. It also provides a template for linking technology to products and markets. Unlike spider charts (see the previous section), technology roadmaps include an explicit time dimension.

You should have cross-functional teams build technology roadmaps (see Chapter 10 for more on cross-functional teams). The best maps include knowledge from different parts of the company. When cross-functional teams update the roadmaps over time, they turn them into repositories for a corporation's knowledge and a key element in strategic and tactical planning. Technology roadmaps are often used to make short-term, tactical decisions. The good thing is that they also provide the strategic context within which tactical decisions are made.

## General roadmapping steps

Your organization needs to take the following actions to make sure that your technology roadmapping efforts are successful:

- ✔ **Identify the projects, products, platforms, or technologies to roadmap.**

- ✔ **Secure management's support.** Management will both sponsor and review the team's work.

- ✔ **Assemble the cross-functional team who will build the map.** Select team members who have a diversity of experience as well as expertise with the roadmap topics.

- ✔ **Identify the roadmap owner.** Each roadmap should have a person designated as the "owner." He or she is the go-to person for questions, and is responsible for keeping an eye out for changes in technology or market and for scheduling reviews when the map needs to be updated (see Chapter 12 for more on reviews).

  The roadmap owner is usually an executive or director who has interest in and is committed to the team's work. The owner may participate on the team, or he or she may be a member of the management support group.

- ✔ **Schedule a series of sessions, with time between sessions for homework.** We find it works best to schedule four or five sessions, each one a week apart. Each session should have at least two uninterrupted hours. This schedule allows time for homework and reflection, but the project doesn't take too long. You want employees to be ready and willing to take on another project, so be reasonable with the time/work requirements.

- ✔ **Identify technology building blocks.** We describe a method for executing this step in the following section.

- ✔ **Draw the first map, placing the building blocks in a timeline.** See the section "Drafting your first roadmap" later in this chapter.

- ✔ **Review and revise the draft of your map.** Review the map with members of management to get their input. We recommend that you also share the map with customers, suppliers, and other stakeholders to get many types of opinions and input. Be sure to remove or disguise sensitive information when you share maps with outside people.

The more audiences you review your map with, the more information you can include. Also, when groups participate in map review, they develop a commitment to and agreement with the map, which encourages people to make use of it.

You've built a map, but your mapmaking job isn't over. Technology changes, markets change, and you always strive to uncover new information. A critical part of good technology mapmaking is to schedule regular review meetings to revise your maps and to call special meetings when unexpected changes occur.

### Mapping your technology building blocks

*Technology building blocks* are the technical capabilities that enable your company to develop and maintain products, and they're vital parts of the technology roadmap. For example, the technology building blocks of a chocolate manufacturer would include the know-how and processes that enable melting, mixing, forming, coloring, and flavoring, as well as packaging. Some of these building blocks would be unique to the individual candy company and give it its unique flavor, so to speak, and some would be common to the industry.

Here are the steps you follow to identify and map the technology building blocks you'll use to draft the technology roadmap. We illustrate each step with an example from the HVAC (heating, ventilating, and air conditioning) industry:

1. **Select the focus of your building-block map.**

   The team's job is to list and map the technology building blocks for its furnace and air conditioner platforms.

2. **List all the technologies and capabilities in the area you're studying.**

   In our example, we include fans, heaters, and coolers — the basic building blocks needed for the HVAC products.

3. **Assess any gaps in your collective knowledge and assign homework before the next meeting.**

   The HVAC team needed to do more research between meetings, so it divided into research pairs. The areas that needed the most work were user interface and software for each of the platforms, although the team had some questions in almost every area.

4. **At the team's next meeting, add any technologies and capabilities that turned up in the homework. Eliminate from consideration duplicates and technologies or capabilities that aren't relevant to the area you're working on, and be sure to clarify any questions that arise within the group.**

   Up to this point, you're bringing as much to the table as possible. Now you have to narrow down so that your map focuses on the area you're responsible for. The HVAC team found all sorts of neat stuff about user interface but decided to include only a bit of it. The members discussed some of the issues they uncovered in the area of fan technology and came to an agreement about which building blocks were most important in that area.

5. **Write the remaining technologies on sticky notes — one technology per note.**

   The HVAC team selected 30 technology building blocks that its members identified as core elements in this technology area.

6. **Group similar technologies and make a header for each technology group.**

   The team used the grouping that it had started out with and added a new category for software building blocks. You see it on the chart as "New Platform" (see Figure 7-2). The team believes that this new platform could provide a competitive edge for its products.

The categories a team starts out with are only first guesses. Sometimes, as a team explores a field of technology, its members come up with unexpected connections, and the groups look different from the ones the team started with.

Figure 7-2 shows a map of the HVAC technology building blocks. Each platform has similar icons — musical notes for Software, circles for Coolers, and so on — which shows that the platforms share similar building blocks. However, the mapping exercise also reveals that some of the platforms use building blocks that are associated with other platforms. The line that connects Fans with the first block in the Cooler platform is an example of this. The lines that connect the platforms with their building blocks suggest which technologies are currently key to those platforms.

**Technology Building Blocks**

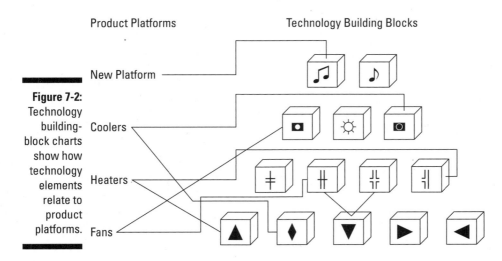

Figure 7-2:
Technology
building-
block charts
show how
technology
elements
relate to
product
platforms.

After you build the first chart, you can use it to build a technology roadmap. (***Note:*** The building block chart doesn't include a timeline; that enters the picture when you get to roadmapping.)

Some companies expand their building block charts to show which technologies are most important to fulfilling customer needs, which technologies they possess in-house, and which they plan to develop. In this way, a chart can lead to a technology action plan.

### Drafting your first roadmap

The technology building blocks are the ingredients you need to draft your first technology roadmap. In the following steps, we show you how the drafting works, and we illustrate the steps by looking at a roadmap of possible technologies for a car engine (shown in Figure 7-3).

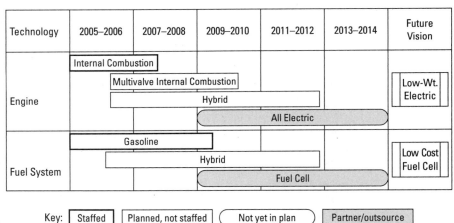

**Figure 7-3:** A technology roadmap that shows the technology evolution of the powertrain engine.

| Technology | 2005–2006 | 2007–2008 | 2009–2010 | 2011–2012 | 2013–2014 | Future Vision |
|---|---|---|---|---|---|---|
| Engine | Internal Combustion / Multivalve Internal Combustion / Hybrid / All Electric | | | | | Low-Wt. Electric |
| Fuel System | Gasoline / Hybrid / Fuel Cell | | | | | Low Cost Fuel Cell |

Key: Staffed | Planned, not staffed | Not yet in plan | Partner/outsource

Co-author Beebe Nelson and Richard Albright created this roadmap illustration for *The PDMA ToolBook2* (Wiley). In this fictitious example, the key driver for the planning effort is the engine manufacturer's concern over new fuel technologies. Senior management charged a team with coming up with technology plans to address the changing landscape.

To prepare for the first roadmap team meeting, hang a couple of pages of 2'-x-3' paper on the wall. You also need a ruler (if you're picky about straight lines), some felt-tip pens, and plenty of sticky notes.

1. **Decide on a time frame for your roadmap, and divide the map into columns that depict equal lengths of time.**

   You can use your ruler to make the columns equal. Technology roadmaps always include a time dimension, and time generally runs from left to right. In the engine map in Figure 7-3, you see dates written at the top that run from 2005 to 2014. The mapmakers have also left room for "Future Vision" — what may happen after 2014.

Be aware of your industry when you decide on a time frame. If you work with software or fashion products, your whole map may run less than five years; if your company develops new drugs, your map will have to include ten or more years.

**2. Divide your technology into subcategories.**

You can start with the technology building-block groupings you create (see the previous section).The engine team has divided the powertrain into two elements: the engine and the fuel system. The technology in both of these areas is related, but the division into subgroups allows the team to get a closer look at the technology the company needs for each.

**3. Put your existing and planned technology onto the map.**

A good place to start is with the building blocks. Adding the time frame in the map may lead you to eliminate or add elements.

You can indicate projects that are underway, planned projects, and projects that are possible but not yet planned. Use different shapes or colors to denote the different projects. In Figure 7-3, staffed projects have a heavy line, planned projects have a thinner line, and possible projects not yet in the company's plan have an oval.

A company may decide to outsource or partner on some of its technology. The team indicates this by shading in the bar for those projects. (You can find out more about outsourcing and partnering in Chapters 15 and 16.)

**4. For each technology project, draw a bar that shows how long you expect the project to take.**

Having a clear and explicit map in front of your team and the company's management makes real resource planning possible (see Chapter 11 for more on project resources). You must update the roadmap regularly because it's a map of the future and things will change. However, the map provides a basis for decision-making and accountability that can make a huge difference in your organization's ability to focus resources and accomplish the important projects.

### Reading and using roadmaps

The company that Figure 7-3 illustrates wants to develop technology that will allow the organization to respond to increasing pressure to reduce fuel consumption. What can you learn about the company's technology plans for accomplishing its goals from the roadmap in Figure 7-3? Until 2007, the company will focus its technology efforts on increasing the gas mileage of the internal combustion (IC) engine. Starting in 2006, the company plans to develop a more efficient IC engine, the "multivalve." At the same time, the company plans to develop its hybrid capabilities. It will continue to staff research and development of all gasoline technologies until 2009. The company plans to begin research into fuel-cell technology in 2009. The roadmap shows that the company plans to complete the work on the new multivalve IC engine in 2009. It doesn't expect work on the hybrid to be complete until 2012.

The company's technology roadmap provides management with an understanding of its resource needs now and in the future:

- ✔ Management has already staffed the work on IC development — you can tell that because the outline of the project is heavy.

- ✔ Both the projects starting in 2006 are planned but not yet staffed. These project outlines are thin.

- ✔ The projects to develop technology for an electric engine and for the fuel cell are unplanned. The shaded bar shows that when it comes time to include the projects in the company's plan, the company will be looking for a partner to develop the technology with. Because they have a map, they can start looking for the right one now!

Although the map in Figure 7-3 is in black and white, clever use of shapes and line thickness allows the company to show plenty of planning detail. You can use color to add even more. For instance, you could add information about staffing requirements for each project, as well as detail about the kind of partners the company wants to look for.

# Connecting Technology Capabilities to Products and Markets

Companies develop and acquire technology so that they can develop new products that will fulfill customer and market needs. They don't develop technology just for fun or to keep their R&D departments busy! Connecting technology planning to customer and market needs enables your company to decide just what technologies it needs.

When you embark on a technology research, start by asking yourself some key questions:

- ✔ What are the key drivers in your industry and in your markets?

- ✔ How do the drivers relate to your existing agenda for technology development (see the later section "Creating an agenda for technology development")?

- ✔ Should your technology development agenda look into the future, or is your research and development (R&D) focused only on short-term goals?

In this section, we look at how you can link your business and technology agendas and at the same time balance your focus on long- and short-term projects. The secret is to create maps that link your market and technology drivers in a time frame that's appropriate for your industry.

## Mapping the strategic geography

The *strategic geography* is a visual representation of the most important influencers or drivers in a particular market. Corning, Inc., a leader in effective innovation processes, uses a simple and effective approach called *event mapping* to chart the strategic geography. An event map provides a framework or context for technology mapmakers. For example, it guides the mapmakers to think of technologies that they otherwise may have overlooked.

Follow these steps to create an event map:

1. **Take a huge sheet of paper, divide it into rows and columns, and label the left side (the Y-axis) with trends.**

   For example, you could insert "market/customer/competition," "economic/social," "legal/regulatory," and "technology."

2. **Along the bottom of the paper (the X-axis), show the time from left to right — from a short time ago, to now, to the future.**

3. **Write down all the relevant drivers you can think of within the categories you've listed on sticky notes, and paste the notes in the appropriate spots.**

If you create an event map with a diverse group of people, different people can add their ideas and group members can question each other for elaboration. We recommend that you take a break of several days between sessions so that people can digest, reflect, and do some homework before you complete the map. Like technology roadmaps (see the earlier section "Technology roadmaps"), maps of strategic drivers are most valuable if you update them over time.

What would an event map look like for the food industry in the United States, for example? Here's a list of some of the shifts and changes in the food market:

✔ **Customer/market trends:**

   • Americans are both more obese and more health-conscious.

   • Americans often eat on the run.

   • We still believe in fad diets. Which one is it this month?

   • Consumers want convenience and health in the same product.

   • Global producers are entering the U.S. market at an increasing rate.

✔ **Social trends:**

- The list of ingredients considered either dangerous or desirable is growing.

- There's growing concern about how and where producers grow foods, leading to increased demand for organic and locally grown produce.

✔ **Legal/regulatory:** Federal regulations are making increasing demands on growers and producers to use safe ingredients and to label foods.

✔ **Technology trends:** Food packaging and processing are becoming more sophisticated.

What a bunch of contradictory drivers! One advantage of a sticky-note process (see Step 3 of the previous list) is that you can capture all the contradictions, each one on its own note. You don't have to resolve the contradictions. For example, have you noticed that many food companies produce both healthy and "sinful" brands of the same product types? When you're developing technologies, you may find solutions that address several of the issues, and sometimes you have to go with only one.

## *Mapping product/technology evolution*

Combining technology roadmaps (see the section "Technology roadmaps") with product line maps helps forge a link between your new product planning and your technology development plans.

You may think it's obvious that you should have technology ready when you need it to develop a new product, but you can easily get involved in the rush of developing a product without having a clear idea of the technology you need. You get there and say, "Oops, I guess now we have to invent something." That's a really bad way to go about introducing a new product into the market!

Creating a visual diagram of how technology will link to potential products in the market expedites your product development process. It also keeps your company from spending resources on technology projects that look interesting but don't clearly link with market/product opportunities. Another good thing about this kind of mapping is that it lets you see, at a glance, how your planning shapes up. Before you make a map of your plans, you may think that everything is just great. When you — and others — can see the planning process on a big sheet of paper, you can easily identify the gaps, the problems, and the opportunities.

In Chapter 3, we map product lines so a company can see where it may need new products or product improvements. We use that same mapping process here to link products and technologies. You place the products you intend to develop and introduce on a timeline and then add the technologies that you'll need in order to develop them. Figure 7-4 shows an example of such a map.

A product/technology map needs to be used, communicated, updated, and reviewed. If a team makes a map like the one in Figure 7-4 and then puts it in the closet, the team will just be wasting time and paper. These maps are made to be dynamic, not set in stone.

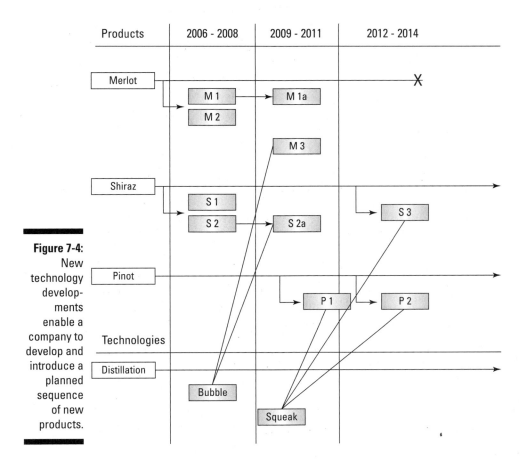

**Figure 7-4:** New technology developments enable a company to develop and introduce a planned sequence of new products.

The following list shows how the company in Figure 7-4 mapped the relationship between technology and products, as well as some interesting details about its product/technology planning:

✔ The map represents the product lines supported by two distillation technologies. We call them "Bubble" and "Squeak."

✔ The company decides to break its timeline into three-year chunks. **Note:** Every industry has its own timing and rhythms. Charlie Fine of MIT has referred to this as an industry's "clockspeed." Three-year chunks may work well for the industry featured in Figure 7-4 but not for faster or slower industries.

✔ The company's planning looks fairly balanced. The Squeak technology seems to focus on fairly significant improvements, including the introduction of a whole new product line.

✔ It looks like the company may phase out Merlot after 2012. Pinot, to be introduced in 2009, continues, as does Shiraz.

✔ The company links each of the technology projects to one or more planned products or platforms.

A platform allows a company to develop a number of different products, using the same technology or architecture (see Chapter 3 for more about platforms).

When companies are in the middle of developing new products and technologies, they can lose sight of the big picture. A product/technology map helps a company assess its agenda. Did the company from Figure 7-4 plan to abandon Merlot, or is that an oversight? Should its researchers be investigating new technologies, or are they comfortable with this rather conservative agenda?

# Developing or Finding the Necessary Technology

You need to be sure that the employees who develop new products in your company work on solutions that are important to your customers. You may have noticed that many of the products you buy have features and functions that you'll never use or that you don't know how to use. For example, we've never met anyone who actually uses all those buttons on a microwave oven. We're not sure anyone even knows what they're all for or how to use them.

Sometimes, product developers add features on purpose. It actually costs less to include all the stuff on a cellphone and digital camera that your kids know how to use than it does to make defeatured products for us older folks. However, the insertion of extra features often occurs because engineers and researchers who develop technology for the products are more interested in their own ideas than in what creates value for the customer and returns for the company. Maybe, in fact, they've never even thought about what the customer values at all.

People who develop technology — the people in your research and development (R&D) department — like to invent new things. They enjoy the technical challenge of making products better and better. Basically, that's what you pay them for, but you need to make sure that they don't go overboard.

A focused agenda for technology development helps R&D employees stay in line with what provides the best returns, and it helps the people who manage R&D employees to judge how well they're doing what they should be doing. A focused agenda also allows you to decide what you should develop in-house and what you may want to acquire from outside partners (see Chapters 15 and 16). We cover technology agendas and outside partnerships in the sections that follow.

# Creating an agenda for technology development

Technology roadmaps, product/technology maps, and spider charts (see the previous sections of this chapter) are all helpful tools for drafting a clear action summary for your organization's technology development. But even if you haven't had time to do all this mapping, we suggest that you create an agenda or action summary for technology development. Drafting an agenda literally puts people on the same page. It pushes you to answer key questions, such as the following: What will you devote resources to? What information do you have or are you lacking? What degree of risk are you willing to take on?

The agenda connects management's decisions with technology development projects. The agenda can be updated and revised as you gather new information.

The following list gives you the steps for creating an agenda, using the spider chart (Figure 7-1) and the technology roadmap (Figure 7-3) we discuss earlier in this chapter. Figure 7-5 shows a sample agenda.

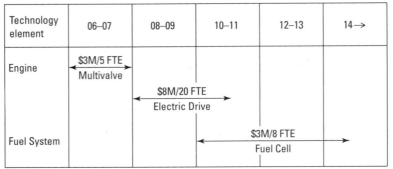

**Figure 7-5:**
A tech-
nology
action
agenda
draws from
many
product,
market, and
technology
maps.

| Technology element | 06–07 | 08–09 | 10–11 | 12–13 | 14→ |
|---|---|---|---|---|---|
| Engine | $3M/5 FTE Multivalve | | | | |
| | | $8M/20 FTE Electric Drive | | | |
| Fuel System | | | | $3M/8 FTE Fuel Cell | |

1. **Decide what the most important customer needs are for your products and rank them in order of importance.**

   The example in Figure 7-1 shows that the car company plans to lead the industry in fuel efficiency. It plans to lag on performance, excel in comfort, and stay at parity on handling, interior space, styling, durability, and safety.

   Scaling back on some drivers is very hard to do, because we all want to be the best at everything! But the purpose of an action agenda is to make sure that you focus resources on the factors that are most important to your business's ability to compete and to create return on new product and technology investments.

2. **Divide your technology initiatives into reasonable chunks that will give you the advantage you seek in the most important areas.**

   The car company focuses its technology resources on the engine and the fuel system to give itself a chance to lead its industry in fuel efficiency. (*Note:* The action agenda in Figure 7-5 shows the company's plans for this effort; it will prepare separate agendas to focus efforts on the other areas if needed.)

3. **Within your technology initiatives, decide on the technology development projects that you must accomplish.**

   To meet its goals, the car company decides to develop two engines — multivalve and electric drive — as well as fuel-cell technology.

4. **Estimate how long each technology-development project will take.**

   To estimate this, you need to understand the *dependencies*. What do you have to complete before you can work on the next thing? What work will contribute to a later project?

   The car company estimates that the multivalve engine will take two years. Development of the electric drive engine will require different technology and won't start until the multivalve engine is complete.

The staff resources for the multivalve engine will be different from the resources needed for the electric drive engine. The company will have to staff up in order to resource the second project (see Step 5). For these reasons, it makes sense to put the second project's start date after the completion date of the first project.

You can see in Figure 7-5 that the company doesn't plan to begin the fuel-cell project until well after it completes the multivalve engine, and looking at Figure 7-3, you can see that the company plans to outsource it.

You should always record the rationale for your decisions. You can do this by providing live links from the action agenda to supporting documents such as technology and product maps.

5. **Estimate the resources, in dollars and in people, that you'll need to accomplish each technology-development project.**

   The multivalve engine will cost $3 million and require 5 FTE (full-time equivalent staff). The electric engine is a much bigger project; it will cost $8 million and 20 FTE. The fuel cell will require $3M and 8 FTE of internal resources to integrate and coordinate the outsourced project into its own technology and product development projects. The outsource cost isn't included on this agenda.

   You should show — either on the chart itself or on a linked chart — exactly what staffing you'll need. If you need employees with specialized skills, you need to be sure that they haven't been assigned to several projects at the same time.

6. **Use the information in this summary to guide your company's technology development efforts!**

   You've created a plan that spans many years. Many things will change. You'll have new opportunities and face new challenges. The action agenda is a plan of action — a contract, really — between R&D and management. It spells out what R&D should do and the resources management will provide. It suggests the rationale for your plan and the context for the team's work. But if anyone assumes that just because it's written down, the future will unfold that way — well, you know what "assume" spells . . . .

## Getting a little help from your friends

Be sure as you develop your technology agenda (see the previous section) that you look carefully for opportunities to avoid unnecessary labor and cost. For example, many companies are now partnering with others who invent and develop technologies for them. Often, you can come up with what you need by putting old things together in new ways. One of your most important goals is to get new products to the market *quickly.* Don't get stuck in the invention stage while someone else brings a successful, high-margin new product to market!

Take a look at the bars labeled "All Electric" and "Fuel Cell" in Figure 7-3. The car company uses a shaded oval bar to indicate that it plans to accomplish these projects with a partner. Even though the development of the fuel cell and the electric engine are extremely important to the company's future, the company doesn't have the necessary resources in-house, and it would take too long to develop the technologies on its own. Furthermore, the company is fairly certain that it can find a partner whose main interest is in the technology itself; therefore, the partner won't present a competitive threat.

In Chapter 16, you can discover much more about how to develop technology and new products with a partner, how to manage your alliances, and how to protect your assets. The better job you do of mapping your technologies and understanding your needs and resources, the more effectively you'll be able to take advantage of partnering and outsourcing.

# Chapter 8

# Focusing Your NPD Efforts

. . . . . . . . . . . . . . . . . . . . . . . . . . . . . . . . . . . . . . . . . . . . . . . . . . . . . . . .

### *In This Chapter*

▶ Pinpointing targets for your NPD efforts

▶ Reviewing the pros and cons of working with outside partners

▶ Measuring progress toward your NPD goals

▶ Constructing an internal communication plan

. . . . . . . . . . . . . . . . . . . . . . . . . . . . . . . . . . . . . . . . . . . . . . . . . . . . . . . .

*H*ere you are at the NPD buffet. Instead of guacamole, fried chicken, and bean salad, you've got technology projects, ideas for radical new stuff, and concepts that will improve your existing products and product lines. And at this buffet, your eyes often are bigger than your stomach, and your plate will hold only so much. You need to set targets and goals for your new product development efforts, and you need to communicate them clearly to employees who work to develop new products. Companies that accomplish this are able to optimize their product development resources.

Different parts of the company — teams, functions, business units, and the company as a whole — have different targets, and metrics are what make the targets precise. You need to design different metrics for different parts of the company. With well-designed metrics, your company can measure how well it's implementing its NPD goals. (Take a look at Chapter 18 for more advice on NPD metrics.)

In this chapter, we show you how to focus your NPD efforts. You discover how to set up targets and how to measure your success in reaching them. We also summarize the logic of partnering — with another firm or with a supplier — and the logic of going it alone. Finally, we introduce a communication plan to put your whole organization on the same page.

# Setting NPD Targets

Developing new products takes resources that business functions could be spending in other ways — for example, to reach new markets, acquire other companies, or expand the company's manufacturing infrastructure. Typically, a company's employees have competing priorities and more than enough tasks to fill their time. Therefore, everyone in the company needs to know how important it is to devote time and resources to new product development.

Executives communicate the importance by setting clear NPD targets and measuring the performance of the business units, functions, and employees against these targets.

Don't make the mistake of setting targets and then not using them to judge performance. Consider this case: A company's executives set a goal of getting a certain percent of its revenue from new products. Co-author Beebe Nelson asked how the company assessed its performance. "We don't," was the answer. "We just say that that's what we want to do, but we never go back to see how we're doing." In this situation, targets and measures have no meaning.

Stock analysts often look at a company's product pipeline to assess the future health of the company. When you set NPD targets, you and the analysts can see — month after month and year after year — how healthy your product pipeline is and how well the company is positioned to grow.

New product development results don't happen overnight. Your targets should extend three to five years or more, depending on your industry.

In this section, we suggest a number of methods that you can use to set your NPD targets.

## Financial targets

Financial targets for new products include both the company's growth targets and targets for replacing revenues that are lost as product lines age. When you look at the lifecycles of products already in the market (see Chapter 3), you see that most of them produce less and less revenue over time. Older products, pressed by competition and plagued by customer familiarity, tend to produce lower revenue and lower margins. How quickly revenues decline depends in part on the kind of business you're in. Products lose value relatively quickly in such industries as fashion, food, and hi-tech. In more stable industries, products may sustain their ability to produce satisfactory revenues over a much longer period of time.

Don't make the mistake of supposing that a product will produce revenue forever. We can't tell you the number of times we've seen business cases for new products that make this assumption.

When setting financial targets, you should take into account the amount of revenue you expect to gain from products already in the market. New products need to make up the gap between existing revenues, expected decline in revenues, and your growth goals. Financial targets for new products include the following:

- **An overall target for the company:** Every company, large or small, should set a financial target for new product development.

- **Targets for business units:** If the company has separate business units, each should have an NPD target. The sum of the business unit targets should add up to the overall company target.

- **Targets for different product lines and product categories:** Setting different targets helps managers make decisions that are appropriate to differing categories. For example, if a company has a line of automobiles that have been in the market for a long time, it will set smaller targets for revenues from new products. If the company manages a newer line — say, a line of hybrids — it can set higher targets for new products as a percent of revenue.

Although financial targets are an important part of the target mix, don't make the mistake of basing all your judgments on them. Researchers consistently find that companies that rely solely on financial measures do worse than companies that use a mix of measures. This is why we tell you later in this chapter about other, non-financial ways of setting new product targets.

### Posting your financial targets

Companies use a number of different ways to express financial targets for product development. The most common are the following:

- Internal rate of return (IRR)
- Return on investment (ROI)
- Net present value (NPV)

You calculate IRR and ROI as percentages: If we spend this much now, what can we expect to get back later? For example, you can look at the ROI over one calendar or fiscal year. If you invest $1,000 in a new product, and in the first year it earns $50, your ROI is 5 percent. If you invest $100 in another product and it earns $20, your ROI for that product is 20 percent.

You use NPV to calculate the future worth of a current investment, and you subtract the expenditures required to get there.

Many companies also set standards, or hurdle rates, for IRR, ROI, and NPV. Your new product development expenditures must provide better returns than a safer investment. After all, why go to all the trouble and risk of developing a new product when investing in the stock or bond market seems like a safer option? A company's understanding of the economy influences the hurdle rate it chooses. If the executives think that they could get a 15 percent return in safer investments, they may set that figure as the hurdle that new product projects have to meet or clear. Setting a hurdle rate reminds everyone that the resources directed to developing new products could be directed elsewhere. Product developers have to demonstrate that they can make good use of the resources entrusted to them (see Chapter 11 for more on managing resources).

In *Portfolio Management for New Products* (Addison-Wesley), Robert Cooper, Scott Edgett, and Elko Kleinschmidt introduce several other financial measures that companies use to set targets. These measures help you to get a handle on the relative worth of resources expended now compared to their future value. One measure is *expected commercial value* (ECV), which you calculate by using a combination of NPV and risk assessments.

Another measure is the *options pricing theory* (OPT). OPT provides a financial framework for the phase/review process. Reviewers stop projects when the business case starts to look bad. The decision to invest is, in reality, a decision — or option — to invest only until the next review. (See Chapter 9 for more on reviews and the phase/review process.)

How do you decide which financial measure to use? Get advice from members of your financial department, and choose the measure that allows you to take information from different parts of the company and merge it into an overall measure. In other words, if your company is running on NPV, for example, that's a good reason to choose NPV; if you're running on IRR, you should choose IRR.

When you choose a financial measure, you're choosing a template that allows you to put information and assumptions about different projects into comparable form. The value of such a measure is that it allows you to compare projects so you can decide which seem better, and you can compare today's measures with tomorrow's to see how well your projects are doing. Never forget, though, that when you gather the information and the assumptions into a measure, the measure is only as good as the information from which it's built — and the information always includes guesses and projections about the future.

When a company settles on its financial measures, it should use them for all its new product projects. Using the same measures provides a common metric on which to base project comparisons. (We talk more about this in Chapter 12, where we discuss business plans and project reviews.)

### Questions to consider

Setting or reassessing financial growth targets depends on your estimates of several "real world" factors, including the following:

- **What's the potential for market growth?** If the market is likely to be growing, you can target higher returns; if the market is shrinking, your targets should be lower.

- **What's our current share? Can we grow that share?** In markets where your company already has large shares, you may not be able to make much more on new products. If your shares are lower, or if you're likely to be able to grow your shares, the target can be higher.

- **What's the competitive picture? Are competitors strong compared to us? Are they entering or leaving?** The financial returns of a great new entry to the market can be undercut by "fast followers" who come up with similar or even better products. On the other hand, perhaps you've found a market where competitors are moving out and you can take advantage of the leftover space.

- **What's happening to prices? Are they holding steady, increasing, or declining?** Prices often start relatively high when products are introduced, and they decline during the products' lifecycles. If you introduce products into an old market where the prices are declining — for example, the computer market — don't set your targets too high (for the computer at least). If the market is newer, you can expect to charge higher prices and gain better margins, so set your targets higher.

- **If we enter a market that we're not currently in, how will that action change the overall picture?** How are competitors likely to respond? Will your entrance attract more customers or simply create more choices for existing customers? Take these things into account when you set your targets.

If your company's executives respond to all these questions, they'll be able to set realistic financial targets for new product development. But this is no easy process. You need to have a good grasp of your market situations and of your opportunities within those markets, and you need to have expertise in developing financial information.

## Market share targets

A clear market share target presents a picture of what a company wants to accomplish in developing new products. If you specify your current market share and the likelihood of market growth in each of your markets, you'll have a benchmark for projecting your desired market share.

Product developers use market share targets to formulate a strategy for gaining the company's desired share. The strategy to achieve this target may include improving existing products or developing new ones. In some cases, a market is so saturated that further growth is unlikely, no matter what the product developers do. In such a case, a company may turn to entirely new markets in order to find room for the profitable introduction of new products.

Say, for example, that a transistor manufacturer controls nearly half the market for a cellphone part. The company shares this market with one other competitor. To gain more share in this market would be very hard to do — maybe even impossible. The company decides to launch a new business in order to pursue high margin returns from new products in totally different markets. The company still enjoys high returns in the cellphone market, which it shares with its nearest competitor, but the company's growth strategy focuses on other markets.

## *Percent-of-sales targets*

Another popular target within new product development is a percent-of-sales target. 3M, for example, uses this measure. For years the company has set a target of earning 25 percent of its revenue from products it has developed in the last five years.

Your company can express percent-of-sales targets in different ways to capture the particular conditions and strategies of the company. Take a look at the following examples:

- ✔ In a fast-moving industry, such as electronics or software, a target of 50 percent of revenue from new product sales may be appropriate.

- ✔ A mature company that focuses on profitability, such as DuPont, may create a target of 15 percent or less for revenue from sales of new products; the rest of the revenue will come from existing products.

- ✔ Consumer products firms, such as Procter & Gamble, often have a target of 20 to 30 percent of their revenue from sales of products that are less than three years old.

- ✔ Companies with stable product lines may have targets for new products of 10 percent of revenue or less. Big oil companies fit this picture. Most of their revenue comes from traditional forms of oil exploration and production, but they earn some revenue from newer technologies and products in the alternative energy field.

Although percent-of-sales targets can be useful, they're subject to gaming. We've known product developers who count the tiniest changes in their tallies of new products. Not only does this derail the intention of the percent-of-sales target, which is to assess the impact of new products, but also contributes to a culture of deceit in which employees pretend to fulfill the company's objectives in order to hide the fact that they haven't.

# Including Partners in New Product Development

An integral part of focusing your NPD efforts is being clear about where your resources are coming from. Are you limited to the resources you have in-house, or can you draw on outside support from partners or suppliers to achieve your product development goals? Working with partners and making effective use of your supply chain can add greatly to your capacity to develop new products. Outsourcing and partnering are important issues for product developers. We devote Chapters 15 and 16 to these topics.

In this section, we address three important questions: What should you keep inside your company? What can you get from a partner? And what could (and should) you buy from a supplier?

## What should you keep inside?

The best way to keep your development efforts protected is to keep your work in-house. The overwhelming agreement among companies is that you shouldn't partner on or outsource your *core competencies* — the things that you do especially well, that give you competitive advantage, and that attract your customers. Generally, firms should identify no more than three to five competencies that they consider to be core.

However, it can be hard to agree on what your competencies are. The International Association for Product Development came up with three important characteristics:

- A core competence provides a significant customer benefit that constitutes a long-term competitive advantage in performance or cost.

- A core competence gives you access to a variety of markets.

- A core competence includes physical and intellectual assets that competitors have difficulty imitating.

Asking the following questions will help you identify your company's core competencies:

- **What knowledge do you have that's better than the knowledge possessed by your competitors?** For example, Corning's knowledge of how to work with glass is its defining core competency.

- **What are the chief intellectual assets that a competitor would want to acquire from your organization (and that you wouldn't want to give** up)? For example, what competitive advantage would Intel have if others figured out how to make its processors?

✓ **What intellectual assets does your organization have that, if lost, would threaten your existence?** Pharmaceutical companies protect patents on drugs they're developing and drugs or compounds that they want to keep from their competitors. Without such protection of intellectual property, the competitive environment in the pharmaceutical industry would be very different; many of the current players might no longer be in the game.

Technology roadmaps and spider charts (see Chapter 7) can be very helpful in your quest to identify your company's core competencies.

Your company's leadership should make its core competencies very clear and should communicate them widely within the firm. You need to protect these assets and nurture them as you develop technologies and products. However, when you need a technology or product that isn't part of the core, you can consider bringing in a partner or buying from a supplier.

## What can you get from a partner?

Often, the best route to the quickest return is to find a partner for your product development efforts. Partnering provides the following benefits:

✓ A partner may provide the resources that allow you to achieve success in certain technologies and markets — success that you wouldn't be able to achieve on your own.

✓ If a partner has already developed a technology, or has more expertise than you, you get to a market and a profit quicker than you would on your own.

✓ Partnering can provide access to new markets and can fill product line gaps.

✓ Partnering can reduce the costs of development.

✓ Partnering can provide competencies that you may lack.

Partnering can be a risky proposition, however. Consider the following pitfalls:

✓ Partnerships often fail for organizational reasons, including cultural differences, misaligned objectives, and failure of leadership.

✓ Partnerships can fail for some of the same reasons that cause internal technology projects to fail: unanticipated market changes, failure to understand the market, and technology failure.

✔ Partnerships expose your company to losses of knowledge assets and intellectual property.

✔ Partnerships always mean that you have less control over the whole enterprise.

When your company needs to decide whether to enter into a partnership, make sure management asks and answers the following questions:

✔ **Could we lose core competencies if we partner on this?** If the answer is yes, don't enter into a partnership.

✔ **Can we get the technology we need from a licensing or supplier arrangement, where we don't have to enter into complex development relationships and we can hold onto our intellectual assets?** If the answer is yes, don't enter into a partnership.

✔ **Does this represent a significant opportunity that we couldn't pursue on our own and that doesn't threaten our core competencies?** If the answer is yes, partnering may be your best option.

If you decide to take on a partner, be sure to read Chapter 16 for more information on finding and managing partnerships.

## What can you buy?

If you need outside assistance to develop and profit from a new product, the cheapest option with the lowest risk usually is to buy from a trusted supplier. In contrast to a partnership arrangement (see the previous section), your company retains control over the relationship. You can specify what you need, and you can protect your intellectual property. Of course, the more you keep your supplier in the dark, the less you can expect the supplier to participate in the product development process. There's always a tradeoff.

So, what should you try to buy from a supplier? You'll have the best success purchasing elements that have the following characteristics:

✔ **Parts of products, or even entire products, that are of little value to the customer:** This category includes commodities, things that the customer can easily get from others, and things that the customer can use substitutes for.

✔ **Parts of products that are modular:** Modular products are like building blocks. You can have a supplier produce one of the building blocks that make up your product, and then you can fit the piece into the overall product. Your supplier doesn't need to know about the whole product.

You also can change the product without having to change the out-sourced part.

✔ **Parts or products that you have a weak position in:** If you're the market or technology leader, you should keep the part or product to yourself. If others can do as good a job or better, you won't put your position in jeopardy if you entrust work to a supplier.

If a certain element is high in customer value, but you have a weak position in it, you may consider a partnership, a strategic alliance, or an outright acqui-sition. We give the same advice about highly integrated technologies, because it's difficult to outsource a piece of a complex entity. However, if you can identify elements that

1) Don't contribute very much to the customer

2) You can't do easily yourself

3) Are separable from the rest of your efforts

you probably have good candidates for outsource transactions.

Consider a company that designs and manufactures inhalers. The company is an expert at plastic molding and manufacturing, and it understands the customer and the market very well. It wants to include a metal part in a new product, which will make it easier to calibrate the product. However, the company has no experience or expertise in metal work; the customer could calibrate the product without the metal part; and the metal part is entirely modular — anyone designing and manufacturing it wouldn't know what it will be a part of. Therefore, the metal part is a good candidate for outsourcing.

# Managing Your Business to Achieve Your NPD Goals

Being successful at new product development demands the integration of many activities within a corporation. In order to gauge success and identify areas that need improvement, corporations use sets of measures to chart how well they handle their business in many places and at many levels.

The following list presents the four areas of business your company needs to manage and measure to be sure you're doing all you can to achieve your NPD goals:

✔ You need to track your corporate and business level targets.

✔ You need to be sure that your new product development teams — the people who actually do the work — have the company's support and are producing what you're counting on them for.

✓ You need to make sure the functions are playing a helpful role.

✓ You need to know that the processes you count on to produce new products are working well.

## Corporate/business measures

After you set your targets (see the section "Setting NPD Targets") and decide whether to buy, to partner, or to develop products alone (see the section "Including Partners in New Product Development"), you need to start keeping track of how well you're measuring up.

The predicted earnings of new products in the development pipeline, taken together with what products are earning in the market, should equal your growth goals.

We recommend that your company executives meet to review and update your target and revenue numbers frequently. If you aren't meeting your targets, you need to find out the source(s) of the problem and take corrective action as quickly as possible. Maybe the targets are unrealistic, or maybe things have changed in the market. Maybe your company is expecting too much from the product development teams, or perhaps your outsource partners aren't providing as much as you expected.

You have two choices:

✓ **You can change your targets.** Executives base their targets and goals on the best information they can gather. If new information changes the picture, you need to change the projections.

✓ **You can change how you're attempting to meet the targets.** Your targets are based on assumptions about your company's ability to meet them; if you're falling short, you can review those assumptions and revise your approach. You can look at staffing and at whether your projects have sufficient resources. Outsourcing may not be providing as much help as it could. You also can review your new product portfolio and make changes to that (see Chapter 11).

If your company *is* hitting its targets, get the word out. Employees who know they're on the right road function better than people who are unsure of their progress. When the business is succeeding, congratulate yourself and everyone else!

## Team measures

When you're developing products, you need to measure how your teams are performing, and do so frequently. When a team or project is failing with respect to schedule, budget, time-to-market, or meeting its financial targets, you need to find out what's happening on that team and within that project. If you're willing to look for root causes instead of rushing to assign blame, you may find that teams that fall short of their goals can provide occasions for improvement rather than for despair.

Ask the following questions:

- ✔ Do they have the resources they need? The necessary skills and experience? Your teams should have the training, skills, experience, and support they need to be successful (see Chapter 10 for more on NPD teams and Chapter 11 for more on managing resources).

- ✔ Are the project goals realistic, and have the team members participated in setting goals and targets for their project (see Chapter 12)?

- ✔ Are they working well as a team?

- ✔ Do they understand the "best practices" they should be using, including understanding customer needs (see Chapter 4), project management (see *Project Management For Dummies,* 2nd Edition, by Stanley E. Portny [Wiley]), and the phase/review process (see Chapter 9)?

Management may have to intervene with an underperforming team. Maybe members of the team are slacking off, or maybe they just aren't up to the assignment. Most often, however, a team's failure points to organizational needs, such as lack of training or skills. A team's failure may even point to organizational patterns — for example, the tendency to overload teams with too many projects.

## Functional measures

Your company's success at NPD depends very much on how well your organization's functions support the development effort. You need to make sure that each functional area has the personnel in place to support NPD and that the functions are willing to devote their resources in order to fulfill the NPD agenda. The following sections outline some measures that will highlight the strength of your functions as they relate to NPD.

### Project resources

New product development doesn't have its own resources. The success of new products depends on the ability of your company's functions to provide needed resources. Your functions are "centers of excellence" in the company. One of their jobs is to have resources for the timely and effective development of new products. The ability to see what's needed now and to plan for what you'll need in the future is critical to your company's NPD success.

## To cancel a project is not to fail!

Sometimes, during the phase/review process (see Chapters 9 and 12), management cancels projects. When this happens to a project, you shouldn't necessarily consider it a failure. What *is* a failure is when a project keeps going when it deserves to be cancelled. Not every project that starts down the development pipeline should reach the market. In fact, in many companies fewer than 50 percent of the projects that start ever reach the market. Your NPD resources are too valuable to squander on projects that, on the way to market — or, even worse, *in* the market — turn out to be mediocre.

So, do the functions within your company have the resources needed to support your NPD effort? Ask the following questions to find out:

- ✔ Does your research and development (R&D) function have the resources it needs to staff new product teams? Does it have plans to build resources in anticipation of new skills that may become necessary?

- ✔ If new product targets involve new technology, is your R&D division working on developing, acquiring, or outsourcing the technology so that it will be ready for the new product? (Refer to Chapter 7 for more on planning for technology resources.)

When new technologies enter a market, they can change how companies develop products and can impact the functionality that customers expect. A company's R&D function must anticipate and build the new expertise that will be needed. Consider how many manufacturers were caught napping when software was included in almost every product except hammers! Too many product development teams had to put development work on hold while the company's few software experts ran from project to project.

- ✔ Can your marketing function support product introduction in the planned markets?

Marketing functions have expertise and relationships in a number of markets. If a new product is planned for a market the function is unfamiliar with, members of the function will have to do a lot of extra work to prepare for the product introduction. You can't assume that the marketers in your company can work their magic anywhere and everywhere. Be sure to plan for marketing's role in product introduction. (See Chapter 13 for more on launching new products.)

- ✔ Are your packaging, service, and other functions set up to do what they need to do? At a minimum, these functional members need to be involved in up-front planning for new product projects (see Chapter 10 for more on cross-functional NPD teaming). In addition, the functions should include expertise in new product development efforts. For example, the functions should be able to provide skill and experience in designing packaging, service, and so on for new products.

✔ Will your manufacturing division be able to develop the processes and resources needed for the new product(s)? If any new products require manufacturing changes, will the manufacturing part of your company be ahead of the curve or be left dragging its feet? Manufacturing must also play a role in ensuring that your company designs products with an eye to manufacturing — in other words, the manufacturing function must provide "design for manufacturing" expertise.

In order for the functions within your company to know what's needed to succeed in NPD, you need to keep them in the loop with respect to the product development agenda (see the section "Uniting Your NPD Efforts with an Internal Communication Plan").

### Functional process alignment

Another important aspect to consider is whether your functional processes are in sync with your company's product development agenda. For instance, functions often reward people — monetarily and in terms of career path — in ways that don't jibe with participation in NPD. If this is the case in your company, team members may be more loyal to their functional goals than to their NPD goals. Your human resources department can help fix this problem by aligning functional and project rewards.

Problems also arise when functional calendars make it hard to achieve success in NPD projects — for example, when yearly budget cycles get in the way of the project-based timing of NPD. Some companies sidestep this problem by assigning project resources that teams can tap into when needed.

Your company must take the time to look at functional issues to see whether you can align the functional processes and schedules with your NPD efforts.

## Process measures

Your NPD processes — including the portfolio process (see Chapter 11), the phase/review process (see Chapter 9), and customer visit and roadmapping processes (see Chapters 4 and 7) — are the engines that power your organization to meet its growth targets. A variety of process measures show the effectiveness of your product development processes in delivering value to the organization over time.

Process measures help your organization look at systemic issues that may be preventing projects from succeeding. The failure of a single project or team may be the result of a company's poor decision making, a lack of resources, poor planning, and so on. You need to resolve these systemic issues at the level of the processes rather than at the level of individuals and teams who don't have the leverage to fix the issues themselves.

Here are some questions that should be included in your process assessments:

- ✔ **How robust is your front-end process?** In particular, do you routinely have more good ideas and opportunities than you can resource and fund? You should. Take a look at Chapters 4 and 5 to find out how.

- ✔ **How quickly do your processes move projects from idea to commercialization?** If your *cycle time* — your time to market — isn't competitive with or better than your competitors', you have some work to do. (Take a look at Chapter 9 for more on cycle time.)

- ✔ **Do your processes deliver a product on time or ahead of schedule while staying on or under budget?** If your projects routinely fail in this category, you should look to the process rather than at individual projects to find a fix.

Your schedule and budget projections need to be as accurate as possible so that your executives can make good decisions about which projects to resource. Coming in ahead of schedule and under budget means that there's slack in the system. See Chapters 9 and 12 for ways in which product teams can work with executives to make accurate predictions.

- ✔ **Do your projects routinely meet the financial targets you predict for them at the beginning of the pipeline?** If not, look to the process to find the reasons.

# Uniting Your NPD Efforts with an Internal Communication Plan

You can't achieve focus in your NPD efforts by writing a document and then crossing your fingers. You have to have a plan — more specifically, an *internal communication plan*. This plan is a process for exchanging information about your company's goals and objectives. This exchange will make the intentions of top management clear; it will allow the different parts of the company to coordinate their efforts; and it will permit the actions and expertise of your NPD teams to be integrated into both planning and delivery.

The internal communication plan isn't a document (though there may be documents involved). It needs to be a living process that engages the people involved. And like any living thing, the plan changes. You need to plan to update it frequently.

In the following sections, we outline a number of methods for documenting and updating the plan and making sure it keeps everyone on the same path.

## *Making sure your plan starts at the top*

Your company can't set product development targets in a vacuum and expect employees to accomplish them. Ongoing dialogue — from top management to business units and from business units to new product teams — is an essential ingredient. And it's up to top management to formulate the company's overall goals.

Harvard's Steven Wheelwright and Kim Clark conducted research that shows that many senior managers get involved in new product development too far along in the process. What often gets them involved is a breakdown that occurs during the development process. The managers jump in, act like heroes, motivate the team, and bring in resources. Often, they exercise their considerable project management and technical skills. What these mangers don't do, however, is *lead.* Leading requires a view of what's causing breakdowns and how the organization can learn to overcome them.

If many of your projects need remedial help late in the development process, take it as a sure sign that your senior managers aren't succeeding at their jobs. Senior managers need to do the following to ensure NPD success:

- ✔ Set the direction of the product development effort

- ✔ Be good communicators

- ✔ Be sure that the goals and objectives for new product development are achievable

- ✔ Inspire the commitment of the business and functional heads who will be responsible for resourcing and carrying out plans

## *Assigning a plan leader*

New product development cuts across many other business processes. It both affects these other processes and is affected by them. The internal communication plan needs a "plan leader" who can work across all these internal boundaries.

## The process owner: All the right wares

To provide a little insight into what an NPD process owner does, here's a story about a company that develops housewares. In this company, no one had the job of coordinating the activities of the different business units, functions, and teams. No one was responsible for deciding what projects should get which resources, or even which projects the company most wanted to pursue. To make matters worse, the company's marketing function was in North America, but its product development and manufacturing functions were in Asia. When the company finally took a look at what was missing in coordinating its NPD efforts, its leaders came up with three critical needs:

✔ A person who could communicate plans (short- and long-term)

✔ A person who could make sure that senior management decided what products the company would develop

✔ A person who could make decisions that crossed boundaries

Recognizing these needs spurred the company to create the role of NPD process owner. The process owner enabled the company to focus its NPD activities, to eliminate waste and rework, and, consequently, to enjoy more success in focusing resources on its NPD goals and targets.

Many companies have an NPD *process owner* who acts on management's behalf to manage and improve the product development practices of the company. The process owner is the best choice for "plan leader," since he or she is already working across these boundaries with the large variety of people who participate in the development of new products.

The key role of the process owner is to coordinate the needs and the activities of the players in your NPD processes (see Chapter 1 for an overview of who those players are). To do so, he or she must

✔ Create dialogue.

✔ Verify that plans are up-to-date.

✔ Make sure that resources are present where and when they're needed (see Chapter 11).

To accomplish all his or her responsibilities, a process owner also must be in charge of the decision-making and delivery processes that surround product development. It's up to the process owner to know what the best practices are, to understand how well the company is doing compared to the competition and to agreed-on benchmarks, and to make sure that the company improves processes and trains personnel to use the processes effectively.

## *Ensuring that team members know their roles and play them well*

New product development teams consist of the people who actually carry out the work that allows companies to meet their objectives (see Chapter 10 for more on these teams). Too often, however, team members don't understand or realize how their work needs to contribute to their company's overall strategy. They just see their jobs, their projects, and their products.

Teams can become very committed to a product — sometimes to the detriment of other projects and to the company's overall business plan. For example, an NPD team (possibly in the R&D division) may be asked to develop a technology or a part that other teams in other projects will use later on. A team that understands the goals of the company will work to make a part that the company can use as widely as possible; a team that's committed to its own vision may produce a part that's great for its product but useless for others.

If NPD teams in your company are ignoring others' goals, you can't fix the problem by chewing out the teams that behave this way. You need to improve company-wide communication. The teams need to have frequent and meaningful briefings on the company's goals. They need to have a chance to participate and offer suggestions and solutions that may improve the company's ability to achieve NPD success.

The team's leader (see Chapter 10), working in conjunction with management and the process owner (see the previous section), shares the responsibility for making sure that the team stays focused — not just on a better mousetrap, but on the role that the mousetrap plays in forwarding the company's NPD agenda.

In many companies, formal or informal "product champions" work at the executive level, play an important role in explaining the benefits of NPD projects to management, and help team members understand management's concerns and expectations.

# Part III
# Navigating the River of Product Development

"I don't think I have to stress how important it is that we all get along on this team."

## In this part . . .

*H*ere's where you move from the ocean of opportunity into the river of development. Now the work gets very disciplined. Product development teams have real schedules and real budgets, and missing timelines or budgets means serious consequences for projects and for the company.

Part III gives you precise information about the role of the product development process; how to organize, lead, manage, support, and work on cross-functional teams; how to facilitate meaningful and appropriate dialogue between executives and team members when they assemble for new product reviews; and how to make sure that all your hard work pays off as you launch your products into the market.

In the middle of this part is Chapter 11. In this chapter, we present what you could call the Master Control Program — the processes and practices that enable companies to control the many opportunities, issues, and problems that product developers have to deal with every day. The chapter has a simple title: Managing Your Corporation's NPD Resources. However, by managing its resources, a company can put its ideas, strategies, dreams, and visions into action. If we could require you to read one chapter in this book, Chapter 11 is the one!

# Chapter 9

# One Foot in Front of the Other: The Product Development Process

*In This Chapter*

▶ Recognizing the parts of the product development process

▶ Tailoring the process to work for you

▶ Getting the company working together

▶ Building knowledge and managing risk

**M**ost companies have some kind of formal process to get new product ideas developed and into the market. Developing new products pulls people together from all over the company — marketing, R&D, manufacturing, and elsewhere. A formal, explicit new product development (NPD) process enables these people who come from such different backgrounds to work together, to assess and manage development risk, and to use common terms to communicate. The process also ties the work of new product development teams to the activities and objectives of the wider corporation — to functions, business units, and upper management.

If your company has a new product development process in place, you may think that your process is special or unique. And why not? It may even have a special name, such as the "Idea to Business Process," the "Commercialization Process," "FastTrack," or whatever. But after you look at many product development processes, you realize that the most important parts and elements of an NPD process are the same from process to process, from company to company, and even from industry to industry. In this chapter, you get a clear view of these important parts and elements. You may even be able to trim off some things you've added to your process — things that get in the way and slow you down.

If you work by yourself or in a very small company but you want to be able to play with the big guys, you need to understand how the larger organizations define and manage their product development processes. Visit your customers to see what they do (see Chapter 4 for tips on visiting customers), talk with them about how they organize their product development work, and take advantage of the networking and resources for NPD professionals by hooking up with organizations like the Product Development and Management Association (PDMA; www.pdma.org).

In this chapter, you discover the basics of the new product development process — a process that outlines the *phases* of product development (sometimes called *stages*) and combines them with *reviews* (sometimes called *gates* or *decision diamonds*). Structured phases and reviews help NPD teams manage their work, ensure that teams are meeting project goals, and help teams and managers make sure that NPD projects stay aligned with the company's goals. You also figure out how to tailor the NPD process so that it fits your company's special style, and how to use the process to integrate functional objectives in order to navigate the often rocky political terrain. Finally, you find out how the NPD process enables teams and executives to manage risk and to anticipate issues that may show up as a product gets closer to market (see Chapter 13 for more on that).

# Connecting Research to Development: The Fuzzy Front End

The *fuzzy front end* is the bridge between the upfront research and brainstorming — exploring market and technology opportunities in the "ocean of opportunity," visiting customers (see Chapter 4), and coming up with ideas and concepts (see Chapter 5) — and the very focused and disciplined process of bringing a product to market.

Crossing the paths that run through the fuzzy front end requires a culture change, because being great at developing new products means that you can work in two different styles. You have to be open, creative, innovative, and divergent in the beginning, and then you have to be disciplined and time-and-budget bound, and you have to work to clear deliverables and clear timetables. The front end of the product development process is the time when the project, the company, and the development team must accomplish this change.

# Phase 1: Navigating from the Ocean to the River

Before an idea can really enter the "river of development" — the product development process — it has to go through several hoops. We call these the Idea Screen and the Concept Review. These hoops begin to take the "fuzziness" out of the initial idea and help the idea to stack up against the business criteria that are all-important to NPD success.

# The Idea Screen and the Concept Brief

The *Idea Screen* is the initial review in the new product development process. The purpose of the Idea Screen is to reduce the large number of ideas for potential projects to a manageable number. Sometimes new product teams narrow down the choices, and sometimes management makes these choices. You can find a lot more about this screen in Chapter 6.

The information that companies usually require to enter the Idea Screen tends to be qualitative and full of "perhapses." Rigor and precision at this stage will kill off any but the most mundane and easy-to-understand ideas. However, before the idea can pass the Concept Review, a team has to write a Concept Brief in order to begin to turn the creative idea into a business proposition. (In Chapter 6, you can read more about the Concept Brief and find a form you can use to draft one.)

In the Concept Brief, the team needs to show how the concept will meet customer needs. You may have gaps in your customer information. For example, if you haven't visited an important market segment, be sure to note that in the brief (and see Chapter 4 for more on how to visit customers and understand their needs). The Concept Brief should outline what technology the concept requires and indicate what technologies are available and which need to be developed (see Chapter 7 for more on linking technology with product development). Be sure to check the assumptions you've made about the market opportunity — the potential size of the market and the attractiveness of the product in that market are critical elements in understanding the business proposition. And in the Concept Brief, for the first time you're expected to include estimates of financial outlay and return — supported by preliminary research.

The team that develops all this information must have sufficient time allocated to the effort Too many companies fail to support the front end of the NPD process. The most successful companies provide defined resources so their NPD teams can create clear and useful product concepts. See Chapter 10 for more on forming a team, and Chapter 11 for the importance of providing adequate project resources.

# The Concept Review

After completing the Concept Brief, the NPD team is ready to hold a *Concept Review,* at which it presents a preliminary business case to the project's reviewers.

The Concept Review is the first time that reviewers will judge an idea for a product against the same criteria that they'll use at every review between now and launch. In this early review, you use ranges and estimates because you still don't have much information. However, pulling the information together in this form allows you to update and revise the business case as you move through the product development process.

At the Concept Review, and at every review after the Concept Review, reviewers do one of three things:

- ✔ **Pass** the project into the next phase.

  If the project looks promising, if reviewers believe it will contribute to the company's goals, and if reviewers can provide the needed resources, the reviewers pass it on to the next phase, where the team will draft the complete business case (see the following section).

- ✔ **Recycle** the project to give the NPD team a chance to develop more information.

  If the reviewers aren't sure whether the project meets the criteria to pass, they may choose to recycle the project. A recycle decision gives reviewers an opportunity to tell the team members what else they need to know and gives the team a chance to develop the needed information. It's far better, in most cases, to ask the team to do more work instead of passing a dubious project into the next phase.

- ✔ **Stop** the project altogether.

  If the project doesn't meet the criteria, it's easy and cheap to stop it early before a team has done much work.

  If reviewers stop a project at the Concept Review, they should return it to the stockpile of concepts that the company may use later on or sell for whatever value it may have. (See Chapter 6 for more on getting value from shelved ideas and concepts.)

# Phase 2: The Business Case Phase

An important part of the NPD team's work in the second phase of the development process is preparing a potential product's full business case. Ohmigosh, you got into product development because you wanted to invent stuff, and we're telling you to act like an MBA! Yup, and here's the reason. If your new products don't earn good returns on your investments, you won't be able to develop any more later on.

The product development process provides a format for the NPD team and members of management to hold meaningful conversations about the business merit of projects. When reviews are done well (see Chapter 12 to find out how), they cultivate an environment where everyone has a chance to shine — in other words, to contribute based on expertise and knowledge — and to work together to create a complete picture of a project's merits and risks.

## Preparing the business case

The business case should include everything your team developed for its Concept Review and more (see the section "The Concept Review"). In this phase, the team needs more resources to do more research. Most business cases include a *Project Overview and Business Strategy* section early on.

Here's what you include in this section:

- ✔ **What the team is planning to develop:** The team describes the new product and the customer needs the new product will fulfill.

- ✔ **Rationale for the project:** How the project is aligned with the company's business, market, and technology strategies.

- ✔ **Resources the team will need to develop the product:** The team estimates what employee resources it will need and includes an estimate of what it will cost to develop the product.

The language of the business case has become rather formal. The team that's developing the product is talking to the executives — the business and financial side of the house. The team's enthusiasm and conviction that the concept will be a great product is important, but the team has to make the dollars-and-cents arguments. Advice to the team: Watch out for the temptation to make those arguments sound better than they are — check your passion with a good dose of reality so that you don't get stuck trying to meet unattainable goals.

The following list presents some of the other pieces of information that most executives ask for in a business case:

- ✔ **Who are the target customers for the new product, and how will the product benefit customers after it hits the marketplace?** See Chapter 4 for more on customer information.

- ✔ **What's the new product's market potential?** Include how stiff the competition is in the proposed market. (See Chapter 3 for more market info.)

- ✔ **What are the details of the technical development and manufacture of the product?** Include as much as you know now. For example, is the necessary technology ready, or do you need to develop the technology? Will you manufacture the product in-house or contract/partner on it (see Chapter 16)? What changes to your existing manufacturing processes will the product require? Will these changes require facility or capital investment?

In the Appendix, we outline a business case template that gives an excellent overview of what many companies require. You can copy the template exactly or tailor it to suit your company.

## Conducting the Feasibility Review

The time has come for the team to present the project's business case to the reviewers. Companies often call this the *Feasibility Review* because what the team and the reviewers must establish is that the project is feasible: that the technology exists or can be developed; that the product will meet customer needs; and that there's a sufficient market for the product to ensure a good return on the company's investment.

In other words, the team will present all the reasons it believes a project should go forward — or not. Reviewers want to know about the project's risks and how the team plans to address these risks. They want to know that the team has included an assessment of the competition. The team should indicate how complete its knowledge is, show where the gaps are, and present its plans for filling the gaps.

The team documents these topics in the business case. The team updates and refines this business case when it presents the project status at later reviews.

# Phase 3: The Development Phase

These next three stages of the product development process take the product from concept to the market. You must define and design the product, test it, and manufacture enough of it to be sure you can ramp up production, all in an effort to prepare for launch. Often, companies overlap these stages instead of carrying them out totally sequentially.

The development phase of the product development process is the most variable of all the phases. It depends a lot on the industry and on the kind of product you're developing. If you're developing software, the phases are extremely iterative and loopy, and after the product is designed, it's done — no manufacturing phase needed! If you're developing trucks, though, manufacturing looms. If your project is to develop a modest improvement to an existing product or product line, the development phase can go quickly; if it's a whole new platform or a breakthrough product, this phase can take months or even years. In all these cases, however, if your team has done some good upfront work, you can reduce the time you spend in these phases.

## Defining the product

The first stage of the development phase is defining the product that management has cleared for development. "Haven't we already done this in the

Concept Brief," you say? Maybe. But you need to make sure. Good product definition starts with a clear understanding of customer needs (see Chapter 4). The product concept should meet those needs, and every aspect of the product should contribute to that effort.

You may need to include other requirements in addition to customer needs:

- ✔ The product may have to come in at a particular price point in order to fill out a product line.

- ✔ The product may have to hit a seasonal market or meet other "window of opportunity" timing (for example, launching ahead of a competitor product).

- ✔ The product may have to include technology that works for an entire platform of products.

- ✔ The product may need to meet regulatory requirements.

- ✔ The product (and processes) may have to meet environmental requirements (such as a specified percent of recycled material, or certain chemicals being eliminated from the manufacturing process).

All these needs must be spelled out clearly in the product definition.

One of the most common reasons for product development failure is that the product definition is fuzzy and unclear. Unclear product definition results in serious problems, including the following:

- ✔ **The design changes later in the process.** A change in design is one of the most common results of poorly conceived product definition, and one of the largest contributors to projects going over schedule and over budget.

- ✔ **The product fails in the market because it doesn't meet a clear customer need.** If the NPD team doesn't tie product definition to customer needs, the team is left to come up with something its members think is interesting. The results of this are all too predictable.

- ✔ **The product isn't aligned with strategic objectives.** If you don't define the product early on, the project tends to wander off and depart from its strategic focus.

One of the best ways to nail down a product definition is by generating a *product requirement matrix* (see Figure 9-1). The requirements — the customers' as well as the company's — appear along the Y-axis. Along the top, or X-axis, you label columns for the product requirements. With this setup, the team can be very clear about the requirements so it can design and develop the product in exactly this way.

**Product Requirement Matrix**
for a Saw

| CUSTOMER REQUIREMENTS | PRODUCT REQUIREMENTS | | | | |
|---|---|---|---|---|---|
| **I can...** | Quick blade change | Ergonomic | Storage for blades | Deeper cut | Sloped nose |
| carry the saw around all day | | | | | |
| change blades easily | | | | | |
| cut through almost any material | | | | | |
| cut things in hard-to-reach places | | | | | |

**Figure 9-1:**
A product requirement matrix helps the NPD team stay on course.

The team members who developed this saw used the matrix to make sure that the features they designed really met the needs of their customers. When they designed the sloped nose, they made sure that it helped the customers fit the saw into hard-to-reach spaces. They designed blade storage in the saw itself in a way that made changing blades easier for the customer.

Here's the thing: It's all too easy for a team to get into the aesthetics of a sloped nose and forget what it's for. It's even easier for a team to design really great storage in the handle but put it in a place that actually makes it *harder* to change the blades. We wish you couldn't think of so many products you've bought recently that evidently fail the design-for-customer-needs test.

As the development process goes on, your team will have to make some *trade-offs* — hard decisions about changing specifications. Your initial specifications are almost sure to contain some impossibilities. For example, the product specs may demand a particular ruggedness and a particular weight. During development, you may discover that it's simply impossible to achieve both. A product requirement matrix allows the team to see exactly why that particular ruggedness and weight are requirements, and it enables the members to make sensible decisions about how to compromise, or trade off.

It's a good idea for projects to have clear "out-of-bounds" criteria. If trade-off decisions force a project outside these conditions, it's time to call for a review to make sure the project can still deliver on its promises. (See Chapter 12 for more on out-of-bounds criteria.)

## Designing the product

To turn the concept that your executives have approved into a real product, you need to bridge the gap between idea and reality. Good product design starts with understanding your customers and their needs (see Chapter 4). Product designers bring an understanding of the required materials and technologies, combined with artistic and creative approaches.

For example, when NPD teams first designed toothbrushes for children, they made them smaller, because kids' hands are smaller than adults' hands. But when good designers started thinking about the best toothbrush design for kids, they realized that kids have a hard time grabbing onto small objects. The right toothbrush for kids, paradoxically, features a much bigger handle than what works for grownups.

The design phase of development requires drafting and modeling. It requires that your team move through iterations. If possible, you should create prototypes at this point in the process and test them with customers (see Chapter 17). Michael Schrage of MIT's Design Lab refers to this part of the process as "serious play."

In Chapter 10, you read about the value of having a cross-functional NPD team — a team that represents the perspectives and needs of the many different functions and disciplines that will contribute to a product concept. You need these varying perspectives during the design stage, because this is the time to think about the many requirements that you'll face "downstream" in the process. You need to *design for x* — for manufacture, service, recycling, and so on. Failure to design for x results in costly delays and reworks. And if you anticipate downstream needs, you often can include "extras" in the product design that don't add to product cost. For example, a phone manufacturer roughed up the surface of the phones so that users couldn't cover them with stickers, because phones covered with stickers are much harder to recycle. The extras may even reduce the cost. For example, making a minor change to a product's upfront design may enable you to extend the product's warranty.

In recent years, industrial designers have become a real force in product development. Industrial designers combine design skills with a knowledge of materials — kind of like having an artist whose medium is the stuff you make products from. If you have employees with that combination of skills, do your best to enlist them in your product design process. If you don't have these kinds of people around, you may want to think about hiring them. Another option is to acquire these skills from an industrial design house, which can provide design skills on an as-needed basis.

# Developing the product

Developing the product, as you may figure, is the heart of the "product development" process. If you've done your homework, developed an understanding of customer needs, assembled a cross-functional team, faced and resolved technology hurdles, and so on, the development stage should go smoothly. On the other hand, if you have to answer preparatory questions late in the process, you create a rework cycle that pushes your product beyond schedule and budget and sets it up for failure in the market.

"Managing by checklist" is a good way to ensure that your team moves smoothly through the development part of the process. Figure 9-2 shows a sample checklist used by a manufacturer of small consumer products (this list is similar to the launch checklist — see Figure 13-1 in Chapter 13).

**Checklist for Development Review**

| Development Review Deliverable | By Whom | By When | Percent Complete |
|---|---|---|---|
| ✓ Working prototype for demonstration | | | |
| ✓ Plan for Design for Manufaturability, signed off by manufacturing team member(s), including a description of confidence in manufacturing capabilities | | | |
| ✓ Determination of key suppliers | | | |
| ✓ Plan for manufacturing scale-up | | | |
| ✓ Completion and analysis of Alpha Testing | | | |
| ✓ Determination of quarterly goals for performance and reliability | | | |
| ✓ Marketing and sales commitment to ±30% volume estimate | | | |
| ✓ Comprehensive customer service plans | | | |
| ✓ Documentation of learnings from the Development Stage | | | |
| ✓ Action plan and request for resources needed to proceed through the Launch Stage | | | |

**Figure 9-2:**
A checklist helps your team stay organized as it moves through the development phase.

The checklist in Figure 9-2 was designed for a manufactured product. You can change the list to meet your particular needs. For example, if your product concept is a service, you can use the list to describe how you'll make the service available to large numbers of customers — perhaps by training service providers and making an infrastructure available to them.

In Figure 9-2, in order to complete the deliverables set up for its development phase, the team members have to build a working prototype. Notice that the team also has to make good on its "Design for Manufacturability," including its plans for manufacturing scale-up and key suppliers. The team also outlines its plans for customer service, making good on "design for serviceability." If the team has done its work well in the design phase, this deliverable can be relatively easy; if the team is making up for earlier omissions, this step can be horrible.

A good way to check team progress during the phase is to review the checklist at team meetings, assess how much of a task is complete, and make sure that team members have the resources they need to complete the work in time for the review.

In the development phase, the team has to reconfirm its marketing and sales estimates and assure the reviewers that the team can commit to the numbers in the business case (see the earlier section "Phase 2: The Business Case Phase"). This deliverable usually requires further market research on the part of the marketing members of the team.

Notice that in the checklist in Figure 9-2, the team doesn't have to pinpoint the marketing volumes; it needs to estimate them in a range of ±30 percent. This is, without doubt, a better way to proceed than to ask for an exact figure. First, the exact figure won't be correct. Second, the team may expend far too much time, wasting scarce resources, in an effort to come up with an exact number. The specified range varies from industry to industry, but determining what degree of precision is needed and appropriate at each phase of the development process is a valuable exercise for executives.

## Testing the product

During the testing stage of the development phase, the team determines how well the product meets the goals for the product's performance and reliability. As the team members move from concept, to prototype, to actual product — in other words, as the product comes closer and closer to its final form — they can define the goals more precisely, and the goals become more stringent.

Performance and reliability criteria form the basis for product testing. In the checklist in Figure 9-2, you can see that the NPD team is expected to accomplish Alpha Tests before the next review. In an *Alpha Test,* you give a small number of products to friendly testers — usually company employees — to use. You ask them to report any problems. Better yet, you observe them using the product so you can discover what happens.

Alpha Tests enable you to get the bugs out of a product. During this stage, it's okay if the product doesn't perform perfectly. Your friends will help you by letting you know, perfectly frankly, what works and what doesn't. Later in the process (after you're as sure as you can be that the product is working well), you move to *Beta Tests* — tests with actual customers. At that point, your product better be working close to perfectly. Beta Tests aren't looking for bugs, just opportunities to make a good product even better.

Alpha and Beta Tests help the team to make sure that the product is meeting its performance goals — in other words, that it performs as expected in the customers' hands. Teams also have to run tests to make sure that the product won't break if dropped or that it will withstand normal use over time. Most companies have experts who can help the teams with this. (You can find out more about product testing in Chapter 17.)

The checklist in Figure 9-2 asks the NPD team to document what it learned during the phase it just completed. Documenting your newly found knowledge is an excellent practice. It enables teams and managers to look backward *and* forward. It provides a basis for continuous learning in order to improve the product development process and practices. Each new product project becomes an experiment in how to develop a product from which later projects can learn.

## *Reviewing from development to launch*

The product development process should look like a funnel: More projects should show up at the beginning than at the end. Reviewers have a chance at every review to weed out projects that don't perform as well as expected or that no longer meet the company's strategic objectives. However, after the Feasibility Review, the "funnel" should straighten out. Reviewers should still be on the lookout for projects that don't measure up or projects that meet unexpected market or technical hurdles. However, in most cases, as the project moves from development and testing to launch, the team and the reviewers have enough information to "see" from here to the market. The team should concentrate on moving from development to market as fast and as efficiently as possible.

For low-risk or quick projects, it's often appropriate to set *out-of-bounds criteria* (see Chapter 12). Under these criteria, management allows a team to proceed with few or even no reviews unless the project violates the conditions. Out-of-bounds criteria include the range of acceptable likely market share, project and product costs, and also changes to the product that may make it hard or impossible to meet customer needs.

In some companies, the phase reviews — especially the later ones, when the product is becoming more and more "real" — can become more like technical reviews. If you're an executive who finds him- or herself more interested in the technology than in the business, perhaps you need to focus on the part of the company where your technical brilliance can be appreciated. But please don't use reviews as a chance to tinker with a product's technical subtleties! Some executive insight is appropriate, but you shouldn't oversalt the soup.

# Phase 4: Launch and Commercialization

The launch and commercialization phase is the last phase in the product development process. After all, you can't launch a product into the market until you've designed it, developed it, tested it, and figured out how you're going to produce it.

Ideally, you should be thinking of prospective markets, of your target customers, and of how you'll get the product to your markets and customers from the very beginning of the process. Too many NPD teams leave launch planning until the end of the process. This is a mistake. You should have a launch subteam working with your NPD team from the get-go. This is so important that we devote a whole chapter to it — see Chapter 13.

When a product goes to market, the reputation of the company rides on its shoulders. In addition, when a product goes to market, it takes its place among the company's other products and usually has an effect on them — it might enhance customers' perceptions of them, or do the opposite; it might boost sales of other products, or it might cannibalize them.

Sometimes, even when the reviewers have been following the work of the team closely, the team makes decisions during the late phases that change the product enough that it doesn't meet the reviewers' expectations. For example, a team may discover that it can add a great feature to a product, but not be aware that the executives are planning a whole new product line centered on that feature. For these reasons, we strongly recommend that your company's executives hold a launch review.

The launch/commercialization phase brings the project to another critical juncture. The work of the product development team is nearing completion, but the project is, in some senses, just starting. Now's the time when the product goes to market to be judged by the court of the customer. A marketing manager or product manager — ideally someone who has worked as a part of the NPD team from the beginning — should take over responsibility so that the passage from development to market is as seamless as possible.

# Making the Product Development Process Work for You

Every company we're familiar with has developed its own product development process. The process involves many different people in many different roles. You have to deal with various interests and make various judgments about what's important and what isn't. We strongly recommend that you design a product development process that fits your company. Be sure to involve the functions in the creation of your company's NPD process (see the section "Involving the Functions in the NPD Process"). After you've designed the process, with input from as many different stakeholders as possible, you can call it whatever you want.

Put someone in charge of making sure people are following the process and of making changes (with input from others) when necessary. The person in charge is usually an executive, or at least reports to an executive, and is often called a *process owner*.

Many companies assign process owners for their product development processes. The process owner is responsible for making sure the process is successful and for changing and improving it over time. Check out Chapter 8 for more information on the process owner role.

In this section, we give you some tips about tailoring the product development process so that it fits your company to a T.

If you walk in on Monday morning with a bright and shiny write-up of a new product development process, and you tell everyone it's time to wake up about how to succeed in new product development, we can tell you one thing: You'll fail. If you want to improve how your company goes about developing new products, you need to gather many people to discuss what you need to do. What are your organization's (and process's) strong and weak points? What parts of the process do you need to improve, and what's okay the way it is? The process you develop with your colleagues may look like a camel rather than a horse, but it will get much more care and feeding, and much more use, than the slick thoroughbred that no one likes.

*Note:* If you develop products, you have a product development process. When you design your new one, build on the tacit process that everyone already follows, and improve on it.

---

## Being the product developer of your product development process

Installing a new product development process for your company isn't unlike producing a new product. You need to understand your customers' spoken and unspoken needs (see Chapter 4) — in this case, the customer is your company. You need to generate ideas that can meet your customers' needs (see Chapter 5), and you need to understand the capabilities that you can use as you develop the solutions (see Chapter 7). You need to narrow down the process options and choose the best ones (see Chapters 6 and 8). You may even discover that you can mold a process quicker, better, and cheaper if you go outside your company for help.

---

## *Right-sizing the process for your company*

The right number of phases for your company's product development process equals the number of phases you need to divide the workflow into logical chunks. Well, how many is that? Most product development processes have between four and seven phases. At a minimum, no matter what kind of products you produce or what industry you do business in, you need the following basic phases in your process:

- **A front end or concept phase:** The front end phase is where you develop ideas or concepts. Many companies now have a Phase Zero, because years ago, when they designed their product development processes, they didn't appreciate the importance of the earliest phases. The front end is where a company's leaders select from a large variety of product development options. You need a front end phase; without it, your company will probably end up with few development options.

- **A business case phase:** The product development process allows management to make business decisions about how to invest the company's resources. The business case phase provides executives with critical information so that they can get their jobs done. No matter what type of product you develop — chemicals, crackers, software, or services — your company's leaders must have business case information.

- **A development and testing phase:** The NPD team has to get its work done to design, develop, and test the product concept. This basic phase is where the greatest variability comes in with respect to the phases:

  - If your product is fairly straightforward (for example, an improvement to a product or product line that's already in the market), you may need only one phase to lay out the deliverables for this stage of the process.

- If your product is complex, needs to be manufactured, or requires the development of processes, it may be a good idea to add distinct phases or subphases. An example of this kind of product would be a new product, such as the iPod, that requires new technology to be developed and that meets new customer needs.

- If your product requires extensive testing to meet regulatory or other requirements, you may include phases that tie directly to that requirement. Pharmaceutical development processes, for example, usually include a phase called "Clinical Trials" because conducting clinical trials is such a major issue in getting a drug into the market.

- If you're producing software, your process needs to allow for the iterative "design/test/design" process that typically goes with software development. On the other hand, your process doesn't have to specify a manufacturing phase, because after you design, develop, and test your product, it's good to go.

So, you need at least one phase for your product's design, development, and testing, but the number of phases varies depending on your product and your industry.

✔ **A commercialization or launch phase:** Every product that gets all the way through the development process needs to end up in a phase that precedes its entry into the market — the launch or commercialization phase. You need this phase at the end of your product development process, but you also need to start the activities and planning for launch early — see Chapter 13 to find out what's involved.

## *Deciding how many reviews to hold*

Reviews connect the ongoing work of the NPD team with the business acumen of executives. How many reviews should you include in your product development process? For sure, you need a review that kicks the project off — the review that follows the front end or concept phase (see the section "The Concept Review") — and you need a review that assesses the business merits of the project — the business case or Feasibility Review (see "Conducting the Feasibility Review" earlier in this chapter). Finally, you should hold a review before you launch the product into the market. That's a "point of no return," and both the NPD team and the company's leadership should be comfortable with the decision to go to market.

As long as you complete those reviews, many projects can proceed to market without other reviews — as long as the projects continue to meet the objectives in the business cases. The following list points out when you *should* have more reviews:

- ✓ **You've built a business case, but the project has major uncertainties.** The reviewers may decide to recycle the project while the team gathers more information (see the section "The Concept Review"), or they may ask for a review at the conclusion of the next phase.

- ✓ **The project will cost significantly more as development proceeds.** You may have to pay for expensive testing, for example, if you develop drugs. You may have to cover capital outlays for process or manufacturing facilities. Or perhaps you have to enter into contracts with vendors and suppliers. You should schedule reviews to precede such outlays to give reviewers the chance to make decisions based on "options" — "we'll invest this much, but then we want to review our options."

- ✓ **The project must pass outside hurdles.** If a product has to meet regulatory requirements, such as environmental permits or FDA approvals, you should schedule reviews to make sure that project is on course.

- ✓ **The project breaks new ground.** If you're working on a radical or breakthrough product or technology (see Chapter 2), you should hold reviews after every process phase. Radical products impact your company's infrastructure and capacities. They may engage your company in new markets and in relationships with new suppliers and partners (see Chapters 3 and 16). They may have an impact on your company's brand. Such projects should always move with due diligence through your phase/review process.

Because each new product project has its own particular situation and needs, your NPD team and the company's reviewers should outline the reviews they feel are necessary for the project instead of relying on review guidelines that "fit" all projects. The best time to do this is at the Feasibility Review, when the team has gathered enough information to make an informed decision about which reviews should be required.

The NPD team members or the reviewers should never hesitate to call for a review meeting when, in their opinions, the project's situation has changed since the last review. New information may lead to new decisions. (Also see Chapter 12 for out-of-bounds criteria that may lead teams or reviewers to call for an unscheduled review.)

# *Involving the Functions in the NPD Process*

The product development process doesn't come equipped with its own resources. You must draw on resources that typically are "owned" by the business functions in your company: R&D, marketing, manufacturing, customer service, and so on.

---

# Teams and functions need the big picture

When co-author Beebe Nelson was consulting at Polaroid, one of her first assignments was to compile what she called "The Big Picture Briefing." She wrote the briefing for people who worked as team leaders or team members on new product development projects. Beebe visited all the functional heads in the company to find out how, in their opinions, their functions connected to product development. She also inquired about how product development team members and team leaders should contact the functional heads, and when in the development process the functions played key roles.

It was a fascinating project that delivered two outcomes (in addition to being a terrific learning experience for Beebe). First, it gave the product development teams a better sense of when to go to the functional leaders and what they may expect from them. Second, and equally important, it gave the functions a chance to define their relationships to the company's product development effort.

---

The business functions can be barriers to product development. They have their own priorities, and for many of them, developing new products may not be on the top of the list. Even the "D" in R&D — the research and development function — has to be enrolled into working with other functions to develop new products. The functions provide the expertise and the people power that make the process tick — all the things we collapse together when we talk about "project resources." For product development to work as well as it can in your company, be sure to pay attention to WIIFM — "what's in it for me" — as the functions cooperate to develop new products.

## "How will my function benefit?"

Why should a functional leader provide valuable resources for a cross-functional NPD activity? Functional heads always have important things to do to achieve functional goals, after all, and no one has extra resources to give away.

The members of the management team need to make the necessity and value of supporting the development of new products absolutely clear to the functional heads. Your company's executives must measure the contribution of the functions to its new product development objectives and assess the functions (and the functional heads) based on that evaluation (see Chapter 18 for more on NPD metrics). In addition, executives should tie the ability of the functions to grow and thrive — to get needed resources — to the contributions the functions make to new product development. (For more on obtaining resources from the functions, see Chapter 11.)

Setting clear NPD objectives (see Chapter 3) and a clear technology development path (see Chapter 7) are tasks that link the functions to product development. Without such clarity, the functions can easily ignore the complexities of NPD and sink into the comfort of setting their own agendas. You need to involve the functions in creating these goals and paths so they know how they'll benefit from the process, and so that management can assess the functions and the process by how well the goals and paths are accomplished.

## Tailoring functional processes to support NPD

Each function has its own processes — ones probably designed years ago — that fit its culture and its business needs quite well. You can't just go to a function and ask politely whether the function heads would mind changing everything just to develop a new product. For sure, the functional leader would mind!

You need to involve the functions in the design and creation of the product development process. You should get their suggestions to tailor the development process to fit their needs as well as it can and to tailor the functional processes to support NPD. (That's why you include members from the functions when you're designing a product development process for your company; see "Making the Product Development Process Work for You" earlier in this chapter.)

You'll run into some pitfalls when you address the relationship of the functional processes to new product development. With each pitfall, however, comes an opportunity to put the functions and the NPD efforts on the same page. Here are a few pitfalls, along with opportunities to fix them:

> **Pitfall:** Human resources (HR) has no career path or reward system for employees who participate in new product development.
>
> **Opportunity:** Help HR design ways to recognize and reward employees who contribute to this important enterprise.
>
> **Pitfall:** The finance department has no tools to track numbers that are important to product developers (such as time spent by functional members on new product teams).

**Opportunity:** Work with finance to develop accounting systems that are in sync with product development.

**Pitfall:** Information Technology (IT) doesn't have a flexible Intranet system designed to allow new product team members to communicate and share their data.

**Opportunity:** Introduce IT to some of the many Intranet systems that professionals are developing to work with their existing information processes. (See Chapter 14 for more information about IT's role in product development.)

**Pitfall:** Your budgets are locked for the year, so projects that management approves for development outside of the designated fiscal year have to beg, borrow, and steal to get resources.

**Opportunity:** Work with the finance department to find a creative way to store resources so that you can allocate them as projects make their way into and through the NPD process.

# Relating to Management during the NPD Process

The new product development process ties the work of your product development team to the goals and objectives set by your company's management. The process, from idea to market, requires team members to think like business people *and* like engineers, marketers, and so on. The business case that your team develops (see this chapter's earlier section "Phase 2: The Business Case Phase") puts the argument for developing a product concept in a language that executives can understand, and it offers evidence that shows how the concept relates to the company's business objectives.

In this next section, you read about how to recognize the political activities in NPD. Part of managing the politics is including the voices of all the functions in designing the product development processes. In this way, more of the people involved have a chance to discuss, bargain, and negotiate in ways that encourage them to identify and work toward similar goals.

## How do I manage the politics of NPD?

Of course you don't have politics in your company. You're running a business, after all, and each employee is focused on improving the business, not on jockeying for position. Really? If so, please give us a call; we want to do a research paper on your unique firm!

Remember this: If people are gathered together, politics is involved. This statement is especially true in product development because the process involves so many different groups and interests, and a business has to spend scarce resources that functions may want to keep for their own purposes. The more the processes take the functional differences into account, the better the functions will be able to work together.

Stephen Markham of North Carolina State University and Patricia Holahan of Stevens Institute of Technology have researched the issue of politics in new product development. They make an important and interesting point: Not only is product development "political" — that is, it involves the transfer of power and influence among people and groups — but it also represents the transfer of functional power to the NPD teams, the process owners, and others who are charged with developing new products.

Markham and Holahan describe the following places where product development tends to be politicized. It's in these critical areas that management and product developers need to be alert in order to manage the politics:

- ✔ Differences in goals between the business functions, the new product development enterprise as a whole, and the individual NPD teams

- ✔ The scarcity of resources that management can allocate to achieve the different goals

- ✔ The interdependency of the functions, the NPD enterprise, and the NPD teams, which can cause conflict over resources

- ✔ The ambiguity of product development efforts, which can put leaders and employees in the position of arguing over opinions rather than facts

- ✔ The vulnerability of the product development process, and of product development projects, to organizational change

Understanding and managing these critical aspects within the product development enterprise can help functional leaders and product developers identify the causes of inappropriate political behavior and reach solutions that achieve both parties' goals. (For more on the politics of NPD, see *The PDMA Handbook of New Product Development,* 2nd Edition [Wiley] and take a look at Chapter 10.)

The book was originally published decades ago, but Roger Fisher and William Ury's slim volume on negotiation, *Getting to Yes* (Houghton Mifflin), should be required reading for all businesspeople. If you're enmeshed in the politics of new product development, pick up a copy and read through it to nail down the basics of negotiation. It can help you with your spouse, your tennis partner, and anyone else you want to negotiate agreements with!

## Tailoring business processes to support NPD

The business processes that provide a structure in which companies make decisions — the budgeting process, the strategy process, and so on — can support product development or get in its way. In order to support product development, business processes must accommodate the way in which new product projects create their own time frames, and they must have an urgency for getting work done and making decisions so that products can get to market on time and on budget.

Many companies design business processes to work on an annual calendar. They hold strategic planning sessions annually and review them quarterly. Their budget cycles tend to be annual. They hold personnel reviews yearly. This logic hails from the way our ancestors, who worked in the agricultural business, tied their work cycles to the seasons — you completed tasks at the same time every year, from spring to summer to fall to winter. Seasonal cycles work fine for most business processes, but they don't work well for product development. New product projects can't always wait until the next budget meeting or strategy cycle.

The companies that successfully support product development provide for the eccentricity of new product decision-making by making time for reviews and decisions that fall outside the "normal" calendar.

# Understanding and Managing NPD Risk

The development of new products is one of the riskiest (and most rewarding) activities that a company can take on. Of course, it's not really as risky as *not* developing new products, but the risk entailed in NPD happens today, while falling behind competitors and becoming a nonentity in markets the company used to own happens slowly — maybe even on someone else's watch.

In many chapters throughout the book, we talk about the balance of risk and reward in new product targets and in new product portfolios (see Chapters 3 and 11). In this section, we look at how the product development process helps companies manage and mitigate the risk of developing new products.

## Preparing for risk

Here's a paradox: As a new product team, you want to write the best business case you can (see the section "Phase 2: The Business Case Phase") for management's review. You want to do the best job you can to produce the best product you can. But you also have another very important job: Being aware of the uncertainties and the risks of the project. You have to let management know about the risks to the project that you foresee and how you plan to mitigate those risks. If you come to the conclusion that you can't drive them down sufficiently, you may have to recommend that management stop the project.

The following list presents a simple method for a product development team to get a handle on risk. Like many of our suggestions in this book, it entails a team meeting, a facilitator, a big wall chart, sticky notes, and felt-tip pens!

1. **Brainstorm a list of the possible sources of risk in your new product project.**

   Here's a short sample list:

   - Technology not ready when needed

   - Key resources missing

   - Prototype unable to meet customer needs

   - Product cost too high to meet desired price point

   To read about the rules and processes of brainstorming, see Chapter 5.

2. **Group and label the sources of risk.**

   For example, you may have a category called "technology risk" and another called "possible competitor moves."

3. **Through a group discussion, give each source group a ranking: How *likely* is this to happen, and how *serious* would the consequences be?**

   Usually, the best approach is to use a simple scale. For example, you can rank both likeliness and seriousness as low, medium, and high. It's very helpful to anchor these rankings with more detail. You may say, "A low ranking means that this is very unlikely to happen; a medium ranking means that we have to be on the lookout for it; and a high ranking means that we should be implementing risk management right away."

This method gives you the basics for managing the risk of a new product project. Assign someone to make a document to preserve the team's thinking by, for example, uploading the data to an Excel file. Set up regular times to review the risk-assessment document during the development process, and call meetings whenever something changes. Also, you should use the risk-assessment document when you're preparing for the next review in the development process. If your team has an Intranet page, include the risk document and encourage everyone to refer to it frequently.

## Using the NPD process to increase knowledge and decrease risk

In its simplest form, the new product development process is a way to get from a point where you know nothing except that you want to develop a new product to a point where you've designed, developed, tested, and marketed a product and can now sit back and count the cash. The process takes you from a place of near total uncertainty to the relative certainties of market share, cash flows, margins, and profits — that is, until you decide that the product line needs refreshing or the model needs to be updated, and then there you go again.

In every phase of the process and at every review you conduct, your NPD team has a chance to find out more information to reduce uncertainty. Will this technology work the way we thought it would? Will this additional feature please our customers? Will consumers find our product attractive enough to choose it over competitive offerings in this important market?

Your NPD team uses product testing, market research, and other activities to ask questions about the product, design experiments to answer the questions, carry out those experiments, and improve the product based on the answers (see Chapter 17). Rather paradoxically, one of the most important things the team must gain knowledge about is risk. In the previous section, we give you a way to understand risk. Never, never turn your face from risk! That's the riskiest thing you can do, no matter how tempting it is.

The product development process gives your NPD team an explicit way to understand the risks you should be looking for in each part of the development process. Early on, for example, you need to address technical risk: Will we be able to design and build this product? When you have a sample product, or a prototype, you have to address the risk that it won't appeal to your customers.

Sometimes, you go to market with major risks still "on the books." And sometimes, that's okay. The development process helps you to face the risks; the team members and reviewers must decide, after the team has reduced the risk as far as it can, whether the company is willing to bear that risk in the market.

# Chapter 10

# Organizing the NPD Troops

*T*o be successful at new product development, you need to gather skills, experiences, and insights from all over your organization. This isn't like running a relay race, where people with all the same skills and training can achieve a common goal. No one functional area alone can accomplish the complex task of creating a new product and bringing it to market.

In this chapter, we show you how to assemble a cross-functional team — a team composed of members from different functional areas whose knowledge and expertise are needed in the new product development process. We explain how to recruit members who possess the necessary knowledge and talents; how to help the team work well together; and how to anticipate the changing needs of a new product project as it moves from idea to market. We also address the organizational structures that can help NPD teams realize the most success.

Getting a team — even a cross-functional team — to work together effectively isn't all that hard. More often than not, organizational brick walls, rather than a team's ineptitude, cause new product failures. For your NPD teams to be successful, they must have the support and resources they need from your organization. (For more on involving management in NPD processes, see Chapter 11.)

# What Makes Teams Fly?

People in the business world — heck, even people in the sports or board-game-playing world — have come to a widespread agreement about what makes teams work well. The following list presents the characteristics that most everyone would include:

- ✔ **The team has shared goals and objectives.** The team should have an explicit mission or vision, and its goals and objectives should be expressed so that all members can agree when they've reached an endpoint.

  Here's a good place to bring up SMART objectives. Team goals and objectives should be <u>s</u>pecific, <u>m</u>easurable, <u>a</u>ctionable, <u>r</u>ealistic, and <u>t</u>ime-bound. If the team members follow this rule, they know what to do, that it can be done, and when they've achieved it.

- ✔ **Team members have clear roles and work assignments.** For a team to work well together, its members need to make all the work assignments explicit. Most teams create a project plan that spells out deadlines to achieve both interim and end goals. Team members must agree on the role each team member will play and the specific tasks each team member is responsible for.

- ✔ **The team holds itself mutually accountable for the work of the whole team.** No member whose team is functioning well sits back and says, "I did my bit. Now it's up to the others." Good teamwork depends on a balance of individual and mutual accountability, which may be expressed as both "How can I help?" and "I'm getting behind. Can you help?"

- ✔ **The team, not the individual, succeeds or fails.** If you need a team to accomplish your goal, you need to realize that your success is the team's success, and the team's is yours. All team members need to check their Lone Ranger masks at the door.

- ✔ **The team has effective leadership.** Cross-functional teams may have single leaders or shared leadership. In either case, the leaders keep an eye out to make sure that the team has a clear mission and goals, and that all team members have clear roles and work assignments. The leaders are also responsible for the softer stuff: that the team members are in this together, working not as a collection of individuals, but as a real team.

  Team leaders have a wider responsibility than other team members. They assess the capacity of their teams to accomplish their goals; they provide what's missing; and they bring breakdowns to the attention of their teams or to management if the teams can't solve the problems on their own.

Several other factors allow teams to be as effective as they can be, including diversity, ground rules, good meeting behavior, and the support of managers who commissioned the teams and count on their output. We review all these ingredients as we discuss what's special about new product teams in the next section.

# Understanding Why Cross-Functional Teams Are Special

Unlike new product development teams, most business teams are made up of people with the same or similar roles in the company. Manufacturers work with other manufacturers, engineers huddle with other engineers, and so on. People from similar positions share a language and a common set of concerns. They've had similar experiences in their work and their education. When these types of teams come together, their members find it relatively easy to agree on a mission, objectives, and the work roles of the team members. The group may share common beliefs about what makes a leader effective and how members should behave in meetings. They often have an unspoken consensus about "how it's done around here."

We don't mean to imply that teams with shared experiences are always as effective as possible, but those teams do start with some advantages — especially compared to the hodge-podge of expectations, backgrounds, and so on within a cross-functional new product development team.

Cross-functional teams are different from most business teams in the following ways:

- **Team members have different experiences, different expectations, and different ways of working that they consider "normal."** Here's an example: Marketers stay up later than engineers and manufacturers and may object when the team wants to meet at 7 a.m.

- **The team must draw resources from many different "control centers" instead of being commissioned by a single manager.** When one manager controls the team's resources and is committed to the team's results, the team has one go-to person. On cross-functional teams, the team leader may have to beg, borrow, or steal to obtain the resources the team needs. How hard it is to hear from a manufacturing manager, "No, you can't use our manufacturing line to test the new product. We have to build the inventory for next year's ski season."

 Some companies commission heavyweight or "tiger" teams, teams which control their own resources and often have their own location away from "business as usual." When the project is large and important to the company, this structure helps to ensure that the team will have the resources it needs.

- **The executives commission the NPD team to carry out the task of developing a new product; upon completion of the task, most team members return to their former roles, and the team's output may have**

**little effect on the members' next jobs.** Working on a cross-functional NPD team doesn't always add to a team member's status "back home." We hope the following tale never happened, but we've heard similar stories:

"A team member from packaging staked his career on a new product project he was working on. He did a terrific job. Everyone on the team agreed that the packaging design had made a great contribution to the product's success in the market, even though the company's packaging-as-usual was pretty fair to terrible. After the project ended, the team member returned to his function, where he was penalized for making changes to the way his peers went about designing packaging. 'What have you done?' they asked. 'Now they'll be breathing down our backs and asking for stuff like this all the time!'"

Cross-functional teams are essential to the success of a company's NPD efforts. However, the company has organized itself to accomplish functional tasks. When a team cuts across these organizational boundaries, it needs special "care and feeding." It thrives on all the same practices, such as good leadership, that nurture functional teams, but it also needs special conditions to ensure that the team is effective. In the next sections, we discuss the special and the regular conditions that support cross-functional team success.

# Leading Cross-Functional Teams

Leading a cross-functional new product development team requires a delicate balance of *traditional* leadership skills — setting direction, making decisions, evaluating the work of the team, and so on — and *facilitative* leadership skills — enabling the team members to set direction and make decisions collaboratively, coaching and mentoring team members, and so on. In cross-functional teams, the facilitative skills are critically important because of the different backgrounds of the team members. ***Note:*** Good team leaders sometimes add facilitators if their skills aren't top-notch. This approach can work extremely well because the facilitator can also act as a coach for the leader.

---

## Same isn't always better

Sometimes, teams with the most diversity can be the most effective. Peter Carcia, a new product developer at Polaroid, once led a team composed of Japanese and American workers. He believes that team made the fewest costly assumptions of any team he had ever been associated with because no members assumed that they knew what anyone else meant. The team members constantly pushed to clarify goals, deliverables, work plans, product specifications, and so on. And the work went smoothly compared to the work of teams whose members think they're communicating but in fact are not. As George Bernard Shaw warned, "The greatest danger in communication is the illusion that it has been achieved."

In addition to these skills, the cross-functional team leader must lead the team through the thorny underbrush of competing functional priorities. The leader must have good political skills. Within this political sphere, the team leader's job description includes the following:

✔ Negotiating with forces outside the team to get resources

✔ Aligning the team's objectives with management's objectives and business strategy

Take a look at Chapter 9 for more on navigating the political terrain.

The good cross-functional team leader should possess healthy doses of the characteristics we list here. All good team leaders possess these same characteristics, but the special nature of cross-functional teams makes them even more important:

✔ **Team-oriented:** Good team leaders strongly believe that the *teams* succeed or fail and that their job is to make sure their teams are doing top-notch work. Unlike the superhero leader who rushes in and insists on doing the job herself, the good NPD leader prefers the often more difficult task of facilitating and coaching; she knows that in the end, this approach will produce the best results. (See Chapter 8, where we make the same point about the leadership of the organization!)

A corollary to this characteristic is that good NPD team leaders realize they don't have all the answers. Typically, team leaders are marketers or engineers, although good leaders have come from manufacturing, design, and any number of other functions. No one function can develop a new product alone; therefore, no team leader — no matter her background — can have all the answers. A good team leader knows this in her gut.

✔ **Goal-oriented:** A good NPD team leader is passionately committed to the goals of her team. She'll go the extra mile to make sure her team gets the proper support from management. She'll inspire and push her team, making realistic but ambitious demands for completing tasks and for finding better solutions.

✔ **Nurturing:** A good NPD team leader takes care of her team. She doesn't push the members too far or judge their performances by the number of hours they put in or how many Saturdays she sees their cars in the parking lot. NPD is a critical function for a company — one that needs long-term nurturing. The team leader can't approach the work of her NPD team like a "make-or-break," just-this-once job.

We've seen far too many NPD teams stretched to the point, or past the point, of breaking. When management pushes an NPD team to its limits, expecting team members to work far too many hours to meet unrealistic goals and withholding resources without changing the project schedule, it may bring a project in on time and on budget, but it makes it harder and harder for a company to field excellent NPD teams. The kind of leadership that pushes teams too hard exhausts resources instead of building capacity. Take a look at Chapter 11 for ways to make sure that projects in the product development pipeline are adequately resourced.

✔ **A realist:** An important part of a team leader's job is to continually encourage her team to look at the dark side — the empty half of the glass. Too often, in their enthusiasm for the project and their desire to succeed, NPD teams assume they can produce needed inventions on schedule, or that customers will love their products even though they haven't done the needed market research to make sure that they will. These kinds of assumptions get teams into real trouble as they skate onto the thin ice of making promises to management that they ultimately can't fulfill. (In Chapters 9 and 12 we talk more about why a team needs to understand the risks and make them explicit.) The responsibility of making sure that team members don't sweep difficulties and risks under the rug falls on the team leader.

✔ **Willing to take responsibility:** The NPD team leader takes charge of developing and presenting a business case that will convince management to support a project — or not (see Chapter 12). The team members are integral parts of this effort, but most of the responsibility belongs to the team leader.

The company's top leaders should always be on the lookout for employees who may excel at leading NPD teams. They don't grow on trees, but they can be developed. Executives should recognize people who have the characteristics of good, even great, cross-functional team leaders and nurture them so they can go on to bigger and better NPD projects.

# Taking the "Cross" Out of Cross-Functional Teams

Cross-functional team leaders need to possess the characteristics of good team leaders; we list those characteristics in the previous section. Companies that are committed to NPD success develop such team leaders. They also work at developing employees who will be great team members. Almost anyone in a function can wind up on a cross-functional team, but smart companies understand what makes for really good cross-functional teaming, and they develop people to have the traits that take the "cross" out of cross-functional teaming.

Here are some of the traits of good, even great, cross-functional team members:

✔ **Demonstrated competence in their functional area:** NPD team members bring their function's knowledge and expertise to the cross-functional team, so they need to be good at what they do back home in the function in order to make a contribution to the team. It also helps if others respect their competence so that they don't have to fight to get people to listen and to believe them.

✔ **Ability to work with different kinds of people:** Cross-functional NPD team members have to work with people from different functions, which means they have to be able to work well with different cultures. After all, the engineering culture and the marketing culture are about as different as cultures can get! In addition to cultural diversity — functional and other — NPD team members differ in personality and style. (As you can read in Chapter 5, this diversity is a good thing, because it increases a team's chances of being creative. However, it can also make communication difficult.)

A team leader doesn't have to count on team members arriving with the ability to work in a diverse group. Team training can help its members to practice respecting and appreciating differences and capitalizing on the opportunities that diversity affords.

Here are some things that management can do to develop cross-functional team skills in their company:

- Provide training for people who will end up on teams

- Enlist the human resource function in keeping a record of who has spent time on cross-functional teams

- Make sure that every team has a balance of experienced, less-experienced, and sometimes even totally inexperienced members

✔ **Independent thinkers and doers:** Because NPD teams often include only one member from each function (marketing, manufacturing, and so on), each team member has to be the voice of his function; if he allows other team members to drown him out, the team misses his function's contribution, and the project suffers.

✔ **Good listening skills:** In addition to being able to clearly and effectively represent their points of view, NPD team members need to use active listening skills so they can understand other members' points of view. Good listening skills are a key feature of being open-minded!

✔ **Ability to negotiate:** Standing for personal convictions and listening generously to the convictions of others are prerequisites of having good negotiation skills. Team members use negotiation skills in order to effectively present a functional point of view and argue for its place in the NPD team's plans. Negotiation skills also are necessary because team members have to make their functional resources available to the team's project. (We talk more about the importance of negotiation in Chapter 9.)

# Preparing for Engagement: Assembling and Equipping Your NPD Team

Like most athletes or scholars, good product development teams are made, not born. The people responsible for chartering NPD teams need to pay attention to the skills, talents, and personalities of the people whom they appoint to carry out a project.

Who's responsible for chartering NPD teams? This question has almost as many answers as there are companies that develop new products. The issue is a thorny one. In Chapters 8 and 11, we cover how companies select and resource new product projects. A critical responsibility of the corporate leaders who select these projects is to be sure that they also charter a team to carry the project out — or that they have clearly designated someone to carry out that important task.

Although the best teams include all the characteristics of good leaders and members that we talk about in the previous sections, you can't find a substitute for experience. Don't forget that you're also building the competence to carry out NPD projects, and that each time an employee participates on an NPD team, he or she should come away better prepared to be an even more effective member of the next one.

In this section, you discover how to put together a good NPD team. You also find out how to equip the team you assemble — with information and skills — so it can function as well as possible.

## Commissioning the troops, chartering the team

When should management assemble a cross-functional team to take on a new product project? Take a look at the map of the product development process on the Cheat Sheet at the front of this book. In this chapter, we focus on the cross-functional team that develops the product in the river of development, but knowing multiple places where cross-functional teams should or could be used is also important. The following list gives you this information:

✔ **In the ocean of opportunity:** Savvy executives and functional leaders are willing to put resources behind searching for opportunities. In Chapter 4, you see how cross-functional teams set sail to visit with customers and explore what solutions might work best for them, and in Chapter 7 you find out how cross-functional teams inventory technology.

✔ **In the river of development:** After a new product project passes the Idea and Concept Screens, the company's leaders should charter a full cross-functional team to write the business plan and carry out the development tasks. This team may be the same as the one that sailed the oceans looking for the opportunity, or it may be different. Here are two reasons why the team may be different:

- The personality characteristics of good explorers don't always translate well to the duties of good developers, so some of the explorers may be set free to explore yet another opportunity.

- Almost always, after the project passes through these initial screens, the team needs additional resources in order to do the work of developing the product. We talk a lot more about that in the next section.

✔ **In the market:** The map shows a pretty clear line between product development and the market, but please take that with a grain or two of salt. In Chapter 13, we describe how the team should make plans for launching the new product during the development process instead of waiting until the last phase. In many companies, a product manager, who's responsible for the success of the product in the market, uses cross-functional teams to help discover and act on opportunities for improvements.

We've said it before, and we'll say it again — senior management must explicitly charter cross-functional NPD teams. NPD is a political activity, and people's toes can get stepped on. We cover some of the political issues in Chapter 9, but here we stress that without a clear charter, team members run the risk of being pulled away from their NPD commitment to cover functional priorities.

You *must* charter a cross-functional team to carry out the tasks in the river of development; we recommend that you charter teams in the ocean of opportunity and that you make cross-functional expertise available when the product is in the market.

## Combining necessary skills and experience

New product development teams have to go "where no man has gone before." They have to develop products that don't yet exist. Therefore, we can't give you a simple formula to figure out what skills and experiences you need for each and every team you assemble.

However, you can ask yourself the following questions; the answers will help you identify the people resources you need:

✔ **Does the product concept have to be designed, developed, tested, and manufactured?** If so, you need designers, engineers, quality personnel, and manufacturing members on the team. But not all products need the full gamut. When the new product is a service, you need to design and test it; when it's a software product, you can skip manufacturing.

✔ **When it gets to the market, will the product need to be serviced?** If so, get service technicians on the team.

✔ **Will the product need special packaging?** If so, someone from packaging should be on the team.

✔ **Does the product concept include software?** If so, include an employee with the skills to design the software.

✔ **Are you developing a software product or service?** If so, you can forget manufacturing, but be sure to include an employee who will understand the user interface or ergonomics.

✔ **Do you expect complex channel or distribution issues?** If so, include someone from distribution on the team.

✔ **Do you foresee complex regulatory or legal issues?** If so, you need a legal or regulatory expert on your team.

✔ **Will you have to deal with a supply chain to provide parts of the product?** If so, you should include someone from purchasing on the team.

Every NPD team should include a marketing member. Every team needs someone who has leadership skills and can lead the team. The team should also have someone with good product planning skills and someone with good facilitator skills (see the earlier section "Taking the 'Cross' out of Cross-Functional Teams" for more on general characteristics). Any of the functional members can take on any, or even several, of these roles if they have the skills. Some companies develop project management skills and assign someone with those skills to the more important teams.

Not all these NPD resources have to be on the core team (see the section "The core team"); however, you need to be sure that their skills are available when you need them so a delay won't hold up the work of the team.

## Getting everyone acquainted

On an NPD project, you can't afford to leave "getting to know you" to chance. Even if your team is made up of people from all over the world — and it may very well be (see Chapter 15) — gathering everyone for an extended period of time near the beginning of the project to get acquainted is usually worth the expense.

A kick-off meeting is the perfect time to complete the following tasks:

✔ Create the project plan (explained in the next section) and the team's communication system.

✔ Discuss all applicable ground rules and protocols.

✔ Hold any team training you think is important. For example, diversity training is a great icebreaker for new teams and will help team members work well together as they get into the project.

✔ Clarify any questions the team members have about how the project fits within the business, technology, and market strategies of the company. You can show the team what the company's strategic drivers are, and you can have representatives of business, technology, and marketing on hand to answer questions. (See Chapter 3 for more on how a project relates to strategy.)

✔ Introduce members to their customers. The customers don't have to show up in person, but make sure your team has a chance to steep itself in everything you know about the customer. (See Chapter 4 for advice on gathering customer information.)

The new product project's executive sponsors should attend a part of this first meeting. The team members need to hear how committed management is to the project and get to know the sponsors. How involved will they be? How should the team members communicate with them? Sponsors can address all these questions at the first meeting.

Every new product project exists because leaders in the company have given it their blessing. The larger and more important the project is, the more important it is to make sure that those leaders stay involved with the project. Some companies explicitly name "champions," while others call on project "sponsors." But in your company, even if these people don't have a name, hold their feet to the fire when it comes to making sure the team knows why this project is important to the company.

During this meeting, you should try to build in as much informal time as possible. The team should certainly stay together around the clock so they can spend mealtime together. Can you also arrange for the members to attend a ball game in the company's suite? Can you go for a boat ride on a nearby river? Can you set up leadership training in a nearby wilderness area? Use resources you have available to try to mix in some fun.

## *Putting people on the same page with a project plan*

A project plan includes the project mission, its key goals, and a time-based schedule of activities for achieving the team goals. Good plans also include an explicit assessment of project risk.

A good project plan provides a great way to actively coordinate the work of the NPD team. At every team meeting — that may mean as often as once a week — the team reviews the status of the plan. This keeps all the team members updated on the status of their work toward the team's goals.

To build a project plan, follow these steps:

1. **Review everything you know about the mission of the project.** This will include the following:

   • The product concept or idea

   • The customer requirements the team must meet in developing the product

   • The product definition, including any specifications that you've identified at this point

   • The relationship of the product to existing and planned technology

   • The market information, including segments you'll address, key competitors, and marketing targets

   • The strategic role you expect the product to play, including its place in the product line and in the company's product portfolio

   • Key indicators of product quality to use when designing tests (the indicators will include the identified customer requirements)

2. **With a clear understanding of what the team wants to accomplish, you can draft a team mission statement from the elements in Step 1.** Here's an example:

   *"The Tailgater Team will develop a product that warns other drivers when they are tailgating. Customer needs include highway safety and an expressed concern on the part of parents regarding their teens' driving habits. The technology for this product is already developed. Use testing must demonstrate contribution to highway safety, including absence of negative responses from drivers who are 'warned'. The team needs to establish markets for this product outside the Northeast, where the concept has already received good feedback. The product is being developed for after-market use."*

3. **Using sticky notes, have the team members write down everything they can think of that the team will need to do to develop the product.** This is often called *work breakdown structure* (WBS), and includes all the tasks of all the functional areas.

4. **When the team comes up with a hundred or so notes, you can stick them all on a wall board or wall chart and group them based on type of activity.** For example, you can group them based on their relation to marketing, manufacturing, design, and so on.

5. **Have the team add anything they forgot and regroup the sticky notes if necessary (sometimes a whole new area of work shows up in this**

**second round!).** Mark each note to show which group it belongs to, because in the next step you sometimes lose track of the groupings.

6. **Have the team order the sticky notes — or, in other words, the tasks — in chronological order.** To keep the sense of the groupings, you can divide the wall chart or wall you're working on into rows labeled for each group — marketing, engineering, manufacturing, and so on. Even if you do this, it's still a good idea to label each note (see Step 5).

   At this point, the team begins to identify *dependencies* — tasks that team members can't complete until they've accomplished something else. For example, you can't put a prototype product in customers' hands for testing until you've developed and built several of them. These dependencies help to define the project's *critical path* — exactly what tasks have to be done and when. Without that information, you can't manage the complex tasks of developing a new product, let alone complete your project on time and on budget.

In order to display the project plans at meetings, you need to have the plan in a form that allows for displaying. You can use Microsoft Project or Excel to document the plan, and you can display it by using an LCD projector and capture changes as they're made. You also can load the plan to a team Intranet site so that nobody has an excuse for blanking on the status of the project.

 We suggest that, especially on large and complex projects, you include someone who's familiar with the process of project planning and who understands dependencies and critical paths on your NPD team. (The Project Management Institute [www.pmi.org] can guide you through the intricacies of project planning — and see *Project Management For Dummies,* 2nd Edition, by Stanley E. Portny [Wiley].)

# Figuring out how to work, together and apart

NPD teams function in two modes: They do some of their work together, and they do some of their work apart. This may seem obvious, but much of the advice experts give you about how to develop effective teamwork focuses only on the time when a team works together. The following sections break down the two modes of work.

### Embracing togetherness

When product development teams work together, they need to have good meeting skills. Here's what you need to hold effective meetings:

- ✔ A set time and a convenient place (which nowadays might be around computer screens all across the world!)
- ✔ Clear communication to the team of the time and place

> ✔ An agenda that leaders circulate to the members before the meeting so that they can prepare
>
> ✔ A notetaker who circulates the meeting minutes and agreed on action items to the team members after the meeting

NPD teams should meet regularly — preferably once a week. If the team members are co-located, or at least in some geographical proximity, you should have the meetings face to face; if that isn't possible, team members should come together, using some combination of Internet, phone lines, and video lines. They take some practice, but remote meetings can be very effective after members get used to them (see Chapter 14 for more on meeting technologies for dispersed teams).

### Surviving time apart

Two big issues arise during the times when NPD teams work apart: accountability and communication. You want to be sure that team members agree to carry out the necessary tasks — on time. And you don't want your members to lose contact with one another.

Here's what the team needs in order to make sure that its members coordinate their activities and tasks between face-to-face meetings:

> ✔ **Clearly specify actions and accountabilities.** Make sure that every action has a clear doer, a clear by-when schedule, and a clear deliverable: "X will do Y by time Z."
>
> ✔ **Communicate to the team when a team/team members accomplish an action.** When a task is completed, the team member should post this information where the rest of the team can see it, usually on an Intranet site. If the team is meeting weekly to review the plan, members may not need to communicate between meetings. But if you know that Joe down the hall is waiting with bated breath for you to finish a piece of the design so that he can move ahead with his task, by all means send him an e-mail, pick up the phone, or — this is still a valid mode of communication! — walk down the hall to his office and let him know he can go ahead.

The following tools help make sure that your team stays in constant communication:

> ✔ A team list that gives team members' names and contact information
>
> ✔ A written agreement on communication protocols, including document formats and handling of revisions
>
> ✔ If possible (in this century, why wouldn't it be?), an Intranet site that allows team members to deposit and access information

## Acquiring functional support

One of the most common reasons why NPD projects come in over budget or late is that they simply don't have the resources they need — money, manpower, and so on. Team leaders need to make sure that executives know what the teams need, and team members must negotiate with their own functions to obtain the necessary resources. (In Chapter 11, we talk about management's responsibility to resource the NPD pipeline.)

Teams need to be clear about what resources they need, and they need to ask for them. This is no time for hero behavior exhibited by proud silence, or for what psychologists call "co-dependency." When teams are underresourced, the whole company can fall into a tailspin caused by what Nelson Repenning at MIT calls "firefighting." When new product development goes into this kind of tailspin, executives pull resources from early-stage projects to get late-stage projects to market on time and with the expected quality. This action delays the early-stage projects, which then need even more resources in order to get to market on time and meet quality targets. If this cycle repeats, the organization falls into a situation from which it can't recover without drastically cutting its NPD pipeline.

Teams can make another mistake, other than staying silent, that makes it hard to get the necessary resources. They leave too much to be invented or solved late in the process. The point of a disciplined product development process is to enable a team of mere mortals to carry out the innovation of a new product. In Chapter 9, we discuss the importance of defining the product early on in the process — the "fuzzy front end." Don't make the mistake of thinking that a miracle will save you later on. You can't blame management if you agreed to carry out a project with "and then a miracle occurs" embedded in the project plan.

# Defining the Troops' Roles and Responsibilities

How many employees does it take to develop a new product? Maybe not quite as many as the number of licks it takes to get to the center of a lollipop, but quite a few, nonetheless. NPD projects need firm and clear leadership on the team as well as from executives, they need clear shared practices, and they need access to groups that have the expertise needed to carry out the actual work. NPD teams need to get a lot of work done — and it's more complex work than most small teams are expected to accomplish.

Most companies make a distinction between the *core team* (you can call this the "leadership team") and the *extended team* (you can call this the "working team"). We cover the basics of these teams in the sections that follow, including who should make up the teams and what roles they play.

## The core team

Members of the core team should have a big-picture understanding of the new product project at hand — its strategic importance (see Chapter 3), the customer needs it will fill (see Chapter 4), how it relates to the company's technology (see Chapter 7), and so on. The core team must ensure that as its members and members of the extended team accomplish the project work, the project stays on track and aligned with its set goals.

A core team member has three leadership responsibilities:

- ✔ **She's responsible, along with her teammates, for managing the big-picture work of the project.** This includes the following tasks:

    - Making the decisions about the direction and work of the project

    - Keeping the project visible to top management

    - Developing and maintaining the project's business case

- ✔ **She leads the extended functional team, whose members carry out the project work that relates to her function (see the following section).** She must keep the extended functional team working and make sure its work is aligned with the directions and decisions of the core team.

    It's extremely helpful to have clear, visual representations of the project goals to keep extended teams on track. For example, you can incorporate tools that can stop a team from wasting time looking for solutions that don't connect specifically with project goals. One such tool, a *technology map,* shows how technical solutions link to customer needs (see Chapter 7). A *product requirement matrix* shows how product specifications connect to customer needs (see Chapter 9).

- ✔ **She must keep her function "in the loop."** A core team member should stay in touch with her functional leaders to make sure they can resolve any issues before they get out of hand (for example, an unanticipated need for additional functional resources during a part of the project). Before reviews, the functional team member will deliver the executive summary to the functional head at a sit-down meeting to resolve any issues. (See Chapter 12 for more on reviews.)

## The extended team

Each functional area of a company, from marketing to manufacturing, may have significant work to do in order to accomplish a project's goals. These functions have to assign personnel and other resources to the project. The members of the *extended team* work under the direction of the core team members (see the previous section).

Extended team membership varies from project to project, depending on the specific project needs that the core team identifies during its planning process. The following list shows some examples (and see the section "Combining necessary skills and experience"):

- ✔ **Marketing:** Personnel from marketing communications, market research, and product management
- ✔ **R&D:** Software engineers, electrical and mechanical engineers, designers, and optics
- ✔ **Manufacturing:** Personnel from contract manufacturing, purchasing, materials management, and manufacturing engineering

In addition, the extended team may include support functions, such as finance, human resources, and legal. If the function's expertise is critical to the project, the core team should include a member from that function. Often, however, members of these functions can work with a core team member and be "on call" when they're needed. For example, if a project involves major intellectual property (IP) issues (see Chapter 15), the core team should include a legal expert. But all teams should identify a legal expert to help with routine legal issues and to be available should knotty problems arise.

# Organizing Your NPD Teams

Most modern businesses are structured like a series of silos, and each silo controls significant percents of the corporation's resources. Often, these silos fill the corporation's internal needs more than the needs of its markets. To produce value for your customers — which is the goal of product development activities — you have to cut across these silos (in other words, people have to join hands, communicate, and collaborate across the functional boundaries in the company). When you do that, you cut across, and into, stuff (people, money, equipment, and so on) that each silo owns.

In this section, you find out how to organize teams and maintain good working relationships to bandage the cuts that NPD projects can inflict.

We discuss some of the best ways to balance the needs of the team with the needs of the functions. When a company puts too much emphasis on the team, in effect separating it — and its members — from the functions, you can't expect the functions to spend too much energy building the resources needed for NPD. On the other hand, if teams are too much under the many functional thumbs, they have a tough time coming together and putting in the effort needed to accomplish the project. So the key, if the company is committed to growing its NPD resources, is balance between functional needs and team needs.

The following list presents the different kinds of team approaches you can adopt. We explain their relationships to the functions, how they should be led, and what kinds of projects they're best suited for:

- **The functional team:** In the functional approach — often called an *over the wall* team — management divides a project into its functional parts and assigns the parts sequentially to one functional team after the other. The functional approach is almost never a good way to develop any but the most routine of new products, but if the NPD project is limited to a slight change of an existing product, for example, this approach can work.

- **The matrix team:** The leadership (core) team shares responsibility with the functional heads. They work together to establish the team's objectives, manage work flows, and resource the project. The matrix-team format is appropriate when the new product project won't deviate very far from the company's existing technologies and products. For example, you may use this format for a platform upgrade or to revitalize a product line, when the changes are reasonably straightforward.

- **The project team:** The core team and the team leader (see "The core team" section earlier in this chapter) lead the project team. The core team leaders negotiate with the company's functions for resources and turn to the functions for technical expertise. The project team format is the "gold standard" of teaming approaches. It's almost always the best format for a project of any newness, importance, or size. The suggestions for good teaming that we make in this chapter are almost always with the project team in mind. We like this format the best for several reasons, including the following:

  - The project team is more autonomous than the matrix team. Although they negotiate with the functions, the functions expect to turn resources over to them to be used as the team wishes. The team isn't constrained by how the functional leaders would want or expect these resources to be used.

  - The project team can turn to the functions for needed expertise, but they're also more likely than the matrix team to go outside if the functions don't have what they need. This can help overcome the functions' typical negative response to outside expertise, often called NIH — not invented here.

✔ **The tiger team:** Sometimes, a company wants to develop a product that differs greatly from its existing technologies and products. In projects that call for radical or breakthrough products, some companies form special teams that they empower to work quite independently. Like the project team, a team leader and core team lead the team. The teams are often located away from the existing business, which helps the teams be more creative and keeps the companies from trying to rein them in.

The tiger-team approach is sometimes called "ambidextrous." The right hand and the left hand are both up to something, but the right hand (the team) doesn't know what the left hand (the company) is doing — and vice versa.

If your company plans to depend on the over-the-wall team approach to develop new products, you'll probably be a very ineffective and me-too product developer. It's almost impossible to develop a great product that will really please your customers when the team that's responsible for the development isn't communicating. Sorry! If your company uses a balance of the matrix and project team approaches, good for you. You give your new product teams the resources and independence they need, and you still build technical expertise in the functions, where it belongs. With a combination of these approaches, you also build the political base for effective negotiation between teams and functions (see Chapter 9). Both approaches work to build your capacity to be effective — even excellent — at developing new products. And when you launch a *really* new, complex, and risky project, consider the tiger team approach.

If your company is planning to use the tiger-team approach, we suggest you be judicious. This approach often leads to NPD success, due in large part to the commitment and excitement it generates among team members. But for the same reasons, it tends to drain the team members and often has one of two effects on them: Normal life looks boring, and they don't want to return to their day jobs, or project life looks exhausting, and they never want to develop another product. You should use tiger teams the way you use wasabi: sparingly, expecting that it may blow your head off.

On the other hand, if you have a "bet the company" project, or one that has the potential to be a real technology or market game changer, a tiger team may be the best approach. The team has the autonomy and resources it needs to come up with something really "out of the box"; executives and functional leaders have acknowledged the importance of the team's work; and team members are free to invent new approaches instead of being weighed down by "how it's done around here." If a tiger team is really what's needed, we hope your executives will have the courage to charter one — and work hard with it to make sure it's guided and supported more than adequately.

Your functional heads and your product development leaders — the executives and business heads who need new products to grow their business — need to understand that by creating a cross-functional team to develop a product, they're working in an area replete with political traps. Teams and functions can get in each other's way. They have different goals and scarce resources to accomplish those goals. However, an NPD team can't succeed without the help of the functions, and the functions depend on the NPD team to create their future.

Take a look at Chapter 9 for some sage advice on how to help teams and functions navigate the political terrain so they all end up winners.

# Chapter 11

# Managing Your Corporation's NPD Resources

. . . . . . . . . . . . . . . . . . . . . . . . . . . . . . . . . . . . . . . . . . . . . . . . . . . . . . . . . . . . .

## In This Chapter

▶ Assessing how well your company uses its resources

▶ Developing your product portfolio

▶ Supporting the projects in your development pipeline

▶ Reducing the cycle time of NPD

▶ Stretching your resources by becoming Lean

. . . . . . . . . . . . . . . . . . . . . . . . . . . . . . . . . . . . . . . . . . . . . . . . . . . . . . . . . . . . .

*Y*ou may think that coming up with good product ideas, developing products that customers want, and getting those products to markets where customers can buy them are the main ingredients you need to bake up an impressive piece of the profit pie. All those ingredients certainly are important, but they aren't enough.

Too many companies fail at the new product development game because they don't manage their resources well. Product development resources are mostly people, and people provide the needed skills and experience. Resources also include financial outlay — for people, of course, but also for equipment and infrastructure. Some projects require capital outlays — for example, when a new product requires new manufacturing facilities.

No company has unlimited resources for developing new products. In this chapter, you find out how to assess the way your company resources its projects. You discover how successful companies make decisions about which projects to resource and which to shelve. We explain how you can make sure the people who develop your new products are *optimally busy* (not sitting around with nothing to do, but not stretched so thin that they delay important projects). Product developers have discovered how to shorten the time it takes to get from idea to market, so at the end of the chapter, we explore a couple effective ways to do this: the Lean and Six Sigma processes.

# *Is Your Company a Well-Oiled Machine or a Herd of Cats?*

The companies that have the most new product development (NPD) success set themselves up to produce new products like a well-oiled machine. Like a machine, all the parts of the process work together to produce the desired result. These companies have the following characteristics:

- ✔ They understand their new product goals, and they make sure that all their new product projects, taken together, can achieve those goals. (See Chapters 3 and 8 for more on setting new product goals.)

- ✔ They know what resources they need and can tell you what resources they have.

- ✔ They have plans in place to develop or acquire resources they need but don't have. In Chapter 7, you can find out how companies plan to develop technology resources; in Chapters 8 and 16, you can read about partnering to acquire needed resources.

- ✔ They look for synergies among projects, sometimes building technology or product platforms (see Chapter 3) that will produce many individual products.

- ✔ They try to optimize the output of their product development pipelines instead of sacrificing speed and efficiency to gain short-term advantages.

- ✔ They select methods to shorten NPD cycle time with great care, knowing that shortcuts can lead to disaster; however, they use every trick in the book to get as much from their pipelines as they can (see the final section of this chapter for cycle-shortening tips).

So, does your company work like a well-oiled machine? Or are your product developers and business functions more like a herd of cats, running around frantically but not getting enough done? Don't worry, even the best innovators can fall into traps. The following questionnaire helps you assess where your organization stands on the "herd of cats" versus "well-oiled machine" continuum. We suggest that you start this chapter by answering Yes or No to these questions:

1. **Our engineers and new product developers work on between 1.5 and 2.0 projects at a time.**

2. **Most of our projects don't change significantly between Concept Review and commercialization (see Chapter 9). If a change does occur, it happens for a good, and documented, reason (for example, because the market changes or a competitor comes out with a better product).**

3. **We change or stop projects that aren't meeting business goals.**

4. We can see a clear connection between our resourced technology projects (see Chapter 7) and product development projects.

5. Every project has a well-defined place in our product portfolio (see the following section).

6. The strategic criteria for making decisions about what we should include in our new product portfolio are clear and well understood (see Chapter 3).

7. We know what resources we need for NPD, now and in the future, and we have a plan to obtain those resources.

8. We use outsourcing, acquisition, partnering, and other means to obtain resources beyond our borders (see Chapter 16).

If you answer Yes to six or more of these questions, your organization has, or is on its way to having, a well-oiled product development machine. You may even be able to skip this chapter, though you may want to read on to pick up some more useful hints (hey, you can never be too successful, right?). If you answer No or I Don't Know to four or more questions, we suspect that your resources for NPD are more like a herd of cats. You *really* need this chapter. And if you fall somewhere in between with your answers, you have a pretty good base, but you still have plenty to learn. Read on!

We suggest that you distribute these questions to others who are responsible for new product development in your company to get their responses. After you read this chapter, call a meeting to find out what problems and strengths your group has identified, and come up with some fixes and improvements you can make.

# Filling and Balancing Your NPD Portfolio

In the good old days, the resources needed for product innovation seemed less constrained. For example, Edwin Land at Polaroid used to commission several projects to work on the same idea to see which would come out on top. Companies like 3M and GE used to have huge internal budgets for R&D. Today, every company is resource-constrained. Businesses must try to make the most of every dollar spent on innovation and product development. What this means is that every company needs to make tough choices about what projects to fund and what to dump, shelve, or sell.

In the sections that follow, you discover how leading companies figure out just what to develop and what to set aside. The key, they've discovered, is in thinking of product development like an investment portfolio — which, of course, it is. You probably have some really safe investments in your own portfolio — bonds, for example. You probably have some that should perform pretty much the same way the rest of the stock market does — reasonable growth but maybe not great. And you may have a small percent of your investments on the possible big winner; you could lose, but you'll lose only your T-shirt, not your whole shirt.

Companies that manage their NPD resources well do much the same thing. They balance their investments in new and risky projects with investments that are more safe and sound, and they make sure to spread their investments among the different product lines and businesses that make up their companies.

## Focusing your portfolio with disciplined portfolio management processes

Your organization needs to have many new product options to choose from if you want to be a successful new product developer. If you don't have more ideas for projects than you can resource, you're putting yourself in the guaranteed-to-fail situation of sticking whatever projects you have hanging around into your NPD pipeline. Have you ever been in a brainstorming session where desperate people are saying things like the following: "Maybe we could dye it red and sell it at Christmas!" "Maybe we could turn our sippy cup into a device for the medical market?" These kinds of ideas are the NPD equivalent of "Let's run it up the flagpole."

You need to have plenty of options, and you can read Chapters 4 and 5 to make sure you have them, but that's only the starting point for having a successful product portfolio. You also need to devote your resources to the best *combination* of projects in order to meet your strategic objectives (see Chapter 3 for more on your company's objectives). Even a seemingly great idea may not be the best fit when you look at it in the context of your other projects. To select the best options, you need a disciplined decision-making process.

Companies use a *disciplined portfolio management process* to identify the optimal mix of products/projects to develop. The best combination of projects will meet your strategic objectives without overloading your capacity.

Implementing a disciplined portfolio management process turns the decision-making process into an iterative, aggregate, and business-level practice. To implement a portfolio management process, you have to bring decision makers together — you can't do it by yourself — and these decision makers have to have good information on which to base their decisions. If you bring the right people to the table and provide them with the right information, you'll find that the implementation of a disciplined portfolio management process will lead your company to obvious and wonderful improvements in product development decision making.

Here are some of the areas of your NPD portfolio you should discuss with the portfolio implementation team:

- ✔ **What criteria are important for making decisions about what you'll include in your product portfolio?** Portfolio criteria usually include financial, strategic, and balance targets (see the following section).

- ✔ **Who will make the decisions about what goes in?** What level of management is appropriate? For example, will you make decisions at the business unit or the corporate level?

- ✔ **What's the right calendar for portfolio review and decision making?** How often will you review the portfolio? How will your portfolio decisions be tied to your strategic and budget calendars?

  The portfolio review calendar sets the timing for "regular" reviews. Your company also must track the portfolio in real time and call reviews if you notice any significant changes in, for example, the market or technology.

- ✔ **How will you link portfolio decisions to decisions about resourcing projects in the pipeline?** It isn't enough to decide what collection of projects will deliver on your company's goals. The portfolio decision makers have to know what resources they have so that they can resource the projects they select. And they have to monitor the use of resources as the projects move through the pipeline.

- ✔ **How will you get the data you need for making portfolio decisions?** What form will the data be in? How detailed does it need to be? The information you gather about your customers (see Chapter 4), about technology (see Chapter 7), and about markets and competitors (see Chapter 3) will be important in making portfolio decisions.

- ✔ **What tools can you use for gathering and organizing the data?** How can you support portfolio decision-making? How can you streamline the collection of data? (In Chapters 3, 4, and 7, you can read about ways to gather and represent data to support decision-making.)

You shouldn't expect to answer these questions in any particular order. Each answer will influence the others, and you'll have to go back and forth to establish your decision-making process.

Making decisions about how much to allocate to different business functions and product lines is, by its nature, a political process. Expect product managers and functional heads to argue for their own corners. (For some tips on how to deal with NPD politics, take a look at Chapter 9.)

You should put the information that the portfolio decision makers will use into a format that all functions and decision makers can understand. Supporters of Joe's pet project should be able to compare Joe's ideas, apples to apples, to Sally's favorite project by using comparable information and portfolio templates (see the following section for more on this topic).

# Using different criteria to shape your portfolio

Companies use a variety of tools and approaches to shape and manage their product portfolios. The key to successful portfolio management is understanding how these different approaches work and finding the best fit for your company. In the following sections, we outline the approaches available to your organization.

The most successful new product developers don't settle for just one approach; they use a hybrid approach, mixing and matching the tools we describe in this section.

### Financial targets

The products you develop will consume a portion of your resources, from overhead to capital expenses to manpower, so, of course, they also should deliver against your goals for financial growth. Companies use financial measures such as *net present value* (NPV) and *expected commercial value* (ECV) to estimate the likely return of a product portfolio. (You can find more detail on financial measures in Chapter 8.)

Financial targets set a threshold or *hurdle rate* for the new product portfolio. Your company has growth goals, as well as goals for how much it expects developing new products to contribute to those goals. When you add all the projects in a new product portfolio, they should equal or exceed the financial targets your company has set for NPD. If your new product portfolio can't get its chin over the financial bar, you need to go back to basics and develop a better set of new product options. The chapters in Part II are all about that.

People can present many arguments for using one financial measure or another. Our advice is that you use the one that's simple for you. The best thing to do is to use the one your company uses now.

The financial measures allow you to compare the expected financial return of projects and to aggregate the estimated financial value of a portfolio. Just be sure to do all the measures for all the projects in the same manner so you can compare apples to apples. Also, remember to document all your assumptions when you do the financials. If you suppose that the market will grow at a rate of 5 percent per year, or if you suppose that the needed technology is "off the shelf" — in other words, you've already developed it — write that down. If it turns out not to be true, it's time for revisions!

You should review your aggregate financial measures regularly — perhaps quarterly or twice a year. You can update each project in a portfolio with recent information, and you can see how your portfolio performs over time.

Although financial measures are important, research shows that firms that rely exclusively on such measures typically have poorer performing portfolios than those that incorporate the other parameters we discuss in this section. You can easily set financial targets that are out of touch with reality, and you can easily "game" financial projections (for example, by inflating market estimates or likely product price points). You should use a combination of metrics to assess the value of a portfolio.

### Balance of product types

One of a portfolio's most important uses is balancing the types of projects your organization funds. Portfolios help your decision makers balance risk/reward, project types, product lines/businesses, and markets/geographies. Product developers often say that a particular new product project "fits the company's strategy" or "is in line with strategic goals." But even if your company is very small, no single project can achieve the strategy all by itself. Companies that balance their new product portfolios can assess whether their resources are indeed enabling them to meet their strategic goals, including growth goals, goals for their different product lines and business units, goals for demographic and geographic diversity, and so on.

#### Balancing risk and reward

To figure out whether a project portfolio is properly balancing risk with reward, you can use a chart like the one you see in Figure 11-1. The chart indicates high to low market and technical risk on the Y-axis, and high to low "reward" — that is, how much revenue product developers expect the new product to earn during its lifecycle — on the X-axis. In this chart, the size of the circle shows how much developers expect the project to cost overall, and the little pie slices represent how much they expect the project to cost in the current year.

## Project Risk vs. Reward

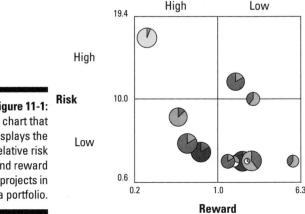

**Figure 11-1:** A chart that displays the relative risk and reward of projects in a portfolio.

When you draw your projects on this type of chart, you can see which ones fall into the low-risk/low-return category (the lower-right corner), which fall into the high-risk/high-return category (the upper-left corner), and which fall in between. Most projects are likely to be low-risk/low-return. In this chart, just one project is high-risk/high-return. This chart has a number of low-risk and high-reward projects. If you find any in that part of your chart, go for them! Notice that two projects are in or near the high-risk/low-return part of the chart. You may decide to resource these kinds of projects, but only if they fulfill other critical strategic objectives.

A portfolio that's balanced between risk and reward has some projects in the lower right-hand corner — no great reward, but not much risk either. It has a few in the upper-left corner — the company wants to be sure to have some risky bets, but it isn't going to "bet the ranch" on them. The "bread and butter" in a risk/reward portfolio is in the middle space — the company is taking risks, but not huge ones, to get good return on its investment.

Although you certainly want to avoid unnecessary project risk, creating a portfolio full of low-risk projects probably won't allow you to achieve your strategic objectives. If a low-risk portfolio does meet your strategic objectives, maybe it's time to rethink your objectives! The goal of a product portfolio to create the balance you need to accomplish your strategy.

### Strategic buckets

In order to ensure that their resource allocations allow their business teams to meet strategic objectives, many companies create *strategic buckets* — set amounts of resources given to different products, product lines, or businesses. A company can also create buckets for high-risk/high-reward projects, for different markets or geographies, or for any other category that leadership deems important for achieving strategic goals.

This is a top-down approach that starts with an articulated strategy for new product development. The strategy specifies targets in different categories. To achieve the best results, companies should combine the strategy with a more bottoms-up approach. For example, you could use strategic buckets at semi-annual or annual portfolio reviews but manage changes to the portfolio at interim reviews.

Bob Cooper, Scott Edgett, and Elko Kleinschmidt, in *Portfolio Management for New Products* (Addison-Wesley), describe how a number of successful companies go about building strategic buckets in order to allocate resources to new product projects. The process goes like this:

1. The company articulates its new product strategy, including a vision and mission (see Chapter 3).

2. The company's executives and business leaders decide on the role that different markets, geographies, products, product lines, and technologies will play in achieving the strategy.

3. They decide how much they'll allocate to each of these strategically important areas.

4. They assign the available resources to "envelopes" or "buckets" — the way you might divide your cash into different envelopes for food, clothing, entertainment, and so on.

For example, the company may decide that an existing product line needs to generate stable revenues compared to the past several years, and that to do that, the product line will require a certain amount of resources. Executives may decide that a promising new market will generate revenue in the future and that a technology will block a competitor from entering a market and conclude that achieving these goals is worth a percent of the company's total investment.

Too often, executives think they have set a strategy when they haven't made the hard resourcing decisions. But Cooper, Edgett, and Kleinschmidt remind readers that "strategy is not real until it translates into spending money on specific activities or projects."

# Resourcing New Product Projects in the Development Pipeline

A product portfolio represents the combination of projects a company's management wants to see developed in order to meet the organization's strategic objectives (see Chapter 3). The projects in the portfolio go into the company's development pipeline, which is where the rubber meets the road. However, too many companies separate portfolio management from pipeline management. In these companies, executives and senior managers make the "strategic" decisions and leave others to make the "tactical" ones. The result is often that the actual work being done does not accomplish the strategic goals.

Allocating resources to strategic buckets (see the previous section) helps to tie strategy with resources. However, the new product pipeline is dynamic, and resource needs of projects tend to change over time. Even if your company's executives have made decisions about which projects will get which resources, resources need ongoing management as projects move through the development pipeline.

A company's executives must oversee and manage the allocation of NPD resources in order to make sure that their teams can complete the approved projects in a timely fashion. It's the team members' job to make careful estimates of the resources they need, project by project. These resources include those the company owns; more and more, resources also include external partners, technologies, and so on (see Chapters 8 and 16). If the team can't acquire the resources it needs, from internal or external sources, executives need to rethink their strategy and trim the project, cancel the project, or spend more to bring the needed resources on board.

In this section, we outline the tasks and responsibilities new product teams and members of management must carry out to appropriately resource projects.

## Managing the product development pipeline

The following list presents the main tasks that lead to successful project resourcing. Some of these tasks are the responsibility of the team members, and some fall under the executives' watch. But in the age-old recipe for success — "manage up and manage down" — make sure you're doing your part, and make sure the people you report to or who report to you are doing their parts, too.

- ✔ **Estimate the people resources needed to support each new product project.** The resources include the number of full-time employees with specific skill sets who will work on the project, as well as the time frame in which they're needed. They also include people outside the company with needed skills that the company may not have.

  Members of management depend on new product teams to give them estimates of the necessary resources for each project. The estimates should be completed by folks who are close to the projects. The manager who's responsible for resourcing the pipeline should provide his or her teams with templates to guide them in making their resource estimates. Otherwise, the manager will get everything from a 20-page project plan to scrawls on the back of an envelope, when what's really needed is data that he or she can use to see what the project portfolio requires. In other words, the manager needs to be able to aggregate the needs of all the projects in the pipeline, so comparable data is essential. (See the following section for a simple template for reporting resource needs.)

- ✔ **Review resource allocations monthly, and make the necessary adjustments to keep your pipeline running smoothly.** No matter how well you've estimated resource requirements at the beginning of a project, as the work progresses the needs will change. The resource manager should make sure that teams use a standard template and report variances on a regular basis.

Don't assign more than 85 percent of your available resources to new product projects. If your pipeline includes projects with high technology risk, you should consider assigning even less of your resources. You need resource flexibility to address emergencies and backlogs — work that "should've been done by now" but somehow isn't (like that stack of paper on your desk that you keep meaning to file). Companies that don't follow the 85-percent rule may fall into firefighting as their projects fall behind and turn into emergency situations.

## *Understanding a project's resource needs*

Each approved project that enters into the product development pipeline must have a clear outline of its resource needs. Projects require both normal resources — people with adequate but widely available skills — and special resources — people or other resources that are in short supply. The company may even need to develop these special resources or find them outside the company (see the later section "Going outside for resource help"). Be sure to note these special resource needs. Management will need to plan for them so that projects aren't held up at critical junctures because they can't get the needed software expertise, or the model shop is jammed with work, or they didn't anticipate the changes to manufacturing processes.

Figure 11-2 gives you a simple matrix that you can use to plot the resource needs of each project. You can aggregate this work into an overall plot of the resources needed for the pipeline.

**Figure 11-2:**
A simple matrix can help you plot a project's resource needs.

| Skill Set | Capacity | Required | Net Available |
|---|---|---|---|
| Software Design | 15 | 10 | +5 |
| Mechanical Engineering | 20 | 22 | −2 |
| Systems Engineering | 5 | 5 | 0 |
| Electrical Engineering | 13 | 12 | +1 |
| TOTALS | 53 | 49 | +4 |

If the manager asks teams to use this matrix, the information will come in a form that he or she can easily compare and aggregate. Of course, you aren't going to know everything right at the beginning. But by predicting resource needs as accurately as possible early on and updating your predictions as situations change, you can avoid a lot of headaches.

## Putting chunks into the pipeline

Some companies use resource chunks rather than headcounts to estimate project needs. The motorcycle company Harley-Davidson, for instance, assigns each project a number from one to six to identify the magnitude of the project. The company determines how many sixes it can have at any time, and how many fives and fours. With these numbers set, team leaders can fill in the gaps with the small-scale threes, twos, and ones. Fairchild Semiconductor, on the other hand, counts intact teams. Until a team completes its current project, it won't receive a new one. The company assigns team members who aren't needed on the project to help out with other projects until everyone is ready to move on to a new project.

## *Securing functional resources*

NPD team members come from the business functions within the company. The team comes together depending on whose expertise needs to be involved, from the fuzzy front end through the launch into market (see Chapters 9 and 10). The team members must assess the resource needs for a project — resources that come from many of the company's functions — and make those needs very clear to the managers who will give the project the green light — or put on the brakes. (See Chapter 12 for more on the relationship between the NPD team and the managers who sit on the review boards.)

Securing functional resources is complex. It isn't like going to your boss and requesting an extra week or three more rolls of tape to complete a project. The members of the NPD team — having formed a clear idea of the resources they need and when they'll need them — must negotiate with the functions. (Take a look at Chapter 9 for some advice on how team members can negotiate successfully with their functions and for more on the politics of NPD.)

Team members should stay within their areas of expertise during negotiations. For example, the marketing team member should negotiate with the marketing function. She can secure market research resources and resources for launch planning and execution (see Chapter 13). The engineering team member should negotiate with R&D for the necessary skills and capabilities and for the equipment and infrastructure required.

An NPD team has great leverage in a company that includes its new product projects in a strategic portfolio (see the section "Filling and Balancing Your NPD Portfolio") and that approves projects in a disciplined phase/review process (see Chapters 9 and 12). In companies with clear new product strategies, if a business function can't provide the team's needed resources, that sends up a flashing warning light for the team and management to see. At this point, the team needs to return to the managers who included the project in the portfolio and renegotiate.

One of three things will happen:

- ✔ **The team can't carry out the project because of a lack of resources.** If management is unable to secure the resources needed, one option is to cancel the project. This has the good effect of making resources available to other projects in the pipeline. Of course, before taking this step, management needs to be sure that the project isn't critical for achieving its strategic objectives.

- ✔ **The project gets delayed.** When projects get delayed because resources are lacking, the products arrive late in the market. When this happens, it should be obvious that the company is slated to lose money. If you calculate what a particular resource may cost — for example, using the services of a software designer for two weeks or outsourcing work to a model shop to build a prototype — you often can show that the cost of the resource is almost insignificant when compared to the revenues lost. Product developers call this calculation *the dollar cost of time* or the *opportunity cost.* (See the following section for help persuading your company that spending money now may be worth it in the future.)

- ✔ **The managers will go to the functions and strengthen the requests for resources with more information and data.** If the project is too critical to be cancelled, and if delay is too costly an option, managers or business leaders may put more clout behind the team requests for resources.

## Going outside for resource help

If your NPD team can show your company that spending on resources now will increase revenue later (see the previous section), you may be able to argue for and obtain outside help. Timely use of external resources can do a world of good to help your team meet or exceed its schedule predictions, with little additional cost and the same or better quality.

If your team has created a well-thought-out plan of its resource needs (see "Understanding a project's resource needs"), you can specify exactly what external resources your team needs to keep a project on track. You may need to farm out the design and development of a whole subsystem, for example, or you may contract with a firm or person who has the skills you need to design or build a part.

Companies count more and more on external resources these days. In fact, as you plan for your resource needs, it may make sense to see not how little you can outsource, but how much. You can look in Chapters 7, 8, 15, and 16 to discover more about how companies are farming out, outsourcing, allying, and partnering on many parts of the product development process.

# Keeping the product development pipeline flowing

The product development pipeline works like a highway. At 10 a.m. on a highway that surrounds a major city, you won't see very many cars. Every car can go the speed limit, and most are going faster. If an online directions service says that it will take an hour for your trip, you may be able to complete it in 50 minutes. These driving conditions are pleasant, but if you always drive at 10 a.m., you may think that the state's transportation department built too many highways and didn't make good use of its resources.

Now suppose that you're making your trip at 4:00 or 4:30 p.m. The highway has some traffic. You go the speed limit, and maybe you curse the jerks in their luxury sedans who dodge in and out of lanes to make better time. On the whole, drivers are using the highway well, and the cars are moving at a pretty optimal rate. But you realize that you left too late. All of a sudden, the traffic slows to a crawl, and you realize that you'll be here, stuck in Friday-afternoon, rush-hour traffic (where'd they get *that* name for it?), for at least another 45 minutes.

What happened? Simple. Material, particles, cars, water, projects — they all flow at the optimal rate for the "highways" they're on until too many cars, too much water, too many projects, and so on enter the picture. At that point, the flow slows to a crawl. When this happens, nothing gets through in good time. In a new product pipeline, when projects compete for resources, they slow each other down and all the projects get delayed. Once in a while, a project — like the guy in the luxury car — finds a hole, speeds up, and makes good time for a while. There may be accidents on the road, but the project in the luxury car gets to the goal (market) ahead of everyone else, and the company's executives cheer and tell the project's team how great it is. Meanwhile, 20 or 30 other projects are still stuck in rush-hour traffic, a few are sidelined by accidents, and the company is no closer to meeting its new product objectives.

If your NPD team and executives haven't had the time or the discipline to examine your projects' resource needs, we recommend that you sideline a few of your projects to see whether the projects that remain in the pipeline start moving faster. Keep taking out projects until the pipeline is moving at a healthy clip and projects are meeting their schedules. By staffing these projects for success and finishing the first set, you'll actually complete the next set sooner than if you staff all the projects at once with less-than-optimal resources.

As you thin out the pipeline, you'll remove the projects that seem less strategically vital than the others. Try to achieve "portfolio balance" even if your portfolio management process isn't all that well-developed (see the section "Filling and Balancing Your NPD Portfolio") by keeping some projects in as many of the important areas as you can (for example, don't remove all the projects focused on one market unless you plan to exit that market).

This strategy works, but it's just so counterintuitive. If you aren't putting enough products into the market, you'll have the urge to put more projects into the pipeline. If you add more, though, you'll slow down the pipeline even more, and you'll put fewer products into the market.

Of course, you don't need to take these measures if you can make more precise estimates of your projects' resource needs and your organization's resource availability. The task isn't easy, but the longer you work at it, the more data and experience you'll build.

# Shortening Cycle Time

One of the most obvious and widely measured results of implementing a disciplined phase/review process (see Chapter 9) is that the process can shorten the time it takes for teams to get new products into the market, or the *cycle time*. Shortening cycle time has many benefits:

- Projects tend to absorb fewer resources (contrary to common belief, which is that shortening cycle time requires more resources).

- Companies can deploy resources to other projects more quickly.

- Products get into the market quickly, where they'll (hopefully) start to earn back the money their companies have spent on them.

In this section, we tell you why it's so important to shorten cycle time, and we give you some of the best ways to go about it.

## Getting to profits within the window of opportunity

When you introduce a new product to the market, be aware that the product has a lifecycle (see Chapter 3). Much as you may want it to, the product won't continue to produce profits forever (unless you have the equivalent of Classic Coke or a commodity product such as bottled hydrogen, in which case the revenue stream may last — at least until you retire).

For most products, teams really need to time their launches for what many call the *window of opportunity* — when the products will bring in the best returns. The more time products spend in development, the more time they lose in the window of opportunity, and after this time is lost, it can't be regained.

For seasonal products such as ski jackets or bathing suits, the window may be the holiday season or summertime. For other products, the window may depend on the following:

- ✔ **Trends or fads** (like hula hoops or fad diets)
- ✔ **How quickly a competitor can launch a product that could steal a part of your market**

  The pace of product development is so fast now that even breakthrough products like digital cameras or the iPod find competitors breathing down their necks.

- ✔ **The length of time patents will protect your product**

  This is critically important for the pharmaceutical industry, which measures its returns on how long a drug will stay on patent.

Poor resourcing is a major cause of delay in getting a product to market (see the earlier section "Securing functional resources"). You need to be sure you provide your time-sensitive projects with adequate resources so that you can get them to market as quickly as possible and gain the most benefit from their best years.

## Spending more time upfront to reduce rework later

It may seem paradoxical, but spending more time upfront in the development process may shorten the time it takes to get to market. Companies that take the time to thoroughly understand their customers and come up with solutions that meet their customers needs, instead of hurrying through the early parts of the product development cycle, not only get to market with products that customers will buy, but also often get there quicker (see Chapter 4 for more on understanding customers).

When teams rush into the projects, they often misunderstand their customers' needs. In addition, they often do things wrong — use the wrong technologies, design parts that don't fit with other parts, design products that are hard or impossible to manufacture, and so on. These kinds of mistakes send the teams into a rework loop where they have to fix things that they could've avoided with better planning.

Executives can get antsy about projects that take longer in the upfront part of the cycle. They're human, and they want to see results. They're happier when they can see a prototype and even happier when they can see the money the product is making. Be sure they read this chapter!

This is a tip for executives: Put more resources into the front end of the product development process. Realize that your teams need to plan in order to work quickly later on and that you'll be saving later in the process. You'll be saving on their ability to get it right the first time — on the rework they don't have to do because they took the time to get it right. Best of all, you'll reap the rewards of a product that meets customer needs and sells well in the market.

### *Planning makes perfect*

Do you really understand your customers' needs and wants (see Chapter 4)? Does your team have a good grip on the technology you'll need and how you plan to get it (see Chapter 7)? Do you understand how the product will be manufactured so that you don't have to fix a whole lot of glitches late in the product development process (see Chapter 9)? Hopefully so if you want to get your product into the market as quickly as possible, make a product that customers will buy, and save your team a lot of headaches, rework, and the finger-pointing that usually goes with making mistakes. And, of course, you avoid the need for additional resources, time, and money; needing these things throws off the business case for your product and often steals resources from other projects in the pipeline.

Team leaders shouldn't push their teams to jump into developing products until they've spent enough time working on their project plans. If team members find gaps, they should go back and get better information. Time spent in preparation should surface assumptions, uncover risks, and help the team members become a focused group.

A product's design and specifications should be set early in the product development process. Late changes can be costly causes of project delay. Take a look at the last section of this chapter for a description of the Six Sigma approach to upfront design, which helps to avoid late changes.

---

## We're so glad we invited *that* guy to the party!

Co-author Robin once worked with a team that was developing a new chemical, along with the process to produce it. Fortunately, the company was using cross-functional teams (see Chapter 10). The R&D members of the team suggested an additive that they were familiar with for the chemical. The manufacturing team member explained to the team that the additive wouldn't scale up well. He suggested a replacement — one that would work better for the scale needed in manufacturing. Because the manufacturing member was a member of the team from the beginning, instead of waiting until "manufacturing issues" arose later in the process, the team prepared itself to produce a chemical that could make a smooth transfer to manufacturing and have a successful launch.

Our friend Professor Jean-Philippe Deschamps of IMD in Lausanne, Switzerland, tells us: "Plan superbly and, only then, run like hell."

### *Working on back-end issues during the front end*

NPD teams shouldn't be tempted to leave the later parts of projects for later. And they can be tempted if the culture of new product development at their companies doesn't include a deep understanding of the importance of planning and upfront work. Even though the work of developing new products is linear — it starts at the beginning with an idea, goes through the phase/review process, and ends up, hopefully, with a product in the market — the planning is not.

Teams need to understand manufacturing issues, legal issues, and regulatory issues. They should be planning early for market development and product launch (see Chapter 13). They need to anticipate technology issues so they can start early to develop or acquire the needed technology. They should consider the impact of packaging and distribution early on.

The more you understand up front, the less you have to deal with downstream issues that hold up projects; the more likely it is that you'll complete the project in the scheduled time; and the fewer resources you'll need overall.

## *Knowing when fast becomes too fast*

Although shortening cycle time is important and beneficial, speed to market can become the only thing that management, or the team leader, cares about. Careful! The goal is to get your product to market quickly, but you want it to be a quality product that your customers will buy.

The following list presents some of the speed traps that NPD teams can fall into:

- **Pushing people or teams with extrinsic rewards or threats.** Most new product team members — and most people in general — respond to the intrinsic reward of doing work they consider worthwhile. Realistic goals to shorten cycle time can motivate NPD teams, but carrots and sticks rarely do.

- **Skipping steps to save time.** You often can skip steps in a phase/review process, but you should think this out carefully in advance. You can't skip reviews if you foresee important questions popping up about the technical or business viability of a project, for instance.

    For many projects, setting out-of-bounds criteria is an appropriate way to speed up a product's cycle time. You can find out more about these in Chapter 12.

- **Compromising quality.** Many speedsters are tempted to cut corners. We've known teams that have eliminated features in a rush to the market, only to find that without those features, the products weren't attractive to customers. Another temptation is to make the product less robust, but that may come back to haunt you when warranty claims skyrocket.

The exception to the quality warning is when your company has a planned sequence of products from a product platform. In this case, the early products could be of lesser quality, or have fewer features, than the later products. See Chapter 3 for more advice on this topic.

To avoid the speed traps, do the upfront work so you don't waste time correcting mistakes you could've anticipated, set conditions that may let teams move quickly through reviews, and, most importantly, value product quality over a senseless rush to get to market.

# Practicing the Discipline of No Waste

Many companies want to cut the waste out of their product development processes and capitalize on the resources they have (or can easily obtain). The approaches most discussed today include Lean development and Six Sigma. This section won't give you the last word on these strategies, but we want you to see how they connect to developing new products.

If you want more information, we encourage you to check out *Six Sigma For Dummies,* by Craig Gygi, Neil DeCarlo, Bruce Williams, and Stephen R. Covey, and *Lean For Dummies,* by Bruce Williams and Natalie Sayer, both published by Wiley. And for a comprehensive look at these types of techniques, you can look at *Quality Control For Dummies,* by Larry Webber and Michael Wallace (Wiley).

## Lean development

*Lean development* is a discipline that has emerged from the quality movement. The quality movement has enabled companies to make impressive improvements in efficiency and quality in their manufacturing enterprises. Although product development differs in many ways from manufacturing, many companies have successfully eliminated waste from their product development processes by using Lean processes.

Follow these steps to follow their lead:

1. **Identify the sources of waste in your new product development efforts.**

   Assign a team to observe your new product teams and processes to see where they're taking unnecessary steps or doing work that could be avoided. Examples could include hand-offs (for example, from engineering to manufacturing), scatter (in other words, making your team members scatter-brained by giving them too many projects — see "Understanding a project's resource needs"), and wishful thinking.

2. **Eliminate waste wherever possible.**

   Here are some methods you can use for the examples in Step 1:

   - To eliminate hand-offs, use a team approach; make sure team members make decisions about the project together ("no decisions outside of this room"); and make a detailed plan for the steps needed to develop the product. You can find more on planning in the product development process in the section "Planning makes perfect" and in Chapter 9.

   - To eliminate scatter, be realistic about the projects you can resource, and don't have a team spend too much time fixing a product that you launched six months ago. Yes, too often people who should be working on new product development are the ones who are diverted to fix problems that should've been taken care of earlier.

   - To eliminate wishful thinking, get serious about what you can accomplish, and don't add more projects until you've completed the most important ones in your pipeline.

## Six Sigma

Like other quality movements, *Six Sigma* was originally introduced to improve the quality of existing products and processes — manufacturing in particular.

### So what's really new?

When executives first hear of Lean or Six Sigma, they often have a missionary glaze in their eyes. They've found the Holy Grail, the silver bullet, the ultimate answer to the ills of their corporations. But you shouldn't be so quick to throw out what you already know.

If you've read this whole chapter, you've seen that many of our recommendations for resourcing your product development efforts are reflected in the Lean and Six Sigma processes. If your executives bring these approaches to your company, by all means use them to link the great processes you already use. The truth is that many of these processes have their initial impetus from the "Japanese Miracle" in which many companies, including Toyota, made impressive changes to their product development processes. These changes scared the heck out of U.S. companies and made them realize that teams, processes, and cross-functional planning are the keys to improvement and competitiveness.

*Design for Six Sigma* (DFSS), however, is a process that seeks to prevent quality problems by focusing on upfront design. Upfront work helps to reduce the number of changes to design as projects move forward. DFSS focuses on developing product requirements by understanding customer needs, using a process similar to the one we describe in Chapter 4. DFSS also focuses on system design in order to identify critical interfaces. This attention to system design reduces rework and frustration later in the process.

Although DFSS can add work to the early parts of the development cycle, companies make up this added time as projects move through the development phases with fewer changes and iterations. See the earlier section "Spending more time upfront to reduce rework later" for more on the need to spend time and resources in the early part of the cycle.

Another benefit of Six Sigma (and one we consider huge) is that companies usually implement it as a system-wide change that includes business, manufacturing, and R&D processes. What this means for a product developer is that the systems and processes that optimize product development won't be so foreign to the rest of the company. You create a common process language that helps employees relate to the other functions and businesses in the company.

# Chapter 12

# Using Reviews to Keep Projects on Track

*M*any things can change between management's initial decision to resource a project and the time when the product development team has the product ready for market. You don't want managers looking over the product development team's shoulder, second-guessing and getting involved in the day-to-day or week-to-week decisions. On the other hand, you don't want your team moving forward without the benefit of management's wider and more strategic view, and its enthusiastic support.

The solution is a reviewing process. At reviews, the product development team updates reviewers on the project status, and reviewers make decisions to supply necessary resources to projects to continue them through development to the next phase — or not.

At the heart of the review process is the business case. It gives the team a way to track key financial and strategic project parameters, and it gives members of management necessary project information that allows them to make "apples-to-apples" comparisons with other projects.

In this chapter, you find out how reviewers strike the tricky balance between focusing on the merits of the project under review and considering the objectives of the entire product portfolio (see Chapter 11). You also discover how reviewers can stop projects and still gain value from the team's work. Finally, we explain how to write a business case to keep reviewers and the new product team on track.

# Understanding the Purpose of Reviews

In the product development process, NPD teams and their projects are *chartered* (authorized, funded, or "given the go-ahead") by management. This authorization happens early in a project's lifecycle, in what people sometimes call the "fuzzy front end." (Turn to Chapter 9 to find out more about the product development process and the fuzzy front end.) From that point on, teams need to be adequately resourced and have autonomy. They should have the ability to be creative in their approaches to turning concepts into products that hit the market.

However, NPD teams shouldn't be so autonomous and so creative that they stray from the business case approved by management. Your company has to strike a balance and also be prepared to deal with unexpected roadblocks or changes in the business and strategic landscape. What looked like a good project six months or a year ago may not seem like such a good bet today.

That's where the reviewing process comes in. In this section, we discuss the main purposes for reviews, and we describe when they should take place.

Phase reviews — the reviews that occur between the phases of the product development process — should focus on business issues, not technical issues. Reviewers and teams need to know whether a project is feasible, but the reviewers don't need to get into the technical details. The key technical issues at a phase review are as follows:

- ✔ Can we make it?
- ✔ How long will it take?
- ✔ How much will it cost?
- ✔ How does this technology relate to the company's technology development strategy (see Chapter 7)?

## Is the project still on track?

One big reason why you have to monitor new product projects as they go through the development process is to make sure they don't migrate from the value propositions managers expect them to fulfill.

For this reason, companies divide the product development process into phases and punctuate the phases with reviews (or what some companies call *gates* or *decision diamonds*). Take a look at the Cheat Sheet in the front of the book to see the major phases and reviews.

During each phase, the development team has a chance to be autonomous and creative; at the reviews following each phase, management gets to see what the team is doing and assess whether the project is meeting the reviewers' strategic and financial objectives (see the following section for financial issues).

The outcome of a review is like a contract between the team members and the reviewers. The reviewers, representing executives and managers, can give the team the resources and direction it needs to go through the next phase and to the next review.

Sometimes, at the beginning of a project, the reviewers and team members decide that the project needs only a few reviews or none at all between the initial Feasibility Review and the final "go-to-market" review. This is especially likely in the case of low-risk or incremental projects, such as a minor improvement to a product that is already in the market. Instead of just assuming that every NPD project has to go through every review in the phase/review process, be sure to consider, at the Feasibility Review, which reviews are important. Then set out-of-bounds criteria — financial and other limits the project has to stay within — so that if things change, the team can call for an unscheduled review (see the section "Creating out-of-bounds criteria" later in this chapter).

You should always hold a review before you launch a product into the market. Every new product affects your company's brand, its competitive position, and, of course, its other products and services. Management should get one last look before you take the fateful step to the market!

## Does the project still make financial sense?

When management approves a project, they base a significant part of their judgment on "What's the return on our investment (ROI) likely to be?" Many companies use hurdles or thresholds — for example, the company might decide that it will seldom approve a project that won't realize 15 percent over its cost.

Don't let company hurdle rates keep managers from approving projects that might have strategic benefits even if their numbers aren't quite up to snuff. For example, a platform project (see Chapter 3) — one that you expect to provide the basis for many products going forward — might have poor financials if you assess it all on its own.

Companies often hold reviews before project phases during which their investments will increase. For example, if the next phase requires expensive investments in special tooling or manufacturing infrastructure, management should make doubly sure that the project is worth the additional resources. This strategy is just good risk management — investing small amounts is okay, but when the sums get larger, the success criteria get firmer.

Each time your company holds a review, the reviewers make a decision to move the project to the next phase, to hold the project for more work, or to stop the project. If management is unwilling to make go/recycle/stop decisions and simply lets most projects move through the review process, your company will spend its scarce resources on many projects that have almost no chance of living up to early promises.

Of course, you have to balance the impact of shutting down a project with the possibility that it will ultimately succeed. 3M had a legendary culture of innovation in part because projects like its Post-it Notes were able to keep on going even though many people in the company thought the product was a bad idea. 3M made room for such projects through its "15 percent rule": Each product developer was able to spend 15 percent of his or her time on whatever he or she wanted. 3M's Post-its survived because of that rule.

Recycled or canceled projects don't signify failure! Reviews allow the team members and the managers to come together and mutually determine the best use of the company's scarce resources. And the responsibility doesn't fall only to the reviewers. If the team has good reason to believe that a project shouldn't continue or should stay longer in its current phase, it should recommend this to the reviewers.

For more advice on stopping or stalling projects, check out the later section "For Reviewers: Knowing When and How to Say No."

# Abiding by the Rules for a Successful Review

Phase reviews in the product development process are an important part of what makes a company successful at developing new products. They are not informal meetings where "the folks" gather to shoot the breeze about the latest new technologies. They are formal occasions, and the best review sessions follow a few basic rules. But don't let this stern warning keep you from enjoying your work! Formal occasions though they are, the best reviews are also places where people who know and respect each other can ask the hard questions and give deserved congratulations for jobs well done.

In this section, we discuss the rules for a successful review, as well as who needs to do what to ensure that you meet these rules.

# Provide clear guidelines for team deliverables

In order to grow your company's competence in holding phase reviews, teams have to follow guidelines so that they prepare appropriately for the reviews. You can make two big mistakes regarding guidelines: leaving the guidelines unclear and overspecifying them. Good guidelines tell team members exactly what the reviewers need to know and what the team has to accomplish before a review for a phase is scheduled.

Who creates these guidelines? It should be someone in management, because guidelines are effective and useful only insofar as they're followed by a large majority of teams. In many companies, the executives appoint a *process owner* for NPD. The process owner's responsibility is to manage the processes, including the review process. This person is also responsible for making sure that processes are changed over time, as his or her company learns what's working and what isn't. (Check out Chapter 8 to find out more about the role of the process owner.)

Having a standard checklist of review deliverables brings uniformity to the product development process. If all of the company's NPD teams use the same checklist, you can weed out what doesn't work and improve the list over time. Your teams will appreciate the guidance that good checklists provide, and reviewers will appreciate knowing what to expect. Your checklist will likely contain plenty of jargon — things that teams always do in your company. That's okay. Just be sure that everyone understands what you mean when you include jargon on your checklist. Don't ask for Beta Testing, for example, if your company doesn't do it or doesn't call it that (see Chapter 17 for info on Beta Testing).

The following is an example of a deliverables checklist for a project that's nearing the end of development. There's another example in Figure 9-2 that you may want to look at. This checklist was used by a company that manufactured cameras. You'll want to change the items to include the things that are important in your company. The cross-functional team leader (see Chapter 10) can use the checklist to manage the work of the team leading up to a review. After each item, write "by whom," "by when," and "percent complete." When you've checked all or most of the items as "100 percent complete," your team is ready for the review.

❑ Beta Tests complete

❑ Pilot production runs complete; manufacturability confirmed

❑ Quality and reliability testing complete

❑ Product launch details complete and committed to by functions

❑ Market research that demonstrates market acceptance

❏ Comparison of manufacturing scale-up plan to marketing launch plan by region

❏ Proposal outlining key issues "cleaned up" and suggests who should be responsible and accountable for each

❏ Proposal outlining how we'll measure product performance over time and who will be accountable for the measuring

❏ Initial order dates set and committed to by functions

❏ Action plan and request for resources needed to proceed to the next phase

## Train the reviewers to know what to look for

Companies usually assume that their teams — the product developers — need the training on how to make reviews effective. This is true, but reviewers need review training, too. What reviewers expect, teams are likely to do. If your reviewers don't know what to expect, though, trying to improve reviews by focusing on NPD teams is like carrying water uphill in a leaky bucket.

An executive should be responsible for making sure that reviewers are trained. The training doesn't have to be a time sink for busy executives. With a well-thought-out plan, most reviewers will get what they need even if the training is limited to "JIT" (just-in-time training) that gives them what they need to know when they need to know it.

When building a training program for reviewers, include an overview of the following points, at a minimum:

✔ You need to know about the project under review *before* the phase review meeting so that you're ready to make sound and informed decisions. If this means contacting functional members of the team beforehand, don't hesitate. For example, if the project is developing technology that is of strategic significance for other projects, be sure to understand how all that is supposed to work.

✔ You should know the role the project plays in your company's overall new product portfolio, as well as the resource implications of the project for the new product pipeline. (See Chapter 11 for more on portfolios and pipelines.)

✔ You should understand the different types of reviews. You need to know when it's appropriate to call a technical review, for example, instead of addressing technical issues at a phase review.

> ✔ You should understand the purposes of the phase review, which are to
> determine the individual merits of a project and its ongoing fit with the
> company's strategic objectives and to make a decision to continue, stop,
> or recycle a project (see the later section "For Reviewers: Knowing
> When and How to Say No").

Co-author Robin's training sessions with review committees include a mock
phase review, where reviewers hear project information, discuss it, and come
to a decision. After the role-play exercise, the reviewers discuss what worked
and what didn't so that they'll know what to expect at the real reviews. For
smaller companies, the JIT approach discussed earlier in this section might
be more appropriate.

## Do the necessary team prep work

Your NPD team needs to complete many tasks to prepare for a phase review.
Preparing for a review includes, but isn't limited to, updating the business
case and creating an executive summary. (You can read about the business
case in Chapter 9, and we offer plenty more later in this chapter. We also provide a template in the Appendix.)

An *executive summary* covers all the information contained in the full report
which the team will present at the review, but in condensed form. An executive summary shouldn't be longer than one or two pages. If your report has
an outline or table of contents, follow that, and write short paragraphs. Write
so that if a reviewer reads only the first sentence of each paragraph, she'll
still get the gist. Think of it this way: If an executive reads only the executive
summary, she should be able to participate in a discussion without revealing
that she didn't do all her homework.

Your NPD team should send the summary and the updated business case to
reviewers several days before a review. In most cases, members of the core
cross-functional NPD team should meet with their functional counterparts
before the review — especially if the reports contain any information that
may be puzzling or controversial for a functional reviewer. (***Note:*** All reviewers should, at a minimum, read the executive summary and review the business plan before the review. They should contact a functional member of the
team if they have any questions.)

Another piece of preparatory work is readying the discussion agenda. The
team leader should prepare an agenda, circulate it to the team members and
to the reviewers, and make sure that the review is scheduled for a convenient
time and at an appropriate location. He should also allocate enough time for
the review (usually an hour, and no more than two).

We recommend keeping the agenda short and sweet. Include an overview of progress since the last review, the team's recommendation and the decisions that the reviewers will make, a comparison of the current state of the project with expected deliverables at this time, and any specific presentations that will add to reviewers' understanding of the project status. Keep these added presentations to a minimum, and include plenty of time for discussion. We recommend including times on the agenda to help the team leader manage the discussion.

If your company's review committee takes on the role of scheduling meetings, your new product team leader should still confirm the details. A new product project belongs to the team, and you don't want the review to fall off the radar.

A team's final piece of prep work can be practice. The team can practice its review presentation ahead of time with some "friendly outsiders" — colleagues who are not working on this project. Through practice, you can make sure that the presentation works well, and the outsiders can help the team to anticipate the questions reviewers may ask.

## Ensure complete review attendance

Having 100 percent attendance seems like a foregone conclusion, right? Not so fast. As companies and new product projects become more and more spread out, it becomes harder to bring a whole team and all the reviewers together for a productive hour of discussion and reflection (see the later section "Inviting the right people to the review" to see who should attend). If you're finding it difficult to gather all required review parties, try some approaches that other companies have found successful:

- ✔ **Set aside a time — perhaps one day per month — when all the reviews take place.** If you have a set time, you can expect all the reviewers and the key members of the core NPD team to attend. The drawback of this method is that it can delay projects if your company has a hard stop at the end of each phase before the next phase can start. It works best if your reviews happen "around the time" of the transitions from one phase to the next. In Chapter 9, you discover more about tailoring phases and reviews to meet your company's needs; you also see that we both strongly recommend allowing for overlapping phases.

- ✔ **Use videoconferencing to "gather" reviewers and teams.** With video-conferencing, you can still display the team slides, the agenda, and any other necessary information for all the participants to see. Videoconferencing works well if your team members and your reviewers are dispersed, which is more and more the case these days.

Be sure that the review participants have a chance to practice with the videoconferencing technology before the review. When you're familiar with the technology, it feels *almost* like being in the same room. If you don't practice, videoconferencing can be very distracting and disruptive. (For more on this tool and the impact of technology on product development, see Chapter 14.)

- ✔ **Create rules of attendance.** No one wants to be called out as the cause of project delay and a waster of company resources. Rules of attendance can instill this fear. At DuPont, for example, the PAC (Project Approval Committee) rules state that if more than one PAC member doesn't show, the review is cancelled. A cancellation can significantly delay a project and upset a team. After DuPont put the rule in place, PAC members made sure they attended the sessions. One PAC member participated in a review from a telephone on the side of the road (he was on a bicycling vacation). Another joined a review from a cruise ship. It can work!

## Communicate review decisions

The reviewers' decision during a phase review isn't really a simple "go, stop, or redirect" decision. That final word is just the output of the decision-making process — the choice the reviewers make after they consider all the options, the information, the debate, and discussion. The decision-making process includes the following:

- ✔ The reviewers' assumptions, values, and concerns
- ✔ What the reviewers know or find out about the project
- ✔ What the reviewers understand about the new product portfolio and the resources that are available to the new product pipeline (see Chapter 11)
- ✔ The reviewers' takes on the company's market strategy, their understanding of the company's competencies, and their assessment of how the current project aligns with these

The review is a conversation in which the team gets to understand the basis for a decision about a project. Team members also get to inform reviewers about their project and correct misunderstandings. The reviewers should walk away with a better understanding of the project; the team should walk away with a better understanding of exactly what reviewers are expecting and how their project aligns with the company's NPD strategies. (See the later section "For Reviewers: Knowing When and How to Say No" for more on decision making.)

One of the most important and helpful parts of the review process is the opportunity that the development team has to listen to and learn from the reviewers. We're not saying that managers and executives are smarter or better than the rest of us. But when it comes to new products, they should have a wider perspective because they must understand the strategic context for a product. Executives often have wider experience than many team members, and they can bring that experience to a review discussion. So it's worth paying attention, and expecting that the review and the discussion on the reviewers' decisions will be useful and productive conversations.

# For Reviewers: Knowing When and How to Say No

Businesspeople are supposed to be hardheaded and unsentimental, but for some reason, members of review committees often have a hard time saying no. Sometimes, we suspect, it's because they aren't sure that there are any better projects to replace the cancelled ones. If that's a problem in your company, read Chapter 5 for advice on how to come up with plenty of great options. Some executives really don't understand that there's room for only so many projects in the development pipeline. If your executives think this way, get them to read Chapter 11 on "Managing Your Corporation's NPD Resources." Whatever the reasons, make sure that the reviewers in your company have a firm grasp on when they should cancel projects and on how they should do so. The following sections show you the way.

## When (and why) to stop projects

Here's a list of appropriate times for reviewers to stop new product projects:

- ✓ **At the very beginning of the process:** The concepts that you review during the Idea/Concept Screens (see Chapter 6) barely qualify as "projects." The team needs to present the review committee with many concepts to choose from. The ones that don't make it into the development pipeline should hit the shelves for later or be licensed/sold if they have value that your company isn't likely to use any time soon.

- ✓ **At the Feasibility Review (see Chapter 9):** After a project passes through the Concept Review, the development team has many questions to answer, including the following:

  - How long will it take to develop or acquire the needed technology, and how much will it cost?

  - Will the proposed product appeal to a large enough market of customers?

  - Will the margins be high enough for the company to make a good return on its investment?

  The Feasibility Review is when reviewers and teams should weed out the projects that can't answer yes to these questions.

  The best-run NPD processes look like funnels up to the Feasibility Review. After that point, you won't mind if your process straightens out and looks more like a tunnel. Be sure, however, that the reviewers aren't closing their eyes to problems that can occur after the Feasibility Review.

✔ **During the phase/review process:** Reviewers have the opportunity to stop a project at scheduled reviews during the development process. For example, they can stop a project whenever

- The team and/or the reviewers determine that the project is so far out of bounds that it no longer makes good business sense to pursue it. (See the later section "Creating out-of-bounds criteria" for more on the topic.)

- You run into resource issues. Perhaps the product pipeline is over-crowded and you have to hold up other projects. When this occurs, reviewers need to determine which projects they should stop or put on hold in order to free up resources for other projects. (For more on resources, see Chapter 11.)

- Competitors have changed the basis of competition by introducing products that make the product your company is developing less attractive. This is particularly true in industries where the market and/or technology are changing rapidly.

- Changes to the company's new product strategy — usually expressed as a portfolio of products (see Chapter 11) — impact the strategic importance of a project.

✔ **Before or just after launch:** No, not lunch. Launch. This should be a last resort. However, if the development team or the reviewers have reason to believe that their expectations for the product were way off, or if it looks like putting the product into market will harm the company's brand or existing products, they should bite the bullet here instead of creating a bigger mess to clean up later.

## *How to stop a project*

Stopping a project is really as simple as saying to the team, "We've decided to stop your project." The advice in this section centers on how to stop a project *well* – how to take care of team members, how to get value from cancelled projects, and so on.

When a project hits the cutting-room floor at a review, be sure the development team on the project is taken care of. Have your human resource professionals and your functions make it very clear in their evaluations that project failure often results from changes in circumstances, discovery of new information, and other stuff that's usually beyond the team's control. Failure shouldn't hurt a team member's evaluation or his or her chances of promotion. In fact, team members who've done an outstanding job on the failed project should be in line to get a great project the next time around.

First, management should take great care of the team. Next, management can turn its attention to the rejected project. You should try to extract all the value that you can from a stopped project. This benefits a company in several ways, including helping the development team recognize that the company values its work. The following list presents some possible sources of value from stopped projects:

- ✔ You may be able to sell or license any intellectual property (IP) you've developed (see Chapter 15 for more on IP).

- ✔ You can shelve the project if it seems like it may be worth developing in the future.

- ✔ You can make the customer visits and other market research the team carried out (see Chapter 4) available to other projects.

- ✔ You can divide the project's resources or what the project has learned among other new product projects. This can be especially useful if a team member's expertise is needed on other projects.

Whenever you stop a project, the development team — and sometimes the reviewers — should do a post-program assessment of what it has learned. The team should consider technical discoveries, information about the market and customers, and process examinations. Often, a process error causes the breakdown that results in the project's cancellation. Stopped projects can provide very valuable information about how well your development process is working and help you to make the process better for future projects.

The review team owes it to management, and to the people responsible for NPD strategy (see Chapter 3), to communicate the reasons for the stoppage, especially if the reasons are strategic and might impact other projects.

# Making Review Meetings Work

Good new product phase reviews should be set up like any good business meeting. They work best when the right people are in attendance, when everyone comes prepared, when the participants follow a clear agenda, and when all parties come away with a clear decision and goal to reach before the next review. We take you through these requirements in the sections that follow.

## Inviting the right people to the review

The new product team leader(s) should attend every review, as should most or all of the members of the new product core team (see Chapter 10 for more on the team leader and the core and extended teams). The team leader should invite any members of the extended development team whose specific knowledge the team needs in order to answer questions from the reviewers.

The other people who attend reviews are, of course, the reviewers. Reviewers are business and functional heads, managers, and executives who can assess the merits of the project under review while understanding the larger strategic landscape. The reviewers oversee the resources that the team needs to keep the project going. Some companies call these people the *Project Approval Committee,* or PAC.

The number of people attending a phase review should be kept small enough to facilitate dialogue. Three to five reviewers can represent functional and business interests; five or so team members should attend the review. Reviewers will generate most of the discussion, with team members presenting the project status.

Some companies have standing committees of reviewers; some call reviewers together as needed for particular projects. Two things to remember:

✔ Make sure your reviewers know what's expected of them (see the earlier section "Train the reviewers to know what to look for").

✔ Make sure your reviewers clearly understand the company's strategic new product objectives (see Chapter 3), along with the company's new product portfolio (see Chapter 11).

## Following a clear meeting plan

A new product review meeting needs a clear agenda. It also helps if you have a facilitator who can lead the group and write key discussion points on a wall chart. An hour is usually enough for presentation, discussion, and decision — but you don't want to waste any of it. For more complex projects, a review may take up to two hours.

A review usually starts with the team leader or the review committee chair calling the meeting to order. The leader or chair reminds the attendees of the purpose of the meeting. The purpose should be a simple variation on this theme: "The purpose of this meeting is to review the status of the X project, to address any questions the reviewers may have, and to come to a decision about the next phase of the project."

The team then updates the reviewers — briefly — on events that have taken place since the last review and presents highlights of the business case. ***Note:*** Usually, the team leader will do the presentation, with team members attending in order to answer questions. However, if a part of the presentation is dicey and clearly in the lap of one of the functional members, he or she might present that part.

Smart companies create standard formats for presenting the information so that reviewers don't have to figure out what the teams are presenting and why. As much as possible, your team should present project information visually and in a format that allows for comparison — both with prior phases of the project and with other projects.

As part of its presentation, the team should make its recommendation to the reviewers to continue, hold, or stop the project. You should also make the necessary decisions very explicit. When co-author Robin facilitated reviews, she would recommend that the teams have a slide at the beginning of their presentations entitled "Decisions Needed." The slide listed all the decisions needed at that review. The teams would show the same slides at the end of their presentations.

Invite reviewers to ask questions at any time, but ask them to hold discussion until set points. Design the presentation so that when you present something that probably needs discussion, you have a slide announcing that.

## Ending with a clear decision

Every phase review should end with a clear decision: The project goes to the next phase, stops altogether, or requires more work in the current phase. Some of the issues that may prompt a review board to "hold" (or *recycle*) a project include the need to clarify customer requirements (see Chapter 4), demonstrate technology feasibility (see Chapter 7), or to make sure that the proposed design can be manufactured (see Chapter 9 for more on "design for x").

In some companies, reviewers send the new product team away after they've completed their questioning to give themselves a chance to discuss and decide alone. Other companies complete the whole process with the teams and reviewers together. Be sure your participants are clear at the beginning of the meeting about how the decision-making process will unfold.

Companies also differ in how they make the decision. You can vote, in which case a simple majority wins, or you can work to consensus. It seems best to us that if any reviewer is firmly opposed to the majority decision, the team should do some further work to answer the questions that would allow the reviewers to come to consensus.

What doesn't work is to have an intermediary communicate the reviewers' decision to the team. Make sure that the team, or at the very least the team leader, has a chance to hear the decision in person and ask questions to understand the reasoning behind it.

## Keeping review records

Every review meeting should have a notetaker present (it's a good idea to tape-record and transcribe the proceedings as well). A team member should have the assignment of circulating the review minutes to the review participants within 48 hours. Every participant should provide additions and corrections, and the team member should create and circulate the final set of minutes and add them to the team's ongoing documentation.

If participants made any explicit requests or promises at the review, the notetaker should clearly include them as part of the review minutes. When the requests or promises are carried out, you should note it in the documentation of the review. Also, if the team and the reviewers suggest a time frame for the next review, include that in the review minutes, too, and have people add it to their calendars.

# The Prose of Finance and Strategy: Writing a Project's Business Case

Companies invest scarce resources in new product development in order to get returns on their investments. It doesn't matter if you think your idea will revolutionize an industry; if it doesn't make good business sense, your company shouldn't invest in it. How you prove that your project makes good business sense is with its *business case* — a document that sets forth the basic market and technology assumptions of the project, along with the financial implications of those assumptions. (We included a business case template in the Appendix which you can use as-is or revise for your projects.)

A business case also can include specific out-of-bounds criteria — metrics, agreed on by the team and the project reviewers, that define the project's key objectives.

In this section, we look at how a new product team moves from an early, preliminary business case to the full-fledged financial justification it will need as it moves into the Feasibility Review. We also explain how to update the business case as the team moves through the rest of the product development process (see Chapter 9).

## Drafting the preliminary business case

The new product team should draft a preliminary, mini business case (sometimes referred to as a *trigger document*) as part of defining the product concept.

The preliminary business case outlines the requirements for the project and includes estimates of likely return. At this early stage, the team should use ranges — "The market for the product is between 100K and 300K," for example. Ranges can accurately represent what the team can know at this point in the project.

The best way to create a preliminary business case is to start with a document that asks for high-level estimates of what you'll include in the full business case. Following are suggestions of what you might include in the preliminary business case:

- ✔ **Project overview:** Include a one-sentence project "mission" or value proposition, a brief description of the proposed project, and a brief description of the product that includes key customer requirements that the team has identified to date.

- ✔ **Estimate of resources needed:** Include the likely skills and material support the team will need, and for how long. This is also the place to outline possible supply-chain or partnership plans.

- ✔ **Strategic alignment:** Include a statement of the project's strategic importance and its alignment with the organization's strategy.

- ✔ **Project timing:** Include the proposed launch date and a description of any known factors that might impact timing.

- ✔ **Market overview:** Include key segments and competitor information to the extent known.

- ✔ **A brief description of technology to be included, plus any foreseen technology hurdles:** Include important manufacturing and operations information here as well.

- ✔ **Overview of legal, regulatory, and other issues:** Include plans for addressing these to the extent known.

- ✔ **Key parameters that will affect the financial value of the project:** Include range estimates of sales units and volume, cost targets, margins, and market share.

Be sure to include the names, team roles, and contact information of key team members, too.

You can't really know, with any certainty, what it will cost to develop your product or how long it will take, not to mention exactly who will buy how many and for how much. Beware of precision without accuracy! As you create the preliminary business case, use range estimates and advertise your degree of confidence. Sometimes, even early on, it's possible to be sure of some information. Other times, you simply put down a guess. Don't pretend to have more information than you really do.

# *Factoring in project financials*

At some companies, the business case is reduced pretty much to financials. If that's the case in your company, we give you some good arguments at the end of this section as to why relying on financials alone isn't such a good idea. However, financials *are* very important. They're based on estimates of market size and share, competitive assessments, and estimated selling prices. These estimates are part of your launch plan and should be included in the business case that the team prepares.

The following list presents some ways that companies judge the financial viability of their new product projects:

- **Net present value (NPV):** The present value of cash inflows minus the present value of cash outflows (or minus initial investment in most cases).

  NPV is a standard method for financial evaluation of long-term projects — like NPD projects.

- **Internal rate of return (IRR):** The return rate that a company expects to earn on the capital it invests.

  In general, if the IRR is greater than the project's cost of capital, or *hurdle rate,* the project will add value for the company.

- **Earnings before interest and taxes (EBIT):** Also known as operating income and operating profit.

  In deciding whether to invest in a new product project, executives sometimes compare the firm's existing earnings potential (or EBIT) with the profit potential of the investment.

- **Shareholder value added (SVA):** Will the investment in a new product return more value to the company's shareholders than it could earn in an alternative and safer investment such as risk-free bonds? If so, it will be an investment that produces a positive SVA.

This alphabet soup includes various ways that companies figure out the likely value of the projects they spend money on. They all have to do with assessing the *cost of capital* — how much it really costs the company to spend its resources today on projects that will not yield results until some time in the future. Businesses, and their investors, tend to want their money now (if not yesterday). New product development forces them to use present money and resources for results that will come in the future. New product teams have to show executives, shareholders, and reviewers that this makes good sense; the formulas in the previous list help to do that.

### Computing/estimating the financials for your project

To compute the financials for your project, you use a combination of estimates. The estimates usually include expected gross revenue, how much the product will cost to produce and distribute (cost of goods sold, or COGS), and other expenses. To figure your expected net revenue, you add the cost to develop the product, any capital expenses incurred, and usually some overhead charge.

Most companies calculate expected revenue over the three-year period when they expect their products to be at peak sales. This time frame varies, however, depending on your industry. (For a discussion of product lifecycles, see Chapter 3.)

### Recognizing why companies shouldn't become too fixated on financials

Financials aren't the whole story. Companies that rely too much on them tend to pull the risk out of their new product portfolios and end up falling behind as product developers. The following list outlines a few problems with the world of project financials:

- ✔ Financial estimates can be very uncertain.
- ✔ The reason for launching a project may be strategic, not financial. For example,

  - You may launch a product in order to block a competitor's entry to a market.

  - You may develop a product in order to build technological capacity or capability.

- ✔ Sometimes projects that don't cost much but won't return much either — for example, exploratory projects — can position a company for success downstream.

Keep an eye on the financials of a project, but remember to be honest — with yourself, your team members, and your reviewers — about how certain you are of your estimates.

## Updating the prelims to draft the full business case

When you start with a preliminary business case that asks for the early version of information that you'll include later, keeping the business case up-to-date becomes a normal part of your team's activities.

Make sure the checklists that teams use in preparing for reviews (see the section "Provide clear guidelines for team deliverables" earlier in this chapter) include the information that's necessary for completing and updating the business case.

In a business case update, your team should make clear exactly what elements have changed since the last review. The team is involved with the project nearly every waking moment (and in some sleeping ones, too) between reviews; the reviewers have had plenty of other tasks on their minds. You should provide a summary of changes to the business case as a part of the executive summary (see the earlier section "Do the necessary team prep work").

Most business cases include three parts:

- ✓ **Program assumptions and resources:** You cover the rationale for the NPD project, the key financial assumptions (see the previous section), an assessment of risks and uncertainties, and the team's request for resources from the company's different functions (see Chapter 11).

  The team should honestly tell reviewers what the risks and uncertainties of the project are, and the reviewers should be able to discuss these risks without blaming anyone. Being able to hold frank discussions of the business case is a good indication that your company has a culture in which new product development can thrive — a culture of openness, honesty, and respect.

- ✓ **Customer satisfaction, competitive landscape, and marketing plan:** You include information about the target market, identified customer needs for the product (see Chapter 4), and the launch plan to date (see Chapter 13).

- ✓ **Product development and production plan:** You provide the project schedule, including target review dates, your plans for research (if any), and your plans for working with partners and/or suppliers (see Chapter 16). You also include environmental issues, patent/legal issues, and standards and quality issues in this part of the plan.

You can find a business case template in the Appendix to this book. Feel free to copy it just as it is, or tailor it to fit your organization's needs. A big part of the difference between the full business case and the preliminary business case is the thoroughness of the information that you should include. To create a preliminary business case, just weed out the more detailed stuff from the full case, and be sure to remind people to use estimates and ranges.

## Creating out-of-bounds criteria

At the Feasibility Review of the development process (see Chapter 9), the review committee makes a decision about whether to fund a project, stick it on the shelf, toss it in the scrap heap, or try to sell it to someone else. The members base their decisions on the information the new product team provides in its business case.

But what if things change? What if, for example, the target market is smaller than estimated, meaning that the company will sell fewer products than the development team was counting on? What if the time and resources necessary are much greater than anticipated? Or, what if it turns out that the technology you had thought would take a year to develop can be acquired cheaply, driving your development time from years to months?

During your Feasibility Review, you should specify certain changes that would affect the business case so seriously that the team would need to call an emergency review. The parameters you specify are known as *out-of-bounds criteria*.

To specify out-of-bounds criteria for a project, the team sets a range for how much the net present value (NPV, the value of the resources being spent on the project) can vary without making a huge difference to the business case. Other criteria include project schedule and expected return.

By setting out-of-bounds criteria, the team members give the reviewers confidence that the product will be developed in a way that meets the review criteria and that the reviewers will be the first to know if that doesn't happen — in time for corrective action, of course. This certainty also motivates reviewers to let projects move ahead without scheduled reviews, which speeds up the development process. As long as the team has set clear out-of-bounds criteria, increasing the speed won't increase the risk. (For more on out-of-bounds criteria, check out Chapter 9.)

# Chapter 13

# Launching Products for Market Success

································································

## In This Chapter

▶ Making preparations for a successful launch

▶ Creating a plan to execute a great product launch

▶ Executing a product launch (with the help of some friends)

▶ Staying on the job after the product gets to market

································································

A new product's market success depends on many factors, and a good launch is certainly one of them. If you've identified what your customers really need (Chapter 4); if you've conjured up great ideas for products that can fulfill those needs and delight your customers (Chapter 5); and if you've assembled a dedicated cross-functional team that has whittled down the ideas and developed a product by using a well-implemented phase/review process (Chapters 9 and 10), all your hard work deserves a well-planned and well-executed launch.

The launch phase is when the company actually releases the product into the market. It's kind of like sending Junior off to college. You know there will be new and different support networks available to him, but you also know that it's a huge transition — for you and for him. At this point, all the launch planning the team has already done and all the new tasks that the team has to carry out become the central activity of the development team. You've executed many duties in direct support of the launch — far in advance of pushing the "Go!" button on the big day.

In this chapter, you discover that you should start your launch planning early and in parallel with all the other development activities. You review the elements of a successful launch. You find out who should complete what tasks and when they should complete them. Finally, you read up on how to support your new product in the market well after it has lost its new-car smell. (Our thanks to Michael Compeau, who provided input, ideas, and edits to this chapter.)

# Preparing for a Successful Launch — You Gotta Start Early

Many phase/review processes in product development name the last phase "Launch." This conveys the idea that the NPD team should work linearly, first on the business case, then on developing the product, then on testing and validating, and then — and only then — launch. No! Postponing launch issues until the last part of the development process is a recipe for disaster. Even though you can't actually launch a product until you complete all those other activities, you can and should start planning your launch right away.

In this way, the launching of a product is no different than the other parts of the phase/review process (see Chapter 9). If the development team keeps the entire scope of work in view and starts on activities as early as possible, it gives the team and the company a much better chance of bringing a successful product to market.

A successful launch requires both administrative tasks and creative thinking, starting at the beginning of the development process and continuing until the product has safely set sail in the market. The sections that follow take you through important steps for planning a successful launch, from naming a "launch leader" to setting the goals for the launch.

## Naming the launch leader

The *launch leader* is a member of the new product team whom the team leader counts on to plan and execute the launch.

Team leaders and managers are responsible for naming the launch leader. When they're assembling a new product team, they should include a team member who has launch experience and possesses the qualities you look for in a successful leader. The team leaders should recruit the launch leader as a team member — a member who has the full awareness that leading the launch is her job. You don't want to be looking around for a launch leader when the project is half over — or worse, a few months or weeks before the end!

Launch leaders often come from the marketing function and have experience in product launches. The launch leader has many responsibilities. She updates the new product team at regular team meetings about how the launch planning is going. She also works with the other team members to make sure their activities and goals stay in sync with her objectives for a successful launch.

For example, launch timing is of critical importance. If the team is developing a seasonal product, they'll have a tight window during which they must launch it. If a competitor is breathing down their necks, speed to market may be essential. To meet an essential deadline, the launch leader may work with the team and the reviewers to eliminate a product feature in order to get the product to the market on time.

## Pulling together the launch team

One of the launch leader's first tasks is to assemble a team of people who can carry out the activities of launch planning and execution — a launch team, which is an extension of the core NPD cross-functional team. Launching a product, like coming up with the idea and developing it, requires a breadth of skills and experience. At a minimum, the launch team needs people who can plan and carry out the following (you can read more about these tasks in the section "Forming the Launch Plan"):

- ✔ Market research (see the following section)
- ✔ Supply chain management
- ✔ Distribution and channel planning and coordination
- ✔ Training for sales and service

Some of the people on the launch team will be members of the core cross-functional team. For the core team members, planning and executing the launch is only a part of their NPD job, but their participation as a part of the launch team is critical. They're the ones who can tie in other aspects of the project — product design, product testing, manufacturing, and so on — with the launch plans.

But for many product launches, the launch leader will need additional skills and experience. These additional people come from different business functions, such as marketing, sales, customer service, and distribution. You can think of them as the "extended" launch team — resources that the launch leader needs to carry out her duties — and their relationship to the new product team is through the launch leader.

In Chapter 10, you find out how to form cross-functional NPD teams and the extended teams that help them carry out the project tasks.

## Understanding marketing's role

Marketing employees are integral to making sure that a new product succeeds in the marketplace. The launch leader must make sure that the launch and core teams are working on marketing issues while they're designing and developing the product. The following list presents the key roles of the marketing members on the new product team.

Although all these roles are important to the launch process, the ones in bold are roles that the launch leader, usually a marketing team member, should lead.

- Participating in customer visits (see Chapter 4)

- Participating in idea generation sessions (see Chapter 5)

- Conducting market research throughout the development process — market segmentation and testing, product use testing (Alpha and Beta), and so on (see Chapter 17)

- Forecasting market and sales projections (see *The PDMA Handbook of New Product Development,* 2nd Edition, edited by Kenneth B. Kahn [Wiley] for more on forecasting)

- **Establishing launch goals (see the following section)**

- **Creating the launch plan (see the section "Forming the Launch Plan"):**

  - Rollout strategy

  - Channel strategy

  - Sales training plan

  - Customer service plan

  - Test marketing and customer trials

  - Pricing strategy

  - Supply chain management

- **Performing a post-launch evaluation (see the section "Factoring In Post-Launch Evaluations")**

- Planning for product obsolescence

## Establishing goals for a successful launch

The launch leader and team members, working with the core team, should use the project's business case (see Chapters 9 and 12) to guide them in establishing what's required for a launch to be successful. The key launch objectives that the team should track include the following:

- Gaining market share and market penetration

- Solid financial performance, including sales

- High quality and customer satisfaction

The goals in the previous list aren't like the final report card you got when you graduated from high school. These are *formative metrics.* The core team and the launch team should develop the product with these goals in mind, and they should track a product's actual performance against these objectives.

## Product introduction versus product launch

At an International Association for Product Development (IAPD) workshop in 2000, Professor Jean-Philippe Deschamps of IMD in Switzerland pinpointed the difference between *introducing* an incremental innovation and *launching* a radical innovation. Introducing a "new-and-improved" version of an existing product should be a smooth process that extends or shifts market demand. On the other hand, launching a completely new product requires mobilization of a company's marketing and sales forces and the creation of new demand in the marketplace. The more radical your new product ideas are, the more you need the advice in this chapter and book as a whole! ***Note:*** From the point of view of launch, *radical* includes both technology newness and market newness.

Often, taking corrective action after a launch can be the difference between success and failure (see the section "Factoring In Post-Launch Evaluations").

Be sure that the formative metrics your team chooses are *actionable.* In other words, the information has to get to the team quickly so members can respond, it has to be accurate so they can respond correctly, and the responses have to be within the team's ability. Tracking sales numbers is a good example of an actionable metric *if* the metric is clear. For example, the metric might include sales volume and sales growth over time, excluding promotional sales.

# Forming the Launch Plan

The *launch plan,* which the launch leader creates (but be sure to involve the rest of the core team!), is a set of strategies that guide the launch team in executing a successful launch. Launching a product has been compared to a three-ring circus — one in which each ring features high-wire acts, jugglers, balancing acts, and wild-animal shows. The core NPD team (see Chapter 10) may feel pressure and confusion as it develops the product, but many people report that that's nothing compared to what the launch team has to deal with as the product moves from the relative protection of the company into the big, wide world.

The following sections discuss the various actions you need to take to create a complete launch plan.

## Creating a rollout strategy

You've finished designing and developing the product, and you've produced enough inventory to support the launch. It's time to open the factory doors and let the product "roll out" into the market (even if your product didn't get produced in a factory). The rollout strategy helps define how your product will get to market. You can introduce the product in one of two ways:

- ✓ **Hard launch:** You introduce the product all at once. With a hard launch, you have to orchestrate it so that you introduce the product simultaneously in all your target markets.

- ✓ **Rolling launch:** You introduce the product in a sequence of different markets. With this strategy, also known as a *soft launch,* you more literally roll out the product into the market in successive waves. Often, you start with one channel or region first, and then you expand into more markets as manufacturing flow and sales build.

Rolling launches can be easier to coordinate, but communication and digitization (see Chapter 14) in today's world make it harder to execute a rolling launch. You may find customers wondering why your product isn't available in their areas or, worse yet, competitors moving in to block your access to certain markets.

The launch leader must help the NPD team determine the right rollout strategy for a product, taking into consideration all the issues in the following list. Notice that the launch leader and the launch team can't decide many of these issues on their own. The NPD core team as a whole should look at the issues these questions raise and decide what makes the most sense for the product to achieve success in the market:

- ✓ **How important is speed to market for the product and "first-mover" advantage in the product or service category?** If you answer "very," you're looking at a hard launch.

- ✓ **Can competitors easily move in after you launch your product?** If so, you may want to protect your position with a hard launch.

- ✓ **Can you stay ahead of the competition by innovating faster than they can?** If you can, the slower pace of a staged rolling launch may work best for you.

- ✓ **How much of the product can you produce in time to support your launch?** Can you produce enough product, get it distributed, and put it on the shelves in order to support a hard launch? If you can't, a rolling launch may be your only option.

- ✓ **How much territory are your sales and service people ready to support?** You should do a rolling launch if you need the extra time to get sales and service up to speed throughout your market.

Here are a few ways that companies take advantage of very small beginnings in order to build up into a larger launch:

- ✓ **Can you target a specific customer group to jump-start your launch?** Sometimes, you can create a buzz and excitement about your product if you soft launch to a particular customer group. The minimal launch will act as a "promotion" for the successive rolling waves.

✓ **Can you start by selling the product through an easy-to-manage channel?** For example, if you can sell the product through your own dealers first, you can conduct a limited launch during which you discover how customers respond to the product. Depending on the response, you can get ready to move to the larger markets. You might also discover changes that would make your product more attractive in the market.

✓ **Can you start by selling the product online?** Some products succeed through Internet sales before their companies start selling in more traditional channels.

You also need to know how much product differentiation you need in order to sell in different markets and how soon you can create it. If your product will be identical in every market in which you plan to launch, a hard launch could work best. If, however, you need to tailor the product — providing instructions in different languages, adjusting for different regulatory hurdles, or changing functionality to serve customers in different markets, for instance — a rolling launch may be your best bet.

Before you can launch your product, you may need regulatory approvals. It is up to the core team, and usually the technical members in particular, to anticipate and secure regulatory approval. However, it's a good idea for the launch leader to make sure that the NPD team gets these approvals in time for launch. And if you plan to launch in different markets or geographies that require different approvals, the launch leader should make sure the team is managing this as well. You can stage a rolling launch so that you secure approvals in time for each successive wave, or you can secure all the approvals in time for a hard launch. Make the decision based on what's best for launch success.

## Determining how your new product will work with (or replace) your existing ones

Launching a new product often means displacing, or *cannibalizing,* existing products. Your company's new product and launch teams don't have a permission slip to launch a new product into a market without first considering its impact on the products you already have there.

How you choose to relate the new product to an existing product depends on the place of the new product in your overall product portfolio (see Chapter 11 for more on product portfolios). Do you want the introduction of the new product to sustain sales in the channel or to contribute to growth of the product line? Do you want to undermine the efforts of a competitor or enhance your brand image? Do you aim to go after a whole new market or technology opportunity?

The answers to these questions will help your team make better decisions about how to place the new product in the ongoing mix of products and sales.

You can use several approaches to dovetail your launch strategy for a new product with your existing products (notice that most of these strategies need to be planned early in the product development process, when you're selecting concepts and designing the product):

- ✔ **Plan for the retirement or the phasing out of the product that you're replacing to coincide with the introduction of the new product.** Your new MP3 player's launch might be just the right time to pull the old one off the shelves. If you've got too much inventory for that, consider moving the old one to some out-of-the-way markets so that the new one can take center stage in your most important ones.

- ✔ **Identify new markets in which the new product could be successful, and launch in those markets.** You may look to different geographies, industries, or even price points. You can keep your new kitchen product from competing with your existing ones if it's pricier (and, of course, has more and better features) or if it's designed for small spaces, summer homes, or trailers.

- ✔ **Price your new and improved product higher than your existing product.** Expect to cannibalize sales of the existing product and to phase it out over time. If you're coming out with a new and improved inkjet printer, for example, take advantage of putting a higher price on it. Some people will buy the old, lower cost one; people who buy the higher priced one will feel they're getting more value because they can compare with the old one; and as you whittle down your inventory on the old one, you'll forestall the inevitable day when your fancy new printer prices will also have to drop to meet price pressure from competitors.

- ✔ **Price your new and somewhat slimmed-down product lower than your existing product.** Expect to attract customers for whom the current product is too pricey. This strategy is the opposite of the one in the previous bullet. Suppose you have a printer on the market with all the bells and whistles; you might introduce one with fewer of these and attract new customers. Do your research to make sure that your higher end customers won't migrate to the lower price product! And be sure that if this is your strategy, you've designed a product platform (see Chapter 3) so that you don't have to reinvent the whole wheel when you develop the new product.

## Flipping through possible channel strategies

Many companies, instead of selling their products directly to the end-user customer, go through *channel partners*. These are the dealers, distributors, and retailers who help to distribute and actually sell your product. They include exclusive dealers, like Harley-Davidson's network, retailers like Shaw's and Stop-and-Shop, and the huge outlets like Wal-Mart and Sears.

Many companies design successful products with the requirements of channel partners in mind. As the NPD team builds its understanding of the customer (see Chapter 4), it also should include market players besides the end-user — and the channels through which the team intends to market the product often play an important role.

Here are a few approaches to channel strategy design. Don't limit your thinking to these alone — here's a good place for your team to be creative!

✔ Many new product launches are successful because their product development teams recruit downstream channel partners as dedicated launch partners well before the launch. These teams carefully coordinate activities to ensure a clockwork-like success when the time comes to launch into the channels. This strategy is particularly common when teams work with large retailers like The Home Depot, Wal-Mart, and Target, but you can apply the logic to any reseller channel.

✔ Many companies recruit dealer networks to distribute and sell their products. Some dealers are exclusive — they carry only products from one company — and some are not. For example, a dealer/distributor of lawn and garden equipment will carry Toro and John Deere and whatever other brands sell well in its territory.

✔ Many companies work with wholesale distributors to make sure that their products get onto the shelves at your local supermarkets or bookstores or into retail shops like K-Mart.

Sometimes, channel partners work closely with the product developers to design products that appeal to their customers and/or fill out their offerings. The NPD team brings its intimate understanding of what the customer wants or needs, and the channel partner brings its understanding of what products may be missing on its shelves and what products it can sell. The channel partner functions almost like a member of the team; however, don't forget that the channel partner holds many of the cards. With this strategy, you give up a degree of independence in exchange for the likelihood — but seldom a guarantee — of a successful launch.

The channel strategy you choose can impact product design, development, packaging, and timing. The launch team members should thoroughly review their recommendations for a channel strategy and do the same with members of the new product team. Otherwise, the team is headed for disappointment when it discovers that the product it has developed cannot be packaged in a way that meets retailers' needs, for example.

## Training your sales and service teams to support the new product

The launch team needs to plan for any necessary sales and service efforts. If your company has a sales force that will drive the sales of the product, the launch team needs to provide for the necessary training. As part of the training, the sales force also needs any manuals, instructions, and other materials that go with the product.

The NPD team may need to complete some actual products that you can use for this training well ahead of the launch date. This is only one of the circumstances that may speed up the need for at least a limited manufacturing run. Others include various kinds of new product testing (see Chapter 17) as well as test marketing (see "Utilizing test marketing and consumer trials" later in this chapter).

If you're launching a new drug, the sales force has to be able to talk to the doctors on the level that the doctors will respect. "Hey, your patients are gonna love this one!" just won't do. The sales force needs training in the results of clinical studies, comparison with other medications, benefits and side effects, and so on. If your new product is a machine for baking bread targeted at high-end restaurants, your sales people had better be prepared to demonstrate to people who already know a lot about bread baking!

In the same way, a service force may need to receive training before the launch. This may include workers who run a call center and the personnel who make visits to the customers. Good use of *Beta Testing* — testing the product in the hands of friendly customers — can help iron out any service issues. The launch team can take responsibility for training a small core team during Beta Site tests, and this team can provide expertise to a larger team when the product is launched. (Take a look at Chapter 17 for more on Beta Testing; the next section talks more about customer trials.)

## Utilizing test marketing and consumer trials

When you use a *test market,* you make a limited amount of the product you're developing available to a small market, and the NPD and launch teams use the experience to improve the product and their launch/market strategies. You benefit from some obvious advantages by dribbling product into the market, including the following:

- If the product fails, only a small portion of your customers will know.
- You can assess consumer response to the product, including packaging, pricing, and use.

> ✔ You get some real stories from satisfied customers to beef up your pro-
> motion and sales when you fully launch the product.
>
> ✔ You can test and improve the logistical aspects of the launch: coordinat-
> ing with suppliers, manufacturing in quantity, shipping, dealing with
> your dealers and distributors, and so on (see the earlier section
> "Creating a rollout strategy" for more).

Test marketing comes with considerable risk. Your competitors may find out about your new product and try to beat you to a wider launch. Because of this, test marketing has become less popular in recent years. We live in an "instant" society where news travels fast and people want everything now or earlier — including your company's investors, who may see test marketing as a way of delaying their share of the goodies.

So how can you decide whether to launch in a test market? If you're one of the big guys, we suggest using these only when you're dealing with an impor-tant customer — one you'd actually like to get involved early. A manufacturer of breast imaging technology placed its brand new technology with a single customer to get early results, for example. After the equipment proves suc-cessful there, it plans to ramp up distribution to other sites.

There are surely other times when a limited introduction may be appropriate. Could you get famous socialites to chew your new bubble gum before you introduce it to the wider public? Go ahead, by all means! But our general rule here is caution.

On the other hand, if you're one of the little guys, limited launch and test mar-keting may be all you can really do. Find the best place to start — perhaps with a customer whose status in the industry will attract other customers — and keep your marketing pace in line with your ability to produce, distribute, sell, and service your product.

You have to support test marketing with adequate amounts of product — including literature, packaging, instructions, and the training of sales and ser-vice people. Don't underestimate the need to be "almost ready" for a full launch when you move into the market in a limited fashion.

Instead of thinking "test market," think "consumer trial." Consumer trials are often called *Beta Tests* (see Chapter 17 for more on these kinds of tests). The next time a Web site offers you a chance to participate in a Beta Test, go ahead. See for yourself how they work, and consider whether a consumer trial could be beneficial as you develop and launch a new product.

## *Establishing a price*

Pricing is a key factor in launch success. Too high and no one will buy it; too low and you've left cash on the table. The problem is, there is no simple way to decide what's "too high" or "too low." Even when the product is in the market, you can't always pin success or failure on price points.

So no wonder pricing isn't a job that most NPD or launch teams want to take on. But achieving the project's goals — the objectives that you establish in the business case (see Chapters 9 and 12, as well as the Appendix) — depend on your pricing strategy. A product's pricing strategy is where the rubber hits the road. Will your new product live up to its financial predictions or fall short?

### Calculating a range

Your first job is to establish a range within which your price will fall. One of the simplest ways to do this is to determine the lowest price at which the company will see return on its investment, and then establish the highest price it could possibly expect because of the product's perceived value in the customer's eyes. To do this, the NPD team, with the help of the launch leader, has to establish two parameters:

- ✔ **Cost:** Be very clear about the cost of the project *and* the product — what it has or will cost the company to develop the product, and what it costs each time it produces and sells one. The cost defines the threshold at which the company will lose or make money on the project.

  Every time you spend more on the project, you add a little to the overall amount that the product must regain in the market. But each time you add as much as a penny to the product cost, you add a financial burden to the product that will have to be figured in over its lifecycle. Beware of adding that cute detail that might skim margin from your product for its entire life!

- ✔ **Value:** Establishing the value of a product starts at the beginning, with customer visits (see Chapter 4). By visiting customers, listening to them, and observing their work processes, you'll begin to understand the benefit — financial or otherwise — that customers get from buying and using your product.

### Setting a price

After you establish a range — the space between *cost* and *value* — you can nail down the actual price you want to set. The launch team and the new product team should consider the following factors:

- ✔ **The competition:** How much are other, similar products selling for? If that's at the high end of your range, you might get away with a higher price; if at the lower, you might have to charge less. If it's in the basement (defined by your costs), shame on you for developing it in the first place!

- ✔ **Distributors/sales force/channel partners:** What percent of the selling price will go to the folks who get your product to the customers? If you can sell your product directly, you'll get 100 percent (but be sure to add the cost to the company of maintaining its sales force and distribution network when you calculate the cost to produce the product).

✔ **Discounts:** Will you offer savings (to large or loyal customers, for example)? How much? Your price might be toward the upper end of the range, but discounts will eat away at profits. Be sure to address this in your calculations. And don't forget: If discounts mean that you're going to sell more, they may well be worth it. Plus, there are some industries, like software, where customers expect a discount nowadays.

✔ **Markets:** Will you offer the product at different price points in different markets? It can be a good strategy, for example, to pin a few dollars or cents onto product that's sold in places where the overall cost of living is higher. Buyers in those demographics tend to be less price-conscious than buyers where a higher price compares unfavorably with other costs in their region.

✔ **Features:** Another variable is product features. Many manufacturers create entire lines of products from low-end vanilla to high-end almond-soy latte. An example of this is blenders. You can get the cheapest one, which will do the trick. Or you can get the most expensive one, which will chop, dice, whirl, heat, bake, set the table — whoops, we're going overboard here. Manufacturers have found that giving customers all these choices pushes them toward the middle of the range, where they probably spend more than if they only had three choices. And a smart product line strategy (see Chapter 3) allows the manufacturer to produce all this diversity with not much added product development time and cost.

✔ **The profit model:** Where and how will this product produce revenue? Some products depend on sales price, and others depend on downstream services or media (think razors/razor blades). Some may even be "loss-leaders," which lure customers to buy your other products. (See Chapter 2 for more on the profit model.)

No one priceing stratregy fits all products or companies. If one does, it's like Plato's "Ideal Forms": there, but unknowable. You should come up with a reasonable price by considering all the issues; and then be ready to alter your pricing strategy if it doesn't work.

You can always lower the price, but you rarely can raise it!

When establishing the launch price, the teams involved should also consider the pricing strategy for the product's lifecycle. Will you introduce the product at a high price point and lower it as competitors apply pressure? Will the product be patented, such as a drug, and have to gain as much revenue as possible before the competition kicks in the door? Is the product a fashion or a fad that will have to make a killing this season? Is the product part of a product line or platform that will reap its return over the course of many related offerings? (Check out Chapter 3 for more on the intricacies and the importance of the product lifecycle.)

## Managing the supply chain

If your company is designing, developing, and manufacturing the whole product, you can skip this section (no, really, we don't mind). Most likely, however, you're developing the product with suppliers and partners (see Chapters 15 and 16), which complicates your launch planning and execution. Not only do you have to make sure your internal teams have the product ready, in sufficient quantity, for launch, but you also have to make sure your external suppliers and partners are coordinated. And by "you," we mean the launch team.

Many of the issues that the launch team has to manage are the direct result of the project's partner/supplier strategy. You can read more about partner/supplier strategy in Chapter 16, and if you're on the launch team, we recommend that you do that. Here are some suggestions for succeeding in this very complex activity:

- **Know exactly who your suppliers are, what their deliverables are, and what the due dates are.** That sounds simple, but with use of international sources growing every day, it's easy for a team to overlook a supplier until it becomes apparent that a needed part is missing.

- **Keep track of your low-cost suppliers.** Make sure they are delivering, and also keep your eyes out for better deals. You can increase a product's chances of success by finding a switch that costs less than the one you were planning on.

- **Be sure that the core team is "overcommunicating" with its suppliers and partners.** Manage that by being willing to ask the "dumb" questions at meetings. "When you say 'switch,' does that mean the switch for the on/off button or the switch for the digital/analog switch-over? Does our supplier know exactly which one it is?" Confusions about things like that have led to the downfall of many product plans.

- **Act quickly if it looks like a supplier or partner won't come through.** As far as possible, anticipate breakdowns instead of letting them surprise you. Here again, asking dumb questions can save the day. "I know you said you'd have that last order in early next week, but can you tell me exactly how much you've done, and whether there's any chance you'll miss the deadline?" And here's also where having a list of alternate suppliers can sometimes help to fill in gaps.

- **Coordinate schedules between the NPD team and the suppliers.** If your launch team works with the NPD team from the beginning, you can avoid having too little inventory or too much inventory.

- **Vet your partners and suppliers very carefully.** You don't want the NPD team to outsource part of the development and production to a partner that may not be able to come through, for example. An advantage of more intimate supplier/partner relationships (see Chapter 16) is that you know the company better, you've developed communication pathways, and it has more commitment to meeting your needs.

You want as little supplies and products in inventory as possible. Try to apply Lean principles (see Chapter 11) to make sure that your supply chain delivers only the amount of raw materials and finished goods that you need. The mantra in business is "just in time," not "just in case."

## Planning for public relations (buzz and chatter)

All too often, development and launch teams postpone public relations work until three days before they're ready to put the product into boxes. That strategy is bad for you and for your product. In an age when the hippest bands — and products! — have Web pages on `myspace.com`, and the buzz online is about the next social media channels, you don't want to fall too far behind. Your marketing team members — and your youngest, hippest team members (even if they're accountants) — should be thinking about how to obtain plenty of free press coverage about your product. And they should be thinking well before, during, and after your launch.

In order to decide what and when information should be made public, the launch team and the new product team have to consider issues like tipping off the competition, getting customers excited too long before product is available, and so on. The timing varies by industry, by product, and by market.

But don't let that warning keep you from creating a buzz. Here are a few ways to go about that:

- ✔ For starters, every industry has a trade journal. These journals often publish announcements of products for free — if you get copy to them by their deadlines, which usually come three weeks before the publication dates. (Of course, they're even more likely to do this "for free" if your company places ads in their journals!)

  Do a bit of research to find a handful of print publications that make good candidates for your launch press release. You also can send information — and sometimes samples — to editors who may review your product.

- ✔ Similarly, scour the Internet for blogs and other social media sites that serve as the mileposts of would-be authorities in your product or service category. Well in advance of your launch, recruit these personalities to serve on an informal product-advisory team. They'll help you identify other places where your product can be promoted, and they'll also be able to identify — perhaps better than you can — what about your product is most likely to bring on the buzz.

✔ Be creative — ply them with T-shirts, free software, key fobs, hats, and so on. Many online mavens who publish blogs spend hours writing and influencing readers with their opinions. If you land a few strong and influential opinions in your corner, you can reap some handsome dividends — not only with great feedback during the development process but also with reader persuasion, all the way through your launch and beyond.

 Get your core team members, and any other people who are working with you on the product development effort, to talk with like-minded people in the media outlets who cover your industry. For example, you can assign a team engineer to contact a journalist who has a technical bent. They speak the same language and may bond over your product features.

## Double-Checking the Details

Before you go public, it's a good idea to make sure one more time that you've covered your bases. Consider the following:

✔ **Revalidate the original value proposition for your product versus the current market and competitive situation.** You've been checking into the market and competitive situations all through the development process, right? At the end, you should make one last check to be sure that the need you want to fill, the fad you want to introduce, or the problem you want to fix is still compelling. Also, make sure your competitors haven't done anything to make your product obsolete, or nearly so.

✔ **Double-check that all your marketing/sales collateral and launch support materials are ready.** Make sure your sales force and your channel support people are fully supported. They need instructional materials — translated into the languages that they'll use when selling your product. They need brochures and flyers, and samples of the product.

✔ **Confirm that all relevant training has taken place or is ready to go.** Your sales and customer-service teams should receive training before the product launch (see the section "Training your sales and service teams to support the new product"). If you need training for customers, that should be ready as well. And if your service teams need to be trained to deliver training, make it so!

✔ **Develop detailed announcements and demo packages, and obtain approval for public notices and advertising.** This isn't the time for general or hazy ideas or last-minute administrative red tape. Right before the launch is the time for putting final ink to paper.

✔ **Make sure that you've tested and trialed all your internal systems (billing, supply, manufacturing, and so on) for full release of the product.** Don't forget how many internal systems have to be up and running to support your product. You don't want your distributors to run out of product, and you don't want customers to complain because they weren't billed on time or accurately.

Try creating a checklist that your launch team can use to coordinate all the complex activities that go on before a launch. You can use the one shown in Figure 13-1; we recommend that you tailor it to fit your team's and company's needs.

**Checklist for Launch Review**

| Launch Review Deliverable | By Whom | By When | Percent Complete |
|---|---|---|---|
| ✓ Beta Tests that confirm product meets customer needs and requirements | | | |
| ✓ Completion and analysis of prototype testing | | | |
| ✓ Pilot production runs complete: Confirmation of Manufacturability | | | |
| ✓ Quality & reliability testing complete | | | |
| ✓ Product launch details complete and committed to by functions | | | |
| ✓ Market research that demonstrates market acceptance from limited sale of product | | | |
| ✓ Comparison of manufacturing scale-up plan to marketing launch plan by region | | | |
| ✓ Proposal outlining key issues to be "cleaned up" | | | |
| ✓ Proposal outlining how product performance should be measured over time | | | |
| ✓ Initial order dates set and committed to by functions | | | |
| ✓ Documentation of learnings from the Development Stage | | | |
| ✓ Action plan and request for resources needed | | | |

**Figure 13-1:**
Use a checklist to manage the complexities of launch execution.

# *Factoring In Post-Launch Evaluations*

Your product is in the market. Your sales force is selling, and your product channels are stocking *and* selling. The service reps are documenting any reported problems, and they're doing their jobs in installation and customer training. Perhaps the NPD team members are looking around for their next jobs or returning to their old ones.

Now, however, isn't the time for the launch team to disband. For the first months after a launch — often for up to a year — the launch team must keep its eye on things. Keep the following questions in mind and be prepared to make changes:

- ✔ Is the product meeting its goals?

- ✔ What problems do we need to iron out?

- ✔ What new opportunities have presented themselves now that the product is in the market?

The launch team can make a huge difference for the company by staying involved as the product moves from the introduction phase to the growth phase of the product lifecycle (see Chapter 3 for more on the product lifecycle).

# Part IV
# New Challenges in Product Development

## The 5th Wave                    By Rich Tennant

"Yes, it's wireless, and yes, it weighs less than a pound, and yes, it has multiuser functionality...but it's a stapler."

# In this part . . .

*H*ere we explore three trends in product development: the digitization of information, globalization, and partnering. These trends are changing the product development landscape and making the job of the product developer even more challenging — and potentially even more rewarding.

One thing we can tell you for sure: The more our world shrinks, the more our work becomes global. And the more we rely on each other to fulfill our business objectives, the more imperative it is to implement the core practices we present in Parts I, II, and III.

Read the chapters in this part to see which way the wind is blowing, and then go back to the other parts to make sure your company has the foundation it needs to stand strong in that wind!

# Chapter 14

# Developing Products in the Digital Age

**C**an you remember way back in the early 1990s when you couldn't communicate by e-mail unless you both used the same software? Have we made you feel old? Sorry! Those days have flashed by so fast. In today's world, anyone and everyone can own a computer and operate a Web site. You can send e-mail to anyone anywhere in the world with at least 90 percent certainty that the message will get there and that the person you sent it to will be able to open it.

The digital age has transformed not only how people communicate, but also how they manage projects and integrate actions with business strategy. We're sure that you and your company are already somewhat "digital" and that digital technology influences how you work — alone and with others.

In this chapter, you find out how companies are developing products in the digital age. We discuss how digital information enables new forms of product testing and experimentation. You find out how digital technology can help your teams come together. And we show you how information technology can help you become organized and efficient.

As you read this chapter, you can expect to broaden your horizons for how "digitization" can help you be more effective in your product development endeavors. However, these days are still the early days of the digital age, and plenty of pitfalls dot the opportunity landscape. You have to move cautiously and think long term. But you also have to realize that without some implementation of the available tools, you aren't likely to be competitive in this day and age. We hope that you come away with some healthy skepticism and some basic rules for avoiding digital pitfalls. (Our thanks to Scott Elliott for his help with this chapter, all of which he provided through digital technologies.)

# Using Digital Technology to Test and Experiment

"Never before," Stefan Thomke tells readers in the introduction to his book *Experimentation Matters* (Harvard Business School Press), "has it been so economically feasible to ask 'what-if' questions and [get] . . . answers." Today's product development teams use digital technology to run tests and experiments that were prohibitively expensive and/or time-consuming in the past. As a result, companies can model early product ideas, test for quality, and simulate system integration long before they actually develop the products. They can get nearly instant customer feedback throughout the product development process. This fast feedback pushes the most critical decisions to the beginning of the product development process, where teams can make changes to design with the least amount of rework and other negative impact.

Modeling, simulating, and prototyping give companies ways to represent things they want to learn more about, to manipulate, to iterate, or to change. The terms cover a lot of ground. They can cover clay models, mathematical models, crash-test simulations, and digital prototypes. What they have in common, though, is that they can provide information about things that are too big or too expensive to be investigated on their own, or that maybe don't yet exist (like a new product). Michael Schrage, in his book *Serious Play* (Harvard Business School Press), tells readers that the three terms — modeling, simulating, and prototyping — have become different "flavors," and that they all point to how people "use technology to re-create some aspect of reality that matters to us."

Tests and experiments can tell you that you're on the right track, that another track may be better, or that you're on the path to failure. Most people prefer to get good news — that their projects are on the right track. However, tests and experiments can be most useful when teams welcome the bad news as well. Leaders and managers need to make the value of uncovering negative results explicit. Knowing upfront that the technology you need to meet a key customer requirement can't be developed within schedule and budget allows you to make other plans — to substitute a different project, or perhaps to change the schedule and/or the budget. To discover the missing technology a month before the scheduled launch leaves you with no good options. To help employees accept the negative, try to lighten it up a bit, maybe by giving rewards or prizes for the teams or people who uncover the negatives.

The following sections present some of the ways that your development team can use digital technologies to test and simulate new products in the development pipeline. Be sure you take note of the limitations of these technologies along with their benefits! (See Chapter 17 for more on prototyping and other kinds of product testing.)

# Computer simulation

*Computer simulation* allows a team to produce a model that behaves — right on the computer — like the product the team is designing. If you've ever played a video game, you know how powerful computer simulations can be in showing the consequences of different inputs to a situation. A team may use computer simulation in the following kinds of situations:

- ✔ **When it needs to model vast amounts of data.** For example, the human genome project is based on computer simulation. It enables scientists to understand the interactions and functions of human genes and has led to whole new industries based on genetically modified or genetically targeted products.

- ✔ **When doing an actual experiment is dangerous or expensive.** Finding out how your product may behave in extreme situations provides great information for your design team. For example, car manufacturers use computer simulations to model car crashes. Face it, you'd rather crash a car in a simulation than wreck a real one. And in fact you can usually learn more about the effects of a crash from a simulation than from a real crash.

Simulation is a powerful tool, but it has limitations. Here are a few things to watch out for:

- ✔ **Not all situations can or should be simulated.** Often, creating a clay model or a prototype is easier (see the following section). But don't give up too quickly. Imagine designing a tennis ball and being able to model its elasticity, the way it bounces in different temperatures and on different surfaces, and the durability of the cover in different situations. It could take you years to develop that kind of information in the "real world"!

- ✔ **Your teams need to have access to a large amount of computer power and know-how.** If you lack either of these, but you really think simulation will provide important information, consulting firms can help you — for a price, of course!

- ✔ **Some of the information a simulation provides may not be accepted by everyone involved.** For example, some regulatory bodies may require "real" rather than simulated experiments. Make sure your stakeholders and customers will accept the results of a simulation before you rely on it.

# Rapid prototyping

In the old days, it took product development teams weeks or even months to build prototypes in order to test their designs. Bottlenecks in a company's model shop often held up product projects because too many teams tried to get their models done at the same time. Today, teams have resources — known as *rapid prototyping* — that enable them to build prototypes easily and quickly. One method, called *stereolithography* (a process in which a computer lays down thousands of tiny layers of material that quickly form a 3-D model of the product), is widely used to create actual models of products in a fraction of the time it used to take. (See Chapter 9 for more information on how prototyping fits into the product development process.)

Teams can use prototypes to show any of the following things:

- ✔ **Form:** showing how the product would look
- ✔ **Fit:** showing how the different parts would fit together in the final product
- ✔ **Function:** showing how the product would work

Be careful! Rapid prototyping is a heady thing. You almost can snap your fingers and produce a viable model of a product that had been just a gleam in your eye. This would seem to be nothing but a great thing; however, teams that use this technology can fall prey to "feature creep." The lure of "just one more" motivates them to add on feature after feature until they've strayed away from the business cases they're supposed to be fulfilling by adding features, cost, and time to the project. See Chapter 12 for advice on how you can keep your projects on the straight and narrow.

## Combinatorial chemistry

Are you in the drug business, or in any industry that requires your company to sort through hundreds and thousands of possible chemical combinations? If so, good news for you: New advances in chemistry experimentation now allow drug companies to synthesize thousands of potential molecules and compounds that are possible candidates in drug development. Scientists can now create vast "libraries" of chemical compounds that drug manufacturers screen to find new drugs. Established pharmaceutical companies often get into *combichem* through an alliance or a merger with a company that has the technology.

Although combichem is a chemical process, we include it here because the methodology requires researchers to handle vast amounts of data. Combichem would not have been possible without advances in computer power gained in the digital age.

Combinatorial chemistry has been a great boon to the pharmaceutical industry among others, but it also brings challenges. The output of combichem often isn't as accurate or as pure as the information that comes from experiments executed in traditional ways. Also, drug companies have had to revamp the rest of their drug-discovery processes in order to deal with the huge number of chemical candidates.

For more information on the uses of product testing in the digital age, take a look at Stefan Thomke's book, *Experimentation Matters* (Harvard Business School Press). It covers the topics we introduce here in much more depth.

# Using Digital Technologies for Team Collaboration

When everyone worked in the same room, or at least in the same building or the same city, managing information wasn't such a big deal. Many teams had "war rooms," where product and project information was displayed permanently on the walls. Big sheets of paper displayed schedules, technology maps, customer requirements, and other important product and project information. Teams held meetings in the war room so everyone could look at the same information. Teams would update information after meetings, and team members could visit the room to check on the latest changes.

Which came first, the chicken or the egg? Did teams start to entrust their information to digital formats because they could no longer count on being physically co-located, or did the rise of digital technology enable teams to work together effectively even though they could no longer shake hands or share a cup of coffee? In *The World is Flat* (Farrar, Straus and Giroux), Thomas Friedman counts "the digital revolution" among "the ten forces that flattened the world." Whichever one got the ball rolling, it's now in full swing, and we suspect that you, too, spend some of your time talking to telephones and computers that connect you with people around the world. And you probably find yourself getting out of bed too early or staying up too late to meet with people whose time zones aren't in sync with yours.

Digital technology connects people with other people and with information that previously would've been unavailable. By using digital collaboration tools, product development teams can communicate in real time and simultaneously, whether they're on the same site or spread out across the world — as many teams now are. When project data are digitized on compatible and readily accessible formats, a product development team can work from anywhere on any aspect of a project. And when company data are digitized, product teams have access to a huge repository of knowledge — technical, market, and so on — that their members can access and use.

Digitization of information has radically changed not only how teams manage product and project information, but also how they work together. In the following sections, we introduce the basics of managing information and managing teams in the digital age — around the clock and around the world. (Take a look at Chapter 15 for more on how product development is going global.)

## Corralling product information

The key to successful management of your new products' information is the standardization of processes, methods, and tools that the development team uses to organize, store, and access information. When product information is well-organized and stored where it can be accessed, the team is able to coordinate work tasks and to make good, timely decisions.

Take a look at the real limitations of the "pen and paper" ways that companies used to collect and store information in the past. If you store the information your development team needs to make decisions and get its work done in a three-ring binder, or if it exists only in drawings that hang on the team room wall, your team will experience trouble, for two reasons:

- Remote team members won't have access to the data.
- The format will discourage team members from changing the data.

Teams in the digital age use CAD (computer aided design) and CAM (computer assisted manufacturing) to create and store their product information digitally. In these forms, all team members can see the information, read it, and — with the right password protections and version controls — change it.

The information inventory you build as your team develops a product should take its place in your corporation's knowledge inventory. Like any inventory, employees can use it, and it can grow in value. Likewise, it can sit there and do nothing! The more your product information is digitized and shared, however, the faster your company will move knowledge through "inventory turns." Company-wide knowledge can contribute to projects today, tomorrow, next year, and the year after.

Be sure your company has good controls in place for who has access to the information, who can change the information, and what information gets sent to whom. The amount of access and flexibility that the Internet provides can turn your careful product plans into a hodge-podge.

## Collaborating with customers

The projects that have the best success rates start with intimate knowledge of the customers (see Chapter 4). However, it can be hard to reach your customers while your team works on the design and development of a product. You're under severe time and budget restraints. (If not, what are your execs thinking?) Also, your team likely will develop an internal focus, which includes a commitment to the solutions developed by the team.

Thankfully, the digital age takes away any excuse you may have for not checking in with your customers in order to test your product during development. You can simulate your product (see the first section in this chapter), and you can reach thousands of customers on the Internet. Here are some methods you can use to collect information from your customers:

- **Questionnaires and surveys:** Some of our favorites are Kano questionnaires and importance surveys. Teams use these tools to validate the importance of different requirements. They can be helpful throughout the development process to answer questions about customer preferences.

- **Online Alpha and Beta Tests:** Teams use Alpha and Beta Tests to find out how the product works in customers' hands (see Chapter 17). If you can simulate the use of your product online, you discover plenty about how your product would really behave.

- **Online sales forecasting:** Use conjoint and other methods (see Chapter 17) to pinpoint your customers' likely buying behavior.

Intelligent use of the Internet can provide your team with scads of useful customer information. Be sure your team plans carefully for what information you need and how you plan to use it. You don't want to have so much information that you ignore certain pieces or find yourself changing directions, missing deadlines, or forgetting what the original project was all about. (See the later section "Developing products in the standard Internet time zone" for more on using the Internet.)

Your company's market research department can be very helpful in setting up and managing these methods. *Note:* These methods work best if your team members are willing to be very frank about their concerns and questions.

## Managing project information

The ability to digitize information should encourage your company to create a virtual space — an Internet or Intranet site, for instance — to store your project information. This space can house many of the project's important pieces, including the following:

- The project mission and vision
- Schedules

> ✔ Action items
>
> ✔ Meeting minutes
>
> ✔ Project metrics
>
> ✔ "Bug" and problem lists

No one on the development team, or elsewhere in the company, has to wonder what the deliverables are for a certain week or who promised to do what at the last meeting, for example. The members of the development team can share the responsibility of updating the information and blowing the whistle when something isn't going well.

## Developing products in the standard Internet time zone

More and more products that hit the shelves for customers are being developed by teams that span the world and include partners from different businesses. When a product development team isn't confined to one place, communication tends to become formal. However, a team needs to "hang out," to inspire each other and have space for complaints. To accomplish all this, new product teams need different modes of communication.

The following sections cover some approaches and some secrets to achieving success in Internet time.

No matter how good your development team gets at communicating over distances, don't under-budget for travel! Teams really do need to meet; managers need to have face time with team members; and at critical times — the beginning of a project, in particular — you can't substitute for having the whole team in the same room. See Chapter 10 for more information on building and nurturing your NPD team.

### Convening formal meetings

Every product development team needs a format in which to conduct a formal meeting — whether the team members are sitting face to face or are spread around the globe. Many teams schedule a regular meeting — usually held weekly — at which they cover an agenda, take notes, make time for discussion, and so on. A team that's spread out in different locations should hold similar meetings.

You may be surprised at how quickly teams can get used to working together through Internet communications programs such as NetMeeting or WebEx, a videocamera (also known as *videoconferencing*), and/or the phone. In Chapter 10, you can read about the basic rules for formal team meetings. The rules are the same for distributed teams: make sure participants receive an agenda before the meeting, take notes at the meeting, and distribute minutes and action items as soon as possible after the meeting. ***Note:*** Many software packages can facilitate meetings on the Internet. We've found that the simplest ones work the best.

The team leader is responsible for convening these meetings and setting the tone. However, the team leader often delegates much of the responsibility for setting up the meetings, arranging the logistics (such as scheduling the videoconferencing or arranging telephone conference calls), note-taking during the meeting, and distributing meeting results afterwards. Often, too, the team leader designates a facilitator to actually run the meeting so that everyone else can focus on the substantive issues.

Working on Internet time often means that teams have to work in many different time zones. Try to hold meetings in a way that's "fair" to everyone. Here's some tried and true meeting advice:

✔ We hate to say it, but most Americans assume that their workdays are what others should conform to. Having that attitude isn't a good way to build a team! Spread out the pain of meeting at awkward times. Meet at 6 a.m. your time one week and at noon your time the next, for example.

✔ Come up with some basic ground rules to facilitate meetings in which participants aren't face to face. Have your members say their names before they launch into their diatribes. If someone forgets, the facilitator — or any member of the team — could say, "It seems awfully dark in here; I'm not sure who's speaking." If people enter or leave the meeting, they should announce their actions to the group.

A number of software products make it easy to share information via spreadsheets, diagrams, or slides. These products allow you to show your images, spreadsheets, and other team data to anyone who has access to the Internet. During the meeting, different people on the team can "control" a presentation by using pointers and highlights to direct attention to certain aspects of the information being presented. Another member can edit the information in real time as the discussion goes on.

### Gathering in informal spaces

Distributed teams should make time for informal communications in addition to the formal meetings. Team members need to get to know each other and to understand each other on a personal level. When team members have real relationships, they can more easily talk together, understand each other's positions, and challenge each other's assumptions. Also, a lot of teamwork can't be done in formal, agenda-driven settings. To be creative, people need to loosen their ties, sit back, and let their imaginations go.

The following list presents some avenues and advice for informal communications:

- ✔ Your team members can convene in live chat rooms on the Internet. These tools can help team members mull over issues that they can't settle in a formal meeting.
- ✔ Team members can brainstorm ideas online and over the phone.
- ✔ Team members can post personal information, such as photos and birthdays, on team-only Web sites. This helps people who don't get the chance to hang out face-to-face to form personal bonds.

### Rockin' around the clock

Can you imagine how fast your team could develop your company's new product if the sun never set on the work that you have to do? Believe it or not, some new product teams have discovered that they can actually make this happen. The following hypothetical narrative presents an example of how it can go:

- ✔ A portion of a product development team based in New Jersey starts work at 8 a.m., eastern standard time. The afternoon before, they had uploaded their work to the Intranet site and called a meeting with their teammates in Palo Alto, California, to get them up to speed. The New Jersey team's first move when they arrive to work is to tap into the Intranet site where the entire team stores its project information to see what team members in other locations have accomplished since yesterday. Here's what the New Jersey members find:

  - • The Palo Alto team worked on the project, and at the end of their day, the team members uploaded their work to the site. Before leaving work, they called a meeting with their teammates in Taiwan, who then worked their whole day on the project.

  - • The Taiwanese team members ended their day by uploading their work to the Intranet site and holding a conference with their teammates in Paris to get them up to speed.

- ✔ At 8 a.m. New Jersey time, the team members in Paris have uploaded their work to the site and are ready for a conference call with New Jersey to review a few issues they couldn't resolve.

- ✔ In 24 hours — from 8 a.m. the previous day to 8 a.m. this day — the entire team has accomplished roughly a week's worth of normal work. Furthermore, the teams haven't had to work overtime. No room for heroes, and no need to miss your kid's little league game.

Sound too good to be true? Usually it is. If you want to experience the bene-fits of "round the world, round the clock" work, be prepared to be extremely organized. You must start with extraordinarily clear product definitions. You have to put processes in place for managing anomalies. And you have to make leadership and decision making very clear. To succeed at this, you have to follow just about every bit of advice we give you in this whole book.

You may have to be super-human to make the process work the way it does in our example, but that's no reason to avoid using worldwide resources to increase your project's efficiency. As you use these resources, you discover what it takes to accomplish more and more of the project on Internet time.

Working in Internet time is very hard on mere mortals. Be sure your leader-ship judges the productivity of your teams, not of your individuals, to keep from burning out your employees.

# Booting Up IT to Organize Your Corporation's Innovations

The opportunities that digital technology provides are huge, and so are the pitfalls. Today's digital information technology opens up the possibility that professionals everywhere can communicate with each other, using common language and common platforms.

Some of the information in this section applies to teams, not to whole corpo-rations. However, if your organization doesn't make decisions at the corpo-rate level about what platforms and tools to use, you miss out on an opportunity to make your systems coherent. In fact, with a piecemeal approach, your company is building in incoherence. Be sure that your com-pany makes decisions from the top down (with plenty of bottom-up input).

## From common to fully integrated: Exploring the best digital technology

Information technologies that can help your organization manage its new product processes and initiatives range from widely available software pack-ages to platforms that promise to automate and integrate just about every-thing within your company. The following list presents some technology options that your company can explore, in order of increasing integration, sophistication, and complexity:

- **Common software packages:** Everyone should be using the same software to create documents, give presentations, assemble spreadsheets, create financial analysis, and so on. You shouldn't put up with the arguments of an accountant who has to have her special spreadsheet or an engineer who can't use Microsoft Excel.

- **Project management software:** Using a common platform for project management helps development teams succeed, and it helps a firm build project management competency over time. Project management software packages are widely available; your organization should get one that allows for Web-based use, even if you don't rely on the Internet at the beginning of the project (see the section "Developing products in the standard Internet time zone" for more on Internet-based development).

- **A common phase/review product development process integrated with project management software:** Your organization shouldn't try to integrate its product development process with its project management software until your teams and managers have a good understanding of both. See Chapter 9 to read about the phase/review process.

- **Communication tools for distributed teams:** Teams whose members are spread around the globe can make good use of phone systems, video-conferencing, and Web-conferencing tools. Make sure your teams have good project and development management processes (common to all of them) before you launch into having them work remotely!

- **Design/development tools, such as CAD and CAM:** Common computer-aided design and manufacturing tools are helpful to teams that manage their projects well but of limited use to teams that aren't good at collaboration.

- **Intranet sites:** After a development team makes its project data digital, it can store the data in a secure, accessible Intranet site.

- **Portfolio management software:** After an organization's management team gets a good grip on the resource needs and timing of projects in its pipeline, it can start to automate the company's portfolio decision making. Many IT tools help to sort projects into strategic buckets, aggregate portfolio worth, and so on. See Chapter 11 for more on managing the product portfolio.

- **Resource management software:** Software that aggregates a development team's available and in-use resources can be helpful when the whole product development process has matured. If you think your company's process is grownup enough, be sure you get a package that's sophisticated enough to identify special versus common resources and flexible enough to illustrate how your resource needs change over time. For more on resource management, check out Chapter 11.

✓ **Corporate repositories or libraries:** When your organization has implemented data gathering and the use of information at the project level and across projects at the portfolio level, you should start creating a flexible, integrated repository that allows project teams to learn from each other and enables executives and managers to oversee and review progress in real time.

## Implementing the technology tools

Selecting and implementing technology tools must be done top-down and company-wide. The benefits come from standardization. The most important lesson we can give you about implementing technology tools is to match the degree of maturity of your product development processes to the tools you install. The list we provide in the previous section appears, roughly, in order of maturity. Your company can't go for the glitz until you have a firm process base. For example, there's little point in installing software for project resource management if your phase/review process doesn't allow you to predict resource needs in the product development pipeline.

---

### Choosing a vendor

Many firms can sell your company software to automate your product development processes. However, *caveat emptor!* Be sure you know what you're getting into before making tool and vendor decisions. Here are a few simple rules:

✓ Try to find an automated system that's similar to the processes you're currently using.

✓ If you have homegrown processes, do some research and find tools that support the processes you have.

✓ If you have no or poorly implemented processes and if your culture is hierarchical, or *top-down,* look for a package that comes with process design and implementation.

✓ If you have no or poorly implemented processes and if your culture is bottom-up, you should first get serious about improving how you develop new products. Realize that it may take more discipline than you usually have. Second, you should establish a working group that can develop processes and select the appropriate IT to support them.

---

Your development team should think through the whole sequence of tool implementation before making choices at the beginning. What kind of resource management process do you want? The answer should impact your choice of project management tools. What data do you want to have available in your corporate repository? The answer may affect *all* the choices you make.

Our next most important piece of advice comes as your team begins to implement the use of digital tools: Be patient! Get each tool fully working before going on to the next. You'll be tempted to rush ahead and build a corporate library that supports full automation of your product development. Only it won't support it. Everyone involved will get frustrated, and your projects will be less efficient.

We recommend that your development team find someone with broad tool-implementation expertise who can help you think through the implications of your choices. The person for this job will probably be a consultant. Make sure that the consultant you work with isn't 100 percent committed to convincing you to buy her technology. Always ask questions before you seal the deal.

# Chapter 15

# Product Development Goes Global

· · · · · · · · · · · · · · · · · · · · · · · · · · · · · · · · · · · · · · · · · · ·

## In This Chapter

▶ Understanding your global opportunities

▶ Being strategic in your approach to globalization

▶ Managing globalization risks

▶ Being on your best collaboration behavior

· · · · · · · · · · · · · · · · · · · · · · · · · · · · · · · · · · · · · · · · · · ·

*W*e'd lay dollars to doughnuts that you outsource some aspects of your company's new product development to other countries. Maybe you buy widgets from China, or a company in Mexico makes your springs. Perhaps you test your new products in other countries before you send them to market. In our highly interlinked world, more and more companies are turning to suppliers to streamline the product development process. Many of these suppliers are located in other countries, and many of them don't just provide widgets — they're becoming partners in the product development process, which turns up the heat on opportunity (and increases the risk).

In this chapter, we introduce you to what leading companies are doing in the global marketplace — including what challenges them and how they meet those challenges. You discover the distinction between "outsourcing" and "offshoring," and you find out why the distinction makes a difference. Companies that approach globalization in a purely opportunistic manner often run into trouble, so we give you some tips to consider as you create your strategy for globalization. Finally, we review some of the basics of collaboration, because collaboration is a key to success in the global economy.

We don't just look at plain vanilla "outsourcing" in this chapter, in which companies use suppliers to gain access to the standard materials they need to run their businesses. Instead, we look at the much higher stakes game of *globally distributed product development* (GDPD). When you develop products with others, you expand your capacities, *and* you put some control into other companies' hands. Companies that succeed at the GDPD game have clear new product strategies (Chapter 3), understand their customers (Chapter 4), know where their technology is headed (Chapter 7), and focus their resources (Chapter 11). They also understand the impact of the digital age (Chapter 14) and how to partner with others (Chapter 16).

# Mapping the Landscape in the Global Development Game

Where in the world might you find partners to join with you in the game of globally distributed product development (GDPD)? Literally anywhere. If you haven't heard yet, let us be the first to tell you: The world is flat. In his book by that title, Thomas Friedman speculates that one of the leading flatteners of the world is the rise of digital technology. In the digital age that has defined the early 21st century, we can communicate with almost anyone anywhere in seconds. So if the world is flat and distance isn't a factor, what does the global product development landscape look like? How can you draw a map and find your way in this new world? Read the following sections to find out.

## Understanding your company's place in GDPD

Where and how your company plays in the global game of product development depends in part on where you are now on the game board. Over the course of the digital age, the global distribution of product development has followed three stages:

**Stage 1: Companies identify strongly with their home bases.** The drivers of globalization are a combination of low-cost suppliers and emerging markets. The game is opportunistic, not strategic. Companies in this stage may outsource some of their product development because countries where they sell products mandate that they spend some percent of their sales on local research and development. Or, companies may look for engineers or scientists in other countries because they can't find the talent in their locations.

Companies that enter the GDPD game in Stage 1 sometimes end up developing products all over the world without any clear strategy. As GDPD is becoming more accessible, common, and strategic, some of these companies are playing catch-up with companies that enter at Stage 2 or 3.

**Stage 2: The strategic nature of the opportunity becomes more apparent.** Companies see more that's attractive in the GDPD game. Former low-cost suppliers — in Taiwan, India, and China, for example — gain technology competence. Risks and advantages are becoming clearer.

In this stage, product and technology strategy direct a company's choices. The company may begin to build specific capabilities that will help it to succeed with partners in GDPD (see Chapter 16 for more).

**Stage 3: Companies are founded as global companies.** Companies seek and find suppliers, markets, and technology partners all over the world. A company's "backyard" is everywhere. Lines of communication and cultural differences are integrated as matters of course.

Some authors call these companies "meta-national." Often, the home base is a country that can't provide adequate markets. Nokia, for example, is a Finnish company. It started out with the goal to become a significant player in the cellphone market by identifying not with Finland, but with the world.

We imagine that you can identify which stage best describes your company. Did you get into the game early? In that case, there's a good chance that your scene is Stage 1. Did your company start global, in Stage 3? The following list presents some detail about the different stages. We include the most important jobs for your company to focus on in order to optimize its global position:

- ✔ If Stage 1 describes your company's GDPD position, you may have woken up one morning to find yourself doing business all over the world. You may be developing products in Alaska to sell in Honduras and in China to sell anywhere you can find a market. Your job is to get a handle on your global assets and use them strategically.

  Stage 1 companies often have very strong identifications with their home base. That identification may be historic ("We were born here, and we grew up here"). Sometimes, it includes brand identity. For example, although Ford has widely distributed development centers and markets all over the world, make no mistake: It's a U.S. company.

- ✔ If Stage 2 describes your company's GDPD position, you may be researching how to get more out of your existing business partnerships and looking around to find new opportunities. You may have legacy projects that focus solely on low-cost or new markets, but you — and your company's leadership — are getting more and more strategic in your approach. Your job is to create a robust strategic plan for GDPD.

- ✔ If you started life as a Stage 3 company, please come on over and help us write the next version of this section! These companies are the lucky ones — except that they have to launch their businesses in a world of high uncertainty and high risk. The most critical job of the Stage 3 company is to take advantage of the wide world of opportunity and to lead the way by implementing new and successful practices.

As you read the rest of this chapter, keep in mind that how your company has evolved in the globally distributed product development story influences what will be important to you and what your next steps will be.

## *Here, there, and everywhere: Figuring out where you can play*

Table 15-1 lists the kinds of supplier and partner relationships your company may have in the GDPD game. The list goes in order from relatively easy and tactical to very complex and strategic.

| Table 15-1 | Supplier/Partner Relationships in GDPD | |
| --- | --- | --- |
| *Relationship* | *Kinds of Tasks/ Activities* | *Ownership* |
| Vendor/Supplier | Simple routines/tasks | No (outsource) |
| Preferred vendor | Limited design/development | No (outsource) |
| "Captive" site | Design/development of parts, modules, whole products | Yes (insource) |
| Partner | Design/development requiring a partner's special competencies | No (partnership) |

The sections that follow discuss these relationships in detail. For more information on partnerships, check out Chapter 16.

### *Outsourcing product development tasks to a vendor*

The lowest level of GDPD is when you outsource product development tasks. In other words, suppliers and vendors that you don't own do some routine work for you — updating drawings, for example. In this chapter, we concentrate on *global* outsourcing, but "outsourcing" also can apply if your supplier does business in the next town just down the road.

Although you don't give away any trade secrets or intellectual property to your vendors, you still have to be careful when you collaborate with suppliers that do business in different countries, with different customs and laws. See the section "Protecting your company's core assets and capabilities" for more information on how to protect your knowledge assets when you work with outsiders.

If you outsource even the most routine parts of NPD, expect to spend time and resources on training. No matter how explicit and clear you think your processes are, even the best partners need to learn exactly how you go about designing, building, and testing if you expect their work to fit seamlessly with yours. Successful companies combine bringing partners in to learn the ropes and sending managers offshore to teach them.

### Building a relationship with a preferred vendor

The next step in GDPD is when you start trusting your suppliers with more complicated and important work. If you've been outsourcing the testing of circuits, for instance, you may move on to outsourcing circuit design. Companies often take this step because they find out that suppliers they're already working with have the skills and experience needed to take on more sophisticated work. This often is work that their product developers are struggling to keep up with on their own.

When you take this step, you probably already have a degree of comfort with your supplier. Taking the next step with a supplier you already know and trust takes some of the anxiety, and risk, out of the picture. Also, it means that your supplier has made some strides toward learning the ropes of your business and industry — the way *you* define them.

When your company begins to give a preferred vendor more responsibility, you have to be even more careful about what work you outsource because the work is getting closer to the core of expertise that creates your company's competitive advantage in new product development. You can give engineers in Beijing drawings to update without giving them enough context to understand the product innovation they're working with, for example. But when you ask these engineers to design a braking system, you're inviting them into your inner world, where the secrets that make your golf cart better than anyone else's reside. Check out the section "Recognizing (And Avoiding) the Risks of Globalization" for more on protecting your company's core knowledge and intellectual property.

### Insourcing

When a company *insources* its product development, it owns product development capabilities away from its central location. For example, Kodak's home base is in Rochester, New York, and its digital camera facility is in Taiwan. Kodak owns the Taiwanese facilities, and the employees there are Kodak employees. That facility is an example of what companies often call a "captive site," or *offshore insourcing.*

The difference between outsourcing and insourcing is critical. When you outsource, you create a situation in which someone else will carry out some of your product development. You need to be sure that your vendor is dependable and that what you outsource isn't a critical competency for your organization. When you insource, you find new places, new competencies, and new capacities for developing products; however, you buy them (acquire them) or build them yourself. In other words, you own them. The "vendors" are part of your company.

Although insourcing limits the risk you take — you can't "lose" assets to another part of your own company — you create even greater issues of culture, communication, and integration than when you outsource. See the later section "Recognizing (And Avoiding) the Risks of Globalization" for more on how to work through the risks.

# Surveying the Benefits of Globalization and Defining Your Strategy

In order to be competitive, most companies need to access global capabilities and global markets. "To be all you can be," you almost certainly need to tread the path of globalization.

In this section, we look at the basics of what globalization offers your organization — in other words, why globalization may have strategic importance for your company. When you decide that a globalization strategy is important for your company to accomplish its goals, you're ready to read further. You also discover how many companies decide where to locate their facilities and where they can find suppliers and partners.

## Going global to add capacity

Perhaps the most common reason companies "go global" with product development is to expand their capacity — in other words, to add skills, knowledge, expertise, and infrastructure that can help them develop more and better products. The following list presents some of the resources your company may want more of and that you may be looking around the world to find; what your organization is looking for should shape your globalization strategy:

- **Finding more skilled hands to do the routine work.** Your skilled product developers — engineers, designers, market researchers, and so on — spend much of their valuable time completing tasks that don't require a high level of skill or integration. Many companies outsource tasks like updating drawings or collating questionnaire results to reduce the burden shouldered by their skilled workforce.

- **Finding resources that can extend and complement your product development work.** Many employees possess skills that your company needs over and over in the NPD process. Pharmaceutical companies need research scientists, electronics companies need electrical engineers, and so on. If you need more skilled people to keep your new product pipeline flowing, you may want to outsource work to a competent supplier or establish a center of your own in another country to insource the work.

✔ **Increasing your access to special competencies.** Many times, your product development projects can be held up because a particular skill is missing in your company. Or perhaps you have too much demand on the limited capacity you possess. This could be true, for example, of special software design skills or of various kinds of product testing. An outside supplier may be able to help you cope with the bottlenecks.

If the problem is acute, and you'll need the resource for a long time, you may want to acquire or establish the competency by using the insourcing model — if adding competency at home isn't an option (see the earlier section "Insourcing").

✔ **Acquiring special skills that out- or insource vendors may do better than you.** Some of the talent and skills you need may be more abundant elsewhere in the world. If so, you should consider establishing relationships that make those skills and talents available. For example, Kodak's digital facility, located in Taiwan, has access to the skills of the "Silicone Valley of the East," skills that tend to be in comparatively short supply in Kodak's home base in Rochester, New York.

# Saving product development costs

Saving on product development costs is the first reason why many companies outsource or offshore their NPD efforts. In the pursuit of bottom-line efficiency — of "doing more with less" — many firms outsource and offshore parts of their product development activities.

The first "bottom line" is that the labor rates are far lower in many parts of the world outside of developed countries. For example, one company increased its capacity, measured by its number of full-time employees, by almost 20 percent by outsourcing a portion of its NPD work. At the same time, the organization lowered its spending on labor by 10 percent and its spending per year per employee by nearly 25 percent.

Wow! But we called this "the first bottom line." Don't be fooled by the appearance of savings. In the previous example, when this company figured in its other costs associated with GDPD, the savings were much lower. Successful outsourcing and offshoring require plenty of support. When you do the math, be sure you add in the unexpected costs, like training, travel, and so on.

Also, you must recognize that the more the developed country exports its work, the more the developing country develops. In this cycle, the developing world's labor supply becomes more skilled — and more expensive. At the same time, its populations become more and more attractive markets.

## Making global products

In order to make products that appeal to customers in different parts of the world, many companies are finding that they need to develop a deep understanding of consumers in different parts of the world. When a company locates design and manufacturing facilities — and its designers, developers, marketers, and so on — near potential customers, it can be much more successful in understanding and meeting customer needs in a wide variety of markets.

In general, European companies tend to be more aware of these market differences than companies in the United States. Nestlé, for example, alters its foods and its brands to suit local populations. The "same" product, such as chicken bouillon cubes, looks and tastes very different depending on whether it's being offered in China, Nigeria, or Poland. Nestlé bases its ability to meet customer needs and expectations in all these locations on a comprehensive methodology of customer understanding backed by a worldwide local training program. (Take a look at Chapter 4 for more on understanding customers.)

Such an "act local" approach runs the risk of creating a fragmented set of product offerings that can be very difficult to manage. Nestlé integrates technology and market strategies to achieve as much consistency as possible. Its byword is: "Optimize on similarities; respect local differences." Take a look at Chapter 3 for information on developing product platforms that can meet differing customer needs.

## Deciding where to go when you go global

Most companies begin to globalize their product development activities in order to exploit low-cost suppliers or global markets. They stick with globalization to reap the benefits of additional skills and capacities. Many of your GDPD activities may emerge from early attempts to outsource lower-skilled tasks. Intel, for example, developed a site in Israel around 30 years ago because of low labor cost and tax incentives. The Israel site has evolved from a low-cost design center to a robust corporate business group.

When deciding where to take your development efforts, scan the world to find different strengths that could attract you to outsource work or locate centers for GDPD. Consider the strengths of the following locations:

- ✓ In Taiwan and Japan, you can find high-tech and electronics capabilities.
- ✓ In China, you can find vendors/partners that can link into your manufacturing efforts and work well with offshore facilities in Taiwan and Korea.
- ✓ India excels in design services and information technology.

✔ Russia and Eastern Europe are big into industrial projects, including aerospace, automotive, and defense.

✔ Canada has most of the talent you can find in the United States for lower — although not low — cost.

Of course, you can find pockets of just about whatever your organization needs in many locations these days, if you devote the time and have the patience to seek them out. By combining your company's existing relationships and a careful review of the different capabilities around the world, you can select the places that will meet your needs.

Making decisions about where to locate is where the hard work begins. You need executive involvement, very careful project planning, and plenty of patience to make GDPD pay off. Your company needs to make globalization decisions strategically. Companies get themselves into trouble when they make opportunistic, short-sighted, merely tactical decisions about globalization. And you need to be aware of the risk from the start (see the later section "Recognizing (And Avoiding) the Risks of Globalization"). Consider the following examples:

✔ Depending on outsourcing to fill an immediate need can weaken a company's resolve to build the capacity in-house.

✔ Outsourcing keeps a company dependent on outside partners.

✔ Insourcing saddles a company with the large responsibility to create and maintain that asset.

From the start, be committed to bringing your globalization decisions to senior management. Make sure that you include the issues in the strategic decision-making process.

# Recognizing (And Avoiding) the Risks of Globalization

Every new product project and every new product strategy brings some risk to the table. In Chapter 11, which deals with managing your company's NPD resources, we recommend that you take on a reasonable amount of risk; otherwise, your new products will turn into commodities, mere ho-hum's, and me-too's that customers won't get excited about or pay for. Along with the opportunity to differentiate your products, globally distributed product development brings risk, and much of it is new risk that you may not have any tried-and-true methods of assessing and managing.

If your organization goes the globalization route, you need to be aware of at least three major risks: losing your core capabilities, giving away your intellectual property (IP), and political conflicts. In this section, you discover how to recognize these risks and avoid, or at least mitigate, them.

## Protecting your company's core assets and capabilities

Your organization's core assets and capabilities are your life force. What distinguishes you as a company? What do customers look to you for? What do you possess that allows you to continue your success into the next year? The next decade? GDPD puts your core assets at risk because you outsource work that you used to do yourself. How far is too far in the GDPD game? We can't give you a simple answer to this question. It's a strategic issue, and you need to ask some tough questions:

- What do you want to preserve?
- How much can you outsource before you become nothing more than a "system integrator" of other people's work?
- Is your distinctive competency exactly that of a system integrator?

You need to be sure that you make strategic assessments of what you can have others do and what you have to keep to yourself before you've gone too far. Some companies — Bose and Corning, for example — identify strongly with their technology competence. Others' identities are tied up in products and/or brands. A company like Caterpillar can outsource a fair amount of development work as long as the end result is a huge, yellow earth-moving machine. Some companies are frankly integrators; Dell has made a great business following this model. Our advice to you is that you *choose* the direction that GDPD opens up for you instead of waking up five or ten years from now and finding that your core identity has changed. (In Chapter 8, you find out how to identify your core technologies. Mapping product lines, which we discuss in Chapter 3, also helps you spot your most important assets.)

## Guarding your intellectual property

The United States and many other developed nations have very clear rules about intellectual property (IP). *Intellectual property* is knowledge that provides competitive advantage to its owner. It includes such assets as technology competence and designs. If you know how to do something or make something that others can't do and it's clear that you own the rights to the process or the design, that becomes your intellectual property. The United States and other parts of the "developed world" have rules in place to protect IP because the countries have so much of it, and it behooves everyone to play by the rules that protect them while also protecting others.

We're not saying that developed countries have ironclad IP protection; think of the impact Napster and other Web-based technologies that enabled consumers to download music for free had on the music industry. What we're saying is that when you do business in countries where IP isn't well protected, you have to take special care. IP protection is improving in developing countries, including China. But you shouldn't count on IP protection in other countries. Many countries don't have laws in place, they don't have the legal infrastructure to enforce the laws they have, and often they don't have a culture that condemns taking other people's IP.

We recommend that you prioritize your intellectual property into three categories:

- ✔ **Very important to you.** Protecting this first category is a critical issue. As much as possible, you should simply keep this IP at home. If you must offshore work with this IP, make sure that you offshore it to a trusted partner (see Chapter 16) and install strong protection procedures and processes.

- ✔ **Important, but not critical.** In the second group, be sure that you assess the risks and put in place reasonable protections, such as making sure that you share only parts of projects that your outsource partner cannot copy. The downside is that you may have no ironclad laws and procedures to protect your IP, and going after offenders may be both expensive and ineffective.

- ✔ **Not all that important.** This IP does belong to you, and "stealing" it isn't nice or right, but it isn't too important. Because protecting IP in many countries is uncertain, difficult, and expensive, many companies identify IP that isn't critical and simply take their chances with it.

Here's a great strategy to follow when you must offshore important IP:

1. **Deconstruct the project into separate pieces.**

2. **Identify parts of the project that separate groups can develop and that don't make much sense individually.**

3. **Give each group a stand-alone piece.**

With this strategy, even if your offshore partners try to cheat, you've given them something that won't lead anywhere.

## *Navigating political landscapes*

The politics of globally distributed product development include the following:

- ✔ The political environments of the countries you do business with
- ✔ The political relationships between your home country and your out-source countries
- ✔ The political/regulatory landscape you work in
- ✔ The internal politics of outsourcing work and working across boundaries

You want to avoid doing business in a country that has an unstable and/or unfriendly political environment. That may be easier said than done, though. As of press time, major oil companies are doing business where the political environment can range from unstable to downright hostile.

When doing business in another country — by outsourcing or partnering with vendors — don't assume that your relationships with its government and local corporations are all that you need. You need to spend time getting to know other parts of the country, including its students, workers, and ordinary people. Setting up an offshore center for GDPD that has a local flavor can make all the difference.

Also, within the previous list, you need to take a close look at the following when you outsource work to other countries:

- ✔ **The regulatory issues:** The countries in which you do business often are very different from the one(s) you're used to. Europe's environmental protection regulations are far more strict (so far) than those in the United States, for example (good for them!). Japan requires researchers to test all medicines on Japanese subjects in order to gain approval for use in Japan.

- ✔ **The general political implications of outsourcing in the first place:** Your stateside employees may feel that your organization doesn't value their work, and they may fear that their jobs are at risk. Beyond that is the brand issue. If you have a brand that's tightly associated with your home country — Harley Davidson is a good example in the United States — you may run the risk of weakening your brand image if you depend on offshore labor (see Chapter 3 for more on brand considerations).

# *Beefing Up Your Social Skills in the Global Economy*

Good communication is a foundation stone of GDPD success, and good communication includes a number of important factors. We consider the following to be critical ingredients of good communication and success in the global arena:

- ✔ The sharing of practices
- ✔ Patience
- ✔ Respect for diversity
- ✔ A commitment to partnership

In the sections that follow, we focus your attention on some basic rules of communicating when you can't depend on sitting down with your team over a cup of coffee to work through knotty problems. We emphasize the need for sharing practices in the last section, but remember that everything we say in the concluding pages of this chapter assumes, even when we don't say it out loud, that you're including patience, respect for diversity, and a commitment to the partnership.

## What time is it there? What language are we speaking?

Even though distance disappears in the age of digitization and globalization, languages and time zones don't. Too bad. Global collaboration puts a huge strain on us mere mortals. Working in different time zones means that you always have to be working in multiple circadian rhythms. In the process, your own rhythm may get totally messed up.

Working with colleagues who speak different languages is fairly straightforward for English speakers, which is a good thing for those of us who live in the United States. Most of us are utterly incompetent in any language but our own — and some of us in that one as well.

As your organization globalizes its product development work, you must account for the fact that employees who usually work from 9 to 5, 8 to 5, or even 6 to 6 will have longer days because of communication to other continents. Most of China and most of the United States are roughly 12 hours apart, for example; just about no time falls within the normal workdays of all the members of a team that's distributed between those two countries.

In this section, we talk about how to facilitate communication on distributed teams. You may be wondering: Isn't this just a matter of sending some work overseas to get it out of our hair? No. You need to form relationships with your outsource and insource partners that allow you to become a cross-functional team. (Take a look at Chapter 10 for more on cross-functional teams.) This is a project, with goals and objectives, a time frame, and a budget. If you just send off information and wait for the results to return, your partnerships are likely to fail.

Following are a few rules you can put in place to make sure that your distributed new product team, as well as the parts of your company that support it, can communicate effectively:

- ✔ **Meet regularly.** Get members of the team used to a regular meeting — every Monday or the second Tuesday of the month, for example. You can vary the times, if necessary, to spread the pain of having to meet outside of normal work hours.

- ✔ **Use a consistent format.** Keep the agenda simple, and keep the agenda format the same. For example, you might include time for the team to greet each other, followed by the status of the project. The team can then work on any problems that have surfaced, as well as any new opportunities. It's a good idea to include a time for new business and to encourage team members to bring up issues that don't fit the rest of the agenda in that slot.

  Be sure to include time for team members to share about what's going on with them during each meeting. A simple and brief "check-in" to start each meeting can encourage team members to inform each other of births and birthdays as well as insights and learning that might forward the team's work.

- ✔ **Create a central location for product documentation.** A password-protected Internet/Intranet site can provide a repository for the team's work (see Chapter 14).

- ✔ **Implement a process for version control.** Make sure that your team doesn't end up in document chaos! This can be as simple as enforcing a format that team members use when they access or change a document. If you have software that allows several members of the team to access documents simultaneously, make sure that software includes version control features.

- ✔ **Use the advantages of a "work-around-the-clock" system.** One team can post its work at the end of the day so a partner whose day is just starting can review it and carry on. Be careful not to go overboard with this; too much 24/7 work can take a huge toll on a team. Take a look at Chapter 14 for an example of 'round-the-clock work.

- ✔ **Familiarize your teams with all the new collaboration tools (see Chapter 14).** Phone conference lines, Web meeting tools (like WebEx and NetMeeting), and videoconferencing allow teams to share information and help to build a sense of team and teamwork.

In Chapter 10, you find out how to make cross-functional teams work. In Chapter 14, you can read up on how digital technologies support the work of distributed teams. Most of what we say there can be applied in spades to teams that work in different locations in our global economy.

Sometimes, the best practices and procedures for making distributed teams work just aren't enough. During these times it can help if you meet face to face. As a general rule, groups should meet face to face toward the beginning of projects and at critical junctures (for example, when the team's work has to be integrated). In addition, an outsourcing team may need to spend time at your home-base facility to get a better sense of how you "do it around here," and managers and team members should plan to spend time with outsource/insource teams — giving oversight, holding training sessions, and keeping the team's work on track.

## *Aligning your processes and practices*

New product developers are using plenty of well-honed processes and practices to roll out great products that meet customer requirements. Even product developers who work in the same location must align their processes. This task becomes even more critical when an organization collaborates across cultures and languages, companies, and continents to produce new products.

Companies that succeed at aligning their processes and practices at home generally have the best success at aligning the work of teams globally. They also have the ability to create an aligned strategy for new product development. You can learn more about most of these important processes and practices elsewhere in this book. The following list reviews them in the context of promoting GDPD success:

- **Understanding customer needs:** The best way to put a team on the same page is to visit customers together to find out what they really want/need. Use the information we present in Chapter 4 to organize a cross-functional, cross-cultural, and international team to carry out a program of customer visits.

- **Linking customer needs to product requirements:** When your teams understand what customers all over the world want, and when they can tie those needs to what the product should do, they can travel a relatively straight and narrow path to the end result. (See Chapter 4 for techniques that make these linkages work.)

- **Mapping technologies, product portfolios, and product lines:** When your teams understand the role their work plays in the company's overall product strategy, they can make good decisions about trade-offs and can hoist a red flag if their work doesn't seem to be in sync. (See Chapter 3 for more on mapping the key aspects of a company's new product strategy.)

- ✔ **Using digital formats for design and drawing:** Make sure you have a standard and well-accepted format for rendering your designs. You don't want to have to translate any drawings into different formats. (See Chapter 14 for the impact of digital technologies on NPD.)

- ✔ **Implementing standard project management practices:** Every member of every team should have some training in, and a great deal of respect for, standard project management (PM) practices. Some teams use project management software, some don't; what makes the real difference isn't the software but the practices themselves. (Take a look at *Project Management For Dummies,* 2nd Edition, by Sydney E. Portny [Wiley] for more information.)

- ✔ **Implementing a robust phase/review process:** Using a phase/review process streamlines the new product development process. A phase/ review process keeps the workflow aligned, forces the teams to pay attention to the business cases for projects, and connects the work of the teams to executive oversight and judgment. (See Chapters 9 and 12 for more advice on conducting the phase/review process.)

If you use these practices and processes for your product development projects, you'll find it much easier to keep your GDPD projects on track. Most of the time, your organization's GDPD projects constitute only a portion of a whole NPD project; your GDPD partners may not need to know all about how your project fits within the related technology, the portfolio, and the product line maps. But you'll be able to connect your in-house work with the work that you in- or outsource, manage that work, and provide consistent formats for your partners and suppliers to work with.

# Chapter 16

# Choose Your Partner! Partners in Product Development

· · · · · · · · · · · · · · · · · · · · · · · · · · · · · · · · · · · · · · · · · · · · · · · ·

· · · · · · · · · · · · · · · · · · · · · · · · · · · · · · · · · · · · · · · · · · · · · · · ·

*M*any companies of different sizes and in different industries take advantage of partnering to boost their ability to bring new products to market. When a company *partners* in product development, it relies on another company to accomplish some of the tasks associated with developing a product.

The partnering trend has accelerated in recent years, in large part due to our shrinking planet. Finding resources all over the world is getting easier (see Chapter 15). Companies often start by working together on more routine tasks, but then they begin to notice opportunities to partner on ever more complex ones, such as product development. Today, virtually all pharmaceutical companies use partners to extend their research and development capacities, and firms that do business in many other industries are discovering how to grow their capabilities and profits.

Of course, with the advantages of partnering come risks — of losing intellectual property, of not developing needed assets in-house, and so on. Your organization must ask a critically important question: What business should we do with partners, and what should we keep inside?

In this chapter, you discover the advantages and the risks of partnering. You look at how to choose the right partner for your business situation, and you find out what kinds of alliances make the most business sense. You'll also see how a leading pharmaceutical company executes another tricky part of partnering — actually managing its partnerships.

We'd like to thank Eli Lilly, and Lilly representatives David Vondle, Global Brand Development Leader, and Mike Ransom, Alliance Manager, for their contribution to this chapter.

# Understanding the "Open Innovation Paradigm"

The new buzz on the NPD campus is *open innovation* — finding and exploiting other companies' *inventions* to create your own marketable *innovations*. It seems obvious that it took a consortium of partners to develop and market just about anything of value that's in the market today — the products and services that are the core of our global economy. Nonetheless, the dominant paradigm in innovation and new product development has been what author Henry Chesbrough calls "closed innovation." Corporations have operated within a world view often characterized as "not invented here," or NIH. Roughly, this translates to "if we didn't invent it, we don't want it."

But why limit your resources to what you can do in-house when a whole world of innovation awaits you?

As Chesbrough convincingly argues in his book, *Open Innovation* (Harvard Business School Press), companies need to give the NIH paradigm the boot. Successful companies in a number of industries have already done so. The open innovation paradigm invites all companies to declare open season on advances in technologies and products, no matter who came up with them or who owns them. The paradigm also invites businesspeople to respect their own and others' intellectual property and to learn how to be good partners.

The go-it-alone approach is fading for a number of reasons:

- ✔ Many traditionally research-focused companies have severely reduced their R&D budgets.

- ✔ Pressures for short-term results — from investors on the outside and executives on the inside — have dampened spending on internal technology initiatives that could create new and breakthrough products.

- ✔ Our world's "technology metabolism" is speeding up. If the metabolism of technology is getting faster and faster, your company's great ideas, your inventions, and your new technologies are becoming old hat at a faster and faster rate. What used to seem like a good plan — inventing stuff and then putting the products on the shelf for later — is becoming less and less prudent.

Convinced? Read on so we can tell you how to navigate the rough seas outside your company.

And if you're an inventor, you should read on, too. The open innovation paradigm has pushed companies large and small to look to the little guys — the inventor who works in his garage, the small start-up company with the intriguing technology and limited resources, and so on. The more you understand about how the big guys operate, the better you can attract their attention.

If you need some convincing that partnering is truly a good way to go, look no further than the following list, where we present some of the benefits your company can generate by working with partners rather than working alone:

- **Accessing new ideas.** You can network with other companies to broaden your perspective and leverage external knowledge.

- **Speeding to market.** You can see beyond your organization's boundaries to find a missing NPD link that may get your new product to market quicker.

- **Meeting a customer need.** You may find inventions that allow your organization to address specific customer needs or differentiate your new products.

- **Getting value from your inventions.** In the open innovation paradigm, you can manage your technology and intellectual property (IP) so that, if you don't have a use for it, you can sell or license it to other companies.

- **Breaking into new markets.** A partner may be able to introduce you to markets your company couldn't have entered on its own.

# Deciding Whom to Partner With

Sometimes, your choice of partner is obvious. Two companies already know each other and may have worked together on previous NPD projects. Perhaps, during your work, you identified some additional ways that you can benefit each other. For example, a company that makes oxygen delivery systems was able to improve its product by working with a company that had expertise in moisturizing oxygen. The second company benefited from the partner's much more elaborate product line and wider reach into the market. Other times, you have a specific need or opportunity, and you must target a company that can make your NPD dreams come true. In the latter scenario, the world is your oyster (or your potential partner).

How will you identify the best companies from the list of maybes? Co-author Robin used a process at DuPont called *Strategic Gap Analysis*. Following are the general steps of the process and how the folks at DuPont used it:

1. **Clearly identify the need or opportunity for which a partner may be appropriate.**

   For example, DuPont identified an opportunity to expand its nylon business globally, and in particular in Taiwan and other Asian countries.

2. **Gather a team of people — preferably employees who are familiar with the NPD area you want to address in your project and who represent different functions and areas of expertise.**

   They formed a cross-functional team (see Chapter 10), which included people with expertise in M&A (mergers and acquisitions), nylon technologies and processes, marketing and market research, and so on.

3. **The team members identify whether their company can be a winner in the market, the processes, and the technology for this project.**

   To do this step, the team should address the following three questions:

   - **Market:** What's the best way to access the target customers with a compelling message?

   - **Process:** What's the best way to develop the new product, including design, development, packaging, launch, and other issues? How can we produce a streamlined flow of new product for our customers?

   - **Technology:** What's the best technology to use in this new product?

   Robin's team members identified DuPont's strengths in the areas that they would need in order to succeed. These strengths included market knowledge, customer access, process and technology, and employees.

   You may want to schedule several meetings for your analysis team. Team members will raise many questions at the first meeting, and you'll do a much better job if you can do some research to answer the questions before you forge ahead to a decision.

4. **With this combined understanding of market, process, and technology, the team identifies what the company can accomplish internally and where the gaps are.**

   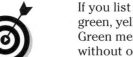

   If you list the questions and answers from Step 3 in a table, you can put green, yellow, and red dots against each element of the winning scenarios. Green means "go" — in other words, your company can go to market without outside help; yellow means there are gaps, but not show-stoppers; red means you'll need help to accomplish your goal.

   DuPont's matrix (see Figure 16-1), not surprisingly, showed they had great strengths in the necessary technologies and processes. What they were weak in, in this case, was market knowledge and employees, and what they need most of all is access to customers in the new market.

**Figure 16-1:** This matrix helps a cross-functional team identify strengths and weaknesses before they select a partner.

| Area of expertise | Green | Yellow | Red |
|---|---|---|---|
| | | | |
| Market knowledge (far east) | | ● | |
| customer access | | | ● |
| Process | ● | | |
| Technoology | ● | | |
| Employees | | ● | |

5. **Create a list of potential partners, and use dots to show their capabilities against each of the required elements.**

   DuPont started a search for a Taiwanese partner. The result was a 50-50 joint venture called DuPont Far Eastern Company, between DuPont Nylon and Far Eastern Textile Ltd. (FETL), which constructed and operated a $100 million nylon fiber plant located in Taiwan, using new fiber-spinning technology from DuPont and local resources and knowledge from FETL. The joint venture successfully introduced products into the Taiwanese market.

You can do a Web search to identify potential partners. Also, employees usually know pretty well who's good at what in their particular fields, so a combination of internal and external approaches works best. Use the red, yellow, and green dots again to show the team's guesstimate regarding the potential partners' capabilities in the areas you're interested in.

# Structuring the Business Partner Relationship

You can join forces with others in the NPD game in many different ways. The approach you choose depends on how serious you want the relationship to be and on your company's and project's business situations. These variables make your organization's decision complex, but if you consider the possibilities before you jump in, you're more likely to come up with a partnering model that works for you. We go through the variables you must consider in the sections that follow.

# Deciding how "serious" the relationship should be

When teaming up with a business partner, the form of the partnership you create determines how involved the relationship will be. NPD alliances run the gamut from the relative simplicity of a vendor or supplier contract to the complexity of mergers and acquisitions. Take a look at Chapters 8 and 15 for more on the spectrum of partner relationships, from just dating to buying your first house together.

The following list reads from least to most complex and from least to most involved — and from least to most risky!

- **Vendor/supplier:** In this relationship, you're the customer, and ending the relationship is easy.

- **Preferred supplier:** In a preferred supplier relationship, you have each made concessions to the other that make the relationship more attractive on both sides but also harder to dissolve.

- **Outsource partner:** In an outsource partner relationship, your company keeps control of the entire project, including any intellectual property. However, the outsource partner isn't just making "stuff" that you could probably get elsewhere without much difficulty. The partner is providing you with key input that depends on your partner's capabilities to develop or produce that input.

- **Joint venture:** In a joint venture, or JV, both parties pony up with equity, and both share in the profits and the expenses. However, their intellectual property and know-how assets are usually not co-mingled.

- **Acquisition:** If one company finds another company that has "just what it needs," and if the price is right, one company may acquire the other. In that case, of course, all the assets and IP of the acquired company are brought into the acquiring company.

- **Merger:** If you find a company that has just what you need, it may be time to consider a merger. In a merger, the two companies come together under common ownership and duke it out over who will do what, whose processes will survive, and so on.

You should choose the partner relationship that allows you to get the job done with the least amount of involvement from the partner. A supplier, for example, gives you more flexibility than a preferred supplier because you can negotiate prices and easily move to another supplier if you find one that will give you a better deal in terms of quality or price. A joint venture has an easier exit path than an acquisition, while an acquisition allows the acquiring company to preserve its company's culture and competencies — things that the company may have to blend, and perhaps lose, in a merger.

On the other hand, you want to choose the partner relationship that gives you a level of commitment on par with the goals you want to achieve. A supplier can easily walk away from the partnership, leaving you with no resources to meet your deadlines. However, you're more likely to lose valuable intellectual property with an outsource partner or a JV than you are in a supplier relationship.

Consider the following factors when making your choice:

- ✔ How much you need the partner, and for what
- ✔ The importance of the project to your goals and objectives
- ✔ How big the project is compared to your entire portfolio
- ✔ How long the partnership is likely to last

We'd love to give you a yardstick to measure all these variables, but in the end, the partnership decision you make is a judgment call. If you consider all these variables, though, you make decisions with your eyes wide open. (Read the section "Unveiling the How-To's and Secrets of Collaboration," later in this chapter, to find out how creating good contracts and managing your partnerships are critical tasks for success in partner relationships.)

## Investigating the different flavors of alliances and partnerships

Partnerships come in many shapes and sizes. If you work for a small company, your choice of a partner may be a life-or-death decision. If you work for a larger company, the decision may affect only an individual project or business unit. For a big company, success is nice, but disaster shouldn't be fatal. However, both large and small players should be thinking about some key factors as they research possible alliances. The following sections point out food for thought.

Understanding your core competencies is at the heart of partnership decisions. See Chapter 8 for more on identifying them, and see the later section "A Line in the Sandbox: Deciding What Assets to Keep and What to Share" for more on how core competencies affect partnership decisions.

### David-and-Goliath alliances

How do the big companies get the technologies they need to provide customer value and to differentiate their products? Instead of, or in addition to, developing the technologies themselves, they often look for little businesses that have the inventions they need. And how do the little companies get technologies and get into markets that, at their size, they wouldn't be able to enter?

They find a bigger company that has the technology and market reach that their innovative new products deserve.

David-and-Goliath matches can come together in several ways:

- A big guy may want to make use of the growing number of brokers who help corporations find the geniuses in their garages — people who just happen to have the solutions the big guys are looking for.

- The little guys may rather be inventors than entrepreneurs. If you fit this bill, get yourself listed on a Web site that helps link businesses like yours to the corporate world. (See the sidebar "Connect and develop.")

- An alliance with a larger company can provide a little guy — who, almost by definition, has limited resources — with the technology support and access to markets needed to take its brainchild to a whole new level. Suppose the little guy can improve the texture of chocolate to rival any chocolate in the world. Where is her invention worth more? In a kitchen in Hackensack, New Jersey, or with a world-class chocolatier like Nestlé or Hershey?

- A big guy can expand its resources by acquiring or partnering with a smaller company that has the technology, product, or market presence the big guy needs. Suppose the big guy who manufactures equipment for the movie industry needs to fill a gap in its product line. What makes more sense — to buy it from the guy in the garage who happens to have invented it several years ago, or to go through the hassles of product design and development more or less from scratch? And how much better if the little guy actually has credibility in that fairly niche market?

## Connect and develop

Proctor and Gamble (P&G), a multinational manufacturer, has coined the phrase "connect and develop" for its practice of locating inventors who can solve the company's technology problems. Have you eaten a potato chip with a trivia question printed on it? P&G acquired that technology after one of its engineers tried to use her ink-jet printer on a piece of potato. Needless to say, neither the printer nor the potato came through the experience very well. But using an innovation broker, the company found someone

who — this is true! — had figured out how to accomplish this amazing feat.

Take a look at the *Harvard Business Review* article "Connect and Develop: Inside Proctor & Gamble's New Model for Innovation" by Huston and Sakkab (March 2006). You'll find more examples of how companies are using brokerage services between corporations and inventors, as well as how to contact some of them.

### Building strength by joining forces: Little + little

Are you a little guy who isn't ready to trust your fortunes to a big partner? Be on the lookout for another small company, possibly a start-up like you, whose capabilities are a good match for yours. The path you choose depends on your business situation:

- ✔ If you have a super technology but not a great way to get it to market, look for a company with good distribution and the need for an influx of new products to feed the market. If there is such a company, you probably are already aware of it. It's not exactly hiding its light under a bushel.

- ✔ If you have good products already in the market, but you aren't strong in innovation, look for a partner who can revitalize your product lines.

### When giants dance: Big + big

Partnerships among the giants usually are focused on particular technologies or markets. When a large company wants to explore a new business, it can get up to speed very quickly by finding a partner who could use what the company has — and whose capabilities could get the company from 0 to 60 in a fraction of the time. For example, when TV manufacturers wanted to produce a high-quality, low-cost TV screen, they didn't develop the technology on their own. They partnered with glass manufacturer Corning, Inc., which had also partnered with GE in the early days to manufacture a high-quality, low-cost glass envelope for Edison's invention.

The old saw about corporate alliances, mergers, and partnerships is that A + B always equals less than the sum of A and B, or what the companies had when they were independent. This has been so true, and the phenomenon of partnership has become so prevalent, that we think the dancers are learning some lessons. So take care if you're in a large company that's thinking of partnering, but realize also that the kinds of experiences you can read about here are revising the chances for success upwards.

# Keeping an eye out for more potential partners

The first time you enter into an alliance, it will probably be because a likely partner appeared on your doorstep or was introduced to you by a customer who thought you'd have something in common. Or you attended a conference and found out about a company that seemed to have exactly what you needed.

That's a fine way to start. But we hope that your approach to partnering is getting more sophisticated. If you run Strategic Gap Analysis sessions (see the earlier section "Deciding Whom to Partner With") with some regularity, you'll identify issues on which you'd like to partner and partners who might fill the gap. If the company takes a position with respect to partnering — for instance, if the company has declared in an annual report that it will grow its reach at least in part through judicious partnering — employees will be on the lookout for partnering opportunities.

We recommend that your company identify a specific person who is responsible for scouting out potential alliances and partnerships. The more potential partners you have in view, the more choice you have when it comes time to get serious. Here are a few tips:

- ✔ **Refresh the list of gaps often.** Use a process like the Strategic Gap Analysis we describe earlier in this chapter.

- ✔ **Assign people to scout for likely partners**. Let them know what the company is looking for — the gaps and the strategic opportunities — and encourage them to keep their eyes and ears open at conferences, in Web searches, and in the many ways that employees relate to the "outside world."

- ✔ **Keep a list of possible partners, along with the gaps they might fill and the strategies they might contribute to.** Update and refresh the list as employees bring in new ideas.

With a nice long list of potential partners, linked to the potential contribution they could make to the company, you'll be able to work with the businesses to identify the ones that should be courted now.

Who does the courting? It depends on the size of the project and the seriousness of the relationship contemplated. In Japan, CEOs often engage in what they call "golf talk" to set up a partnership, even though others are responsible for setting up the actual relationship.

When both parties are looking interested, it's time to talk about contracts. But first, take a look at the next section to make sure you're not giving away the crown jewels. And see the section later on "Writing a contract" to see what to do when it's time to dot the i's and cross the t's.

# *A Line in the Sandbox: Deciding What Assets to Keep and What to Share*

You don't want to give away your company's most treasured secrets. If you do, you'll become an empty shell whose only function is to coordinate the innovation efforts of others. So you have to be cautious about what you partner on.

The answers to tough partnering questions will become apparent *if* you have a good grasp on what your core technologies, products, and processes are.

The following list gives you a pretty simple way of categorizing what you should partner on and what you should guard:

- ✔ **If you have the competency and capacity to develop a strategically important technology, you should keep this asset inside.** For example, Caterpillar has developed the technology to build energy-efficient, clean off-road vehicles. This is a strategic asset for them, especially as emissions regulations seem to be getting tougher.

- ✔ **If you *have* the competency and capacity and the asset isn't strategically important, you may want to outsource work — unless you can do it yourself more cheaply or easily.** Caterpillar designs and develops a lot of the components that make up its vehicles, but it outsources many of the components that it doesn't regard as strategic. (See Chapter 15 for more on outsourcing.)

- ✔ **If you *don't* have the competency or capacity and the necessary asset isn't strategically important, you should outsource the work.** Over time, as you outsource work that's not strategically important, you'll stop building those capabilities — so make sure you've chosen things you don't mind depending on others for. For example, car manufacturers often outsource many aspects of interior design and don't have the ability in-house to do that kind of work.

- ✔ **If you don't have the competency or capacity and the asset *is* strategically important, you should develop a relationship with a trusted partner or acquire the competency by buying it.** You also may consider developing the competency internally, depending on how long and expensive the project would be, or merging with a partner who can fill the gaps (see the earlier section "Deciding Whom to Partner With").

Even though you can easily create four categories and see what makes sense in each of them, the devil is always in the details and the borderline cases. Only through open and frank internal discussion and by using good practices, such as technology mapping (see Chapter 7) and identifying your new product strategies and opportunities (see Chapter 3), can you make tough decisions about what to partner on and what to guard inside.

# *Unveiling the How-To's and Secrets of Collaboration*

You've done all the hard work of deciding what to partner on, researched possible partners, and figured out the right partnership model. You've courted and won a partner. Now comes the equally hard work of making the partnership work. In this section, we stress a few things we've discovered about what makes business partnerships work — whether they're large/small, small/small, or large/large (see the earlier section "Investigating the different flavors of alliances and partnerships"). You can also find some tips about how to collaborate with global partners in Chapter 15.

## Writing a contract

A partnership contract lays out the financial and other agreements that will structure the relationship. Of course, writing a contract for work with a supplier will be much easier than writing a contract for a JV. Supplier contracts should be mainly boilerplate. Contracts for more complex relationships will need to be created to meet the specific goals and circumstances of the partnership.

Writing a good contract depends on the following:

- Making the partnership goals clear
- Specifying who will be involved
- Including contingencies for managing change

A good partnership is seldom static; you can rarely see all the way to the end of the partnership road.

 In light of all this contract talk, here's a piece of very good advice: Write the best contract you can, and then put it aside. The success of your partnership truly depends on how well you build and maintain the relationship. It depends on what the folks at pharmaceutical company Eli Lilly call "alliance management."

If you *don't* have a good contract, you've created a recipe for disaster. But if your strategy for managing the partnership is to point to what the contract says in section 3.a.1, you've lost the chance to develop the relationship that a successful partnership depends on.

## Setting the frame for communication

Who does the communicating in a successful partnering relationship? Everyone who is involved. Imagine that the partnership is two side-by-side tall buildings and that every floor of each building has windows that open toward a window in the other building. On each floor there are different people whose work is affected by the partnership. The CEOs and business leaders are probably on the top floor; on the other floors, you can find R&D, marketing, sales, and so on.

As the partnership progresses, the people behind the windows pay more and more attention to the people behind the windows in the other building. The business leaders hang out at the window during their coffee break, chatting with the business leaders from the other side. The engineers have fixed up a signal system so they can alert their buddies on the other side every time a new and wonderful idea occurs to them. The marketers, of course, have flag-poles — when a marketer runs something up her flagpole, the marketer on the other side comes to his window and the two head out to Starbucks for a chat. The people behind the windows can also signal people on other floors, so they can include marketing in the CEO's strategic chat, or R&D in discussions about target markets or the future of the partnership.

The point of the metaphor is to remind you that communication — the life's blood of the partnership — needs to run through all its available veins, and that good partnerships continually grow new veins through which people can communicate. We get a gold star for mixed metaphor with that one, don't we? Forgive us, but remember the metaphors and heed the "golden rules" we list here:

- **Overcommunicate.** Never assume that a partner understands what you're trying to say. Remember: "The biggest danger in communication is the illusion that it has been achieved."

- **Outline clear goals and objectives for your partnership.** This task is important for people who work alone and for teams, but its importance goes up exponentially with the number and distance of the partners.

- **Set up a clear communication system.** Share e-mails and create an Intranet repository for important documents. This is important for people and teams within a single company; its importance goes up exponentially when you're working between companies.

- **Develop a language for communication.** Each company comes to the partnership with its own way of representing information. You should take the time to create a common language so that the assumptions and knowledge of each partner are transparent. *Note:* The initial lack of a common language can be an asset.

- **Make requests, promises, schedules, and deliverables clear.** Good project management is a critical element of good partnerships — and of successful new product development in general (see *Project Management For Dummies,* 2nd Edition, by Stanley Portny [Wiley] for more on this essential skill). Of course your partnership will have clear goals and objectives (see the section "Writing a contract," for example), but the goals for the partnership don't include all the work the partners will do. That's much more fine-grained. What a bummer when a partnership flounders because one side says, "I didn't know you expected me to come up with that research by today."

# Getting an A+ in alliance management

When pharmaceutical company Eli Lilly decided on a strategy of alliances and partnerships to grow the organization, a board member challenged the company by saying "If alliances are so critical to our success, then what are we doing to improve our alliance management capability?"

In response, Lilly created an Office of Alliance Management (OAM) to build that capacity even as it managed existing alliances. The folks at Lilly's OAM like to say "We don't make alliances — we make them better." Selecting the partner and writing the contract are essential to making good alliances, but too many companies stop there.

David Vondle and Mike Ransom shared these tips at a recent IAPD workshop:

- ✔ **Don't expect alliances to work on their own.** Create guidelines for alliances that provide the stepping stones partners will need.

- ✔ **Help alliance partners develop a common language.** See the earlier section "Setting the frame for communication" for more on this.

- ✔ **Build your alliance competency by keeping track of what works and what doesn't.** In this way you'll improve your guidelines and create a core competency for your company.

The OAM at Lilly provides training for teams that work in alliances. Its members develop and share processes and tools, and they provide facilitation when the partners need to resolve issues. The OAM measures the ongoing health of an alliance with a tool called the VOA, or *voice of the alliance*. By identifying parameters that are critical to alliance health, the OAM often can nip problems in the bud and offer help to alliances that may be headed for trouble.

Our advice to you: Take partnership seriously, and begin to build your own knowledge base. Follow Lilly's lead and collect good practices. Assign personnel whose primary job is to monitor and support the health of your alliances.

# Part V
# The Part of Tens

## The 5th Wave

By Rich Tennant

"I was giving them a rousing motivational speech from my college football days, at the end of which everyone jumped up and butted heads."

# In this part . . .

**A**uthors always have bits of information they want to tell you about that just don't seem to fit in their books. That's why we have *For Dummies* Part of Tens lists! In these two chapters, we give you hints, tips, and some good old facts about how to improve your products with the judicious use of testing and how to select metrics to make sure that all your product development efforts are paying off.

When you're developing products, you're coming up with something new, so it stands to reason that you need to test and measure. Product developers — whatever function they're from — work a bit like experimental scientists. "What if we designed the product this way?" "What would happen if we used this kind of process?" The way to find the answers is by running experiments, or tests, and measuring the results. The information in this part helps you design experiments so you can improve the products you introduce, as well as the practices and processes you use to develop them.

# Chapter 17

# Ten Ideas on Ways to Test Your New Products

*P*roduct testing should start before your development team even has a product concept and continue throughout the product lifecycle. Testing opens doors to many ideas, allows you to make sure that you have a good product concept, and helps you improve on the product even after it's in the market. In this chapter, we give you an outline of tests that follow the flow of the product development process. You can read this chapter top to bottom to get an idea of the sequence of tests product developers use, or you can just skip through and pick out the tests you need for your current projects.

To achieve success with many of the tests we include in this chapter, you need the assistance of experts: marketers, engineers, facilitators, and so on. Some larger companies have a lot of expertise in-house. But if you need to hire it in, you can find these experts in many different ways:

✔ You can do an Internet search for the term Product Testing (you get around 91 million results), select a few firms, and talk with people to get ideas on narrowing down your search for where to find the help you need.

✔ You can network with a local professional group, like a Product Development and Management Association (PDMA) chapter, to ask for references to firms that can address your particular need.

✔ You can ask your marketing department to recommend firms it has used in the past.

✔ You can ask friends in other companies how they found someone to help them with their product testing.

Testing expertise is available at many cost levels. The size of your testing program should correlate to the size of the firm you work with, and to the size of the project. Don't make the mistake of paying more for the test than you expect to gain from the test results (yes, we've seen people do this!). In all cases, you should budget your new product development project to cover the necessary testing.

# Conducting New Product Concept Testing

Long before your new product development team has anything you can call a "product," you can and should start testing. You have two ways to confirm that you have a good product concept: *qualitative market research* and *quantitative market research*. The difference between these methods is that qualitative research tends to be exploratory — it addresses the question "What could we do?" — while quantitative research confirms, in fact, that you should push ahead with a project, modify it, or toss it into the scrap heap.

## Qualitative market research

You should conduct qualitative research with customers way before you even have a product concept. Early research helps your team understand customers' needs so that you can come up with ideas for products that meet those needs. When you ask "What *could* we do?" qualitative research (in effect, the customer) answers the question. Customer visits, interviews with customers, and observation of customer environments and work/play processes reveal what they need and want. (Take a look at Chapter 4 for details on how to conduct this early research.)

After you do come up with a concept (see Chapter 5), you can use a number of other qualitative methods to zero in on the customer's reactions to different possible functions and features of proposed products, for example using con-joint analysis or simple preference statements and surveys.

Qualitative research can guide your product development efforts, but what you discover in a qualitative study can't tell you how many people want a certain feature or how many customers might buy a product at a certain price. In other words, qualitative research may lead your team to develop a great product, but you can't count on it to support your business case. For that, you need quantitative research.

## Quantitative market research

Quantitative research answers the *how much* and *how many* questions your development team needs to answer to develop the business case (see Chapter 12). In other words, you take something that represents the product or the product experience to customers you believe would want that product, and in so many words, ask "Would you buy this?" "How much would you pay for it?" And, "When would you like to buy it?" Quantitative research also helps establish the relative importance of different features. For example, your team may think that the blue whirly-gig on the top of the product is the coolest thing since sliced bread, but it may leave most of your target customers cold.

Quantitative research helps you come up with statistically significant conclusions about the relative importance of the following:

- ✔ The customer needs you identify through qualitative research
- ✔ What difference adding or subtracting a feature could make
- ✔ The number of people who are likely to buy the product you're developing; in other words, how large the total market for a product may be

 The usefulness and validity of quantitative research depends on how well your product development team designs the research. If you ask the wrong customers whether they want a product or how much a product is worth to them, you could kill a potentially successful product or go to market with a product that your target customers don't really want (in terms of features, price point, quantity, and so on). Start with qualitative research so you can identify important questions in your customers' minds, and follow that work with quantitative research to establish the significance of what you discover.

# Checking Your Progress with Prototypes

When your new product development team moves into the design and development phases of the NPD process (see Chapter 9), you'll encounter a time when you need to build a *prototype* — a physical representation of the product or product features that has previously existed only in someone's mind, or as words on a page or sketches in a software program. People often have different interpretations of words, but seeing something in physical form greatly reduces potential confusion over the look, feel, and actions of a product idea or feature. Prototypes differ, depending on the industry and the kind of product. They're hugely important in making sure that the products you design and build actually perform as your test audiences expect.

In the following sections, you discover the differences between fit, form, and function prototypes; you see what kind of prototypes work best in different situations; and you find out how to give rapid prototyping a try.

## Going for fit, form, or function

Building a prototype that includes all the parts of the final product *(fit),* looks just like you expect the final product to look *(form),* and does everything you want the finished product to do *(function)* takes much longer than creating a prototype that meets only one or two of these criteria. A prototype should represent the full fit, form, and function of the product as much as possible, but we all know that budget constraints sometimes require compromises. When you have to compromise, remember what information you're hoping to get from your prototype test. A service product is more function than anything else, for example. A new paint color is more form (color, texture) and function (coverage) than it is fit.

When your NPD team is building a prototype, make sure that all your members are totally clear about the purpose of the prototype:

- ✔ **A fit prototype gives the team a chance to see how all the parts go together.** Different members of the team may be working on different parts of the product. If you don't track how the parts fit, you may find the lens occupying the space that belongs to the shutter, or that the front seat of a car isn't designed in a way that allows the driver to access the glove compartment.

- ✔ **A form prototype makes sure that the beautiful product you designed will be as beautiful in finished form.** A 3-D version of the product may show flaws that the initial sketches hid. A form prototype also can generate very interesting discussions with a focus group.

- ✔ **A function prototype shows how the product will work.** In the early stages, you shouldn't mind if wires.are running all over the place or if the back of the product is made of cardboard. The point you want to prove with a function prototype is that when you push the button, the light really does go on and the bells really do ring.

## Deciding which prototype is best for you

Different businesses use different prototypes during the product development process. The Product Development and Management Association

Glossary defines prototype as "a physical model of the new product concept." However, you shouldn't take the word "physical" too literally. Software developers make prototypes that consist of code. Service developers make prototypes that consist of people walking through routines. And financial developers make prototypes that describe financial transactions in detail.

You have many different kinds of prototypes to choose from, depending on your business and product lines. We cover the basics in the following list:

- **Models of physical products:** When you hear the word "prototype," you probably think of a physical model of a physical product, such as an airplane model in a wind tunnel. A company uses physical prototypes as early in the design/development process as possible so product developers can see and feel what they're working on. Product developers also show physical prototypes to customers to get feedback. Examples of settings where product developers might use prototypes to get customer feedback include focus groups and early Alpha Tests.

- **Software prototypes:** Software is a "virtual product" whose functions can be represented with a series of screens that represent actual functions. The software product is all the code that users never see that's behind the user interface — that is, the screens the users see or the sounds they hear.

  Typically, software designers will develop screens that show what would happen if an option on a screen were selected. An example would be a screen for a new Web site showing multiple options for finding photographs of whales to test for interest in a Web site that searches for photographs. The designer would have collected photographs of whales to show after a selection was made without the necessary code being written to actually go out to the Internet to find them. Using screens allows the product team to test for interest in a search concept without investing in actual product development. Software designers can start testing their products right away without actually building the product. They call the tests they use Alpha, Beta, and Gamma Tests, depending on how "finished" their products are (see the section "Testing Products in Customers' Hands" in this chapter).

- **Service prototypes:** To prototype a service, you really have to create a "life-size" model and test it with your customers. For example, if a hotel chain wants to offer a new way to clean rooms for long-term guests, it has to implement the change in one hotel to see whether it really works and to gauge guest reactions. You can avoid plenty of costly problems by testing your services before you send them out to market.

More and more product developers are focusing on "solutions" rather than products or services alone (see Chapter 5 for more on this topic). If your organization's "product" includes a service component, don't forget to prototype and test the service part of it. For example, a new robot lawn mower may have to include training over the Internet or via CD-ROM to show purchasers how to set up the robot to work on their lawns. Testing the training module, as well as the lawn mower, ensures that purchasers of the lawn mowing "solution" actually have a working product.

## Giving rapid prototyping a try

*Rapid prototypes* are models or full-size representations of physical products built from successive layers of liquid or powdered material that will harden to become the shapes that represent the product ideas. You use a machine to build up the representation from a physical or digital drawing or from a set of instructions from a computer aided design (CAD) system. Not so long ago, many companies switched to CAD because it's faster than paper and pencil and has the ability to generate dimensions and other data that paper models can't. CAD also enables teams that work in different places to share their work.

Product developers can look at and feel these rapid prototypes, turn them over, and share them with customers in idea sessions or focus groups. With their physical information and feedback, developers can revise, correct, and add to their original ideas — quickly and painlessly. (In Chapter 14 you can find out how computer aided design and rapid prototyping connects to the digital revolution in product development.)

For example, a CAD machine may have been used to develop a drawing of the Apple iPhone. A rapid prototype machine would use data to produce a physical model of the phone that developers could use to test how users like the size and feel of the phone. This provides more valuable testing than a drawing alone could accomplish. The instructions that drive the rapid prototyping machine also can drive manufacturing robots that produce the case.

As you may have guessed, rapid prototyping can be very expensive and often isn't suitable for small start-up companies and the like.

Your organization can use the Internet to give consumers the chance to interact with your prototype, or even your product at an advanced stage of development, and give you feedback. This technique works well for software products (such as interfaces), financial products (such as new savings accounts that depend on ATMs or the Internet to capture transactions), and physical products — if you use graphic design software to show the products and how they work.

## Testing Products in Customers' Hands

When your NPD team has sailed around a few of the bends in the "river of development" — when you've designed your product, have the ability to produce at least a small number, and have brought in customers to react to how the product looks and functions — the time has come to put some of your product directly into your customers' hands to see how they get along.

Whether your team has made a sippy cup for babies or a sophisticated software product for bankers, you take a huge chance if you put your product into the market without seeing how your customers will respond to it. When your product hits the market, your team can't tell a baby how to grab the neat handles you designed, and you can't tell a banker how to find certain features. The customers will have to dance without your help, and your product has to be the teacher.

Product developers often talk about three stages of product use testing: Alpha, Beta, and Gamma (this last one is mostly used in software development). They also use Market Tests. This section discusses each of these tests.

## *Alpha Tests*

The *Alpha Test* is the first time you put your "real" product into customers' hands. It isn't a prototype test. You've manufactured or produced your product the way you'll produce subsequent real products. Your finished product may have bugs, which leads to the point of the Alpha Test: to find out about the bugs now, not after you've manufactured and distributed hundreds or thousands of products.

Here's what you need for Alpha Tests:

- ✔ A clear understanding, from the product definition (see Chapter 9), of how the product should perform when in your customers' hands

- ✔ Enough of the product, in its final or near-final form, to run the test

- ✔ "Customers" who will use the product

  Whenever possible, conduct Alpha Tests with people who work for your company or with people who are very friendly and won't spread the word if your new plastic bags break and they get spaghetti sauce all over them.

- ✔ Researchers who will observe and/or interview the customers

- ✔ Continuous reporting to assess how the product works for the customers

The more effective your early testing (see the previous sections of this chapter), the smoother your Alpha Tests will be. Put real effort into testing your concepts and prototypes. Bringing customers in for focus groups or prototype tests beforehand can help to avoid Alpha shocks.

## Beta Tests

*Beta Tests* are field tests of products. By using a Beta Test, you get to see how your customers will use your product, allowing you to make modifications if necessary (although it's unusual — and upsetting! — to have to make major changes during Beta Testing). During Beta Tests, you can discover plenty about how to install your product, how to instruct customers to use it, and what kinds of questions customers may have. You may even pick up valuable tips about how to market your product and support it when it hits its market.

Here's what you need to conduct Beta Tests:

- ✔ Products that you've "debugged" during Alpha Testing
- ✔ Products whose production mirrors the production you intend for your launch products
- ✔ A clear definition of your expectations for the products
- ✔ Customers who will use the products and participate in the research

  Work with customers who seem friendly, but make sure that their desire to please you doesn't prevent them from telling you what's wrong with the products.
- ✔ Researchers who will observe, test, and report on the progress
- ✔ A plan for making the changes to the product suggested by the test results

You need to be innovative to find enough customers to run your Beta Tests. One company, for example, tests its packaging by giving away samples at retirement homes. Its researchers observe whether the residents can open the packages easily. Some software companies offer customers the chance to be "Beta-site customers" on the Internet. If you see one of these offers, sign up to see how the company runs the test.

## Gamma Tests

A *Gamma Test* is the final test phase when a product is in general release. It assesses how well your product performs, whether it addresses the customer needs it should address, and how well it satisfies customers. Often, what characterizes this test phase is the fact that a company will maintain extra staff to deal with problems that come up after a product's general release exposes it to unanticipated user conditions.

Teams in the software industry are more likely to use Gamma Tests. Most software products are so complex and have to operate in so many different technical environments that they're almost never completely bug-free. Often – we're sure you know this from your own experience! – a software firm will release a product to the open market knowing that while it doesn't have fatal bugs, it may have some relatively minor bugs. Finding those bugs, and supporting customers who run into them, is the essence of a Gamma Test. Some people say software never gets out of Gamma Testing.

## Market Tests

*Market Testing* occurs when the new product and its marketing plan are tested together. It gives you a chance to find out how well your whole package works. It also helps you put together a more accurate forecast of how much and how consistently you can sell so you can update your business plan and prepare for launch (see Chapter 13). A Market Test should be carried out toward the end of the product development process.

Here's what you need to carry out a Market Test:

- ✔ Enough product in its final form — complete with packaging, instructional guides, and any other materials that will allow you to put the product in a statistically valid number of users' hands. The sample size is driven by the variability of the target market. If users in the target market are essentially the same, you can get away with a smaller amount of test product; if the users have many differences, you need enough product for a large sample.
- ✔ Advertising and other promotional materials
- ✔ A site, or several sites, where you can carry out the tests
- ✔ Researchers who will assess the test results
- ✔ A plan for responding to the test results
- ✔ Potential customers who represent the conditions in the market you built the product for. Food companies, for example, have to test every region of the target market that has different taste preferences. Software companies have to represent the variety of technical skills and operating systems found in their defined target market.

# Chapter 18

# Ten (Or More) Ways to Track Your Innovation Efforts

## In This Chapter

▶ Marking your NPD team's progress

▶ Assessing the processes you use for product development

▶ Linking projects and processes to the company's strategic objectives

▶ Getting a quick glance at progress with dashboard metrics

*I*t takes a company, with every division, team, and business group working together, to be successful at developing new products. At each level of responsibility, people use benchmarks and metrics to track performance. Here are the three kinds of output, from three different levels of your company, that your team's selection of metrics needs to link:

- ✔ **Team or project level:** The metrics focus on project progress, quality, and output.

- ✔ **Management or process level:** The metrics focus on process quality, strategic balance, and output.

- ✔ **Corporate level:** The metrics focus on strategic balance and financial outcomes.

In this chapter, we describe many ways to measure output in each of these areas. (Kind of like a few Part of Tens chapters in one — aren't you lucky!) Browse through this chapter to pick out three to five metrics that address different areas of performance that will help your company's leaders assess what's important to them. (If you choose more than that, you'll spend too much time measuring and providing reports that members of management won't read.) The goals and the outcomes at each of the three levels of product development are fundamentally interrelated. Choose metrics that assess the impact each of these levels has on the others. You can add more metrics, or replace unsatisfactory ones, after you give your first choices a fair shake.

330 Part V: The Part of Tens

Here's a saying we read on a tea bag: To err is human; to blame the error on someone else is even more human. Some company leaders use metrics to determine who they can blame when things go wrong. That rarely — or never, we suspect — gets at the real causes of the problems. In fact, using metrics for that purpose is more likely to make the problems worse. Beating people over the head isn't a good way to use a yardstick! Instead, you should use metrics to pinpoint what's going right so that you can do more of it, and what's going wrong so that you can fix it.

# Ten (Minus Two) Ways to Keep Track of Your Teams' Progress

During the phase/review process of new product development (see Chapters 9 and 12), the NPD team and its team leader commit to meeting certain deliverables, or milestones, in a specific time frame. If the team falls short, it has either overpromised or underdelivered. Both of these actions send a clear signal that the team needs to make some changes to get in sync with management's expectations.

The following list presents types of metrics that track team and project progress. The team is largely responsible for the first four metrics; a failure to meet any of the second four may signal that the process is broken.

If you're working on an NPD team that doesn't receive adequate support, be the squeaky wheel. The issues that plague you and your colleagues will continue to undermine your efforts and your company's ability to thrive. (See Chapter 11 for more on project resources.)

- **Deliverables completed at each phase review:** The measure to aim for is to complete 100 percent of set deliverables. However, in some cases, a team can allow some deliverables to slide. In such a case, the team should document the following:

  - Specific information about the incomplete deliverables

  - Why the incompletions won't detract from the review

  - Plans for completing the deliverables in the next phase

- **Business case measures:** The business case features a number of measures — such as market size or sales forecasts, which impact financial performance — that the NPD team commits to meeting. The team should update the business case measures at each review, accounting for any slippage or overage and reviewing the impact on the project's business merit. (See Chapter 12 for more on business cases.)

✔ **Schedule:** The target for meeting the proposed schedule should be zero slip-ups. If that isn't possible, the team should shoot for quick recoveries. One schedule slip tends to lead to another, and the impact on the project often is cumulative. Arriving late to market, for example, can blow an entire business case.

If many projects show large numbers of schedule slips, NPD teams may be facing process issues such as underresourcing or overpromising. The managers need to solve these process problems. When teams are stretched to the limit, they can't do much more to fix the problems on their own.

If your NPD team can develop a product quickly and for less money, you should earn a blue ribbon, right? Not necessarily. One of the most important process metrics is predictability. If you can develop a product faster and cheaper, those forecasts should show up at the beginning of the project in your schedule and budget.

✔ **Budget:** The budget for a development project is tied to the business case, so the target for the budget is to never go over. However, the cost of a project can be much less significant than other measures. You may be fine with exceeding the budget if, for instance, you can get the product to market quicker or lower the cost of the product. You can make budget decisions at a scheduled review (see Chapter 12), or you can call a special review if time is pressing. At the meeting, the team resets the budget, with the agreement of the reviewers, and the adjusted budget becomes the new target.

✔ **Percent of turnover within the core team:** When the core development team experiences turnover, it's hard for team members to work together. The commitment of the remaining team members may flag; valuable knowledge walks out the door with the departing team member; and new members need to be brought up to speed. Often, the cause of excessive turnover is systemic, stemming from the team's lack of resources or the company's lack of commitment to the NPD efforts. The problem usually requires the intervention of top management. (See Chapter 10 for more on the core team.)

✔ **Changes to product design:** These changes are often referred to as *engineering change notices,* or ECNs. A high number of ECNs can mean that the process for achieving a stable definition of a product and project is flawed. Perhaps the teams don't spend enough time at the early product definition stage. ECNs also can stem from schedule issues and budget overruns.

✔ **Feature changes:** These changes, often referred to as *feature creep,* can happen when a product team gets more excited about its product and technology than its customers' needs (see Chapter 4) and the business case (see Chapter 12). An example is a team adding road-mapping capabilities to a cellular phone designed for the low-end market, just because the technology is available. Feature changes lead to schedule and budget overruns. Even worse, they can lead to products that don't fit with the team's strategic objectives or the company's market realities. Feature changes should occur only when customer needs change, and should be documented, prior to product release.

✔ **Reuse of product features, or *platformization*:** We're looking for a high score here! Companies can create great leverage by making sure their products and NPD teams reuse work that other products and teams have utilized in the past. The more your NPD teams work from technology or product platforms, the cheaper their projects will be and the quicker they'll get to market. Look at Chapter 3 for a deeper discussion of platforms.

An excellent example of feature reuse is a small battery-driven motor for hand-held drills, screwdrivers, and sanders. Product developers using the same motor and battery design created a family of tools that all work off the same motor and battery. This technique saves on design and production costs and creates a nifty feature that increases customer appeal.

# Ten Ways to Measure the Health of Your Product Development Processes

Your organization needs to measure the health of your product development processes. Companies that have effective processes get products developed faster, spend less money doing so, get more products to market, and generate higher revenues from new products than companies with less-effective NPD processes. This section lists a number of metrics that can help you gauge the effectiveness of your processes and target your process improvement efforts where they'll do the most good.

*Note:* The first four metrics in this list provide a yardstick to measure how well your projects are doing, on average. The second four help you measure the value your processes are delivering. And the last two identify whether your projects are linked to strategic objectives.

✔ **Number of teams fully resourced:** At each review, your company should set a schedule of resources the NPD teams need in the future. Ideally, the teams should have 100 percent of the resources the company commits to them at each review. Not having all the required resources means projects won't get completed on time and will begin to clog up the NPD pipeline.

- **Number of projects that meet schedule and budget targets:** The goal with this metric is predictability. You don't want projects that exceed or fall short of their goals; you want to build the project management skills that allow your teams to estimate, with accuracy, how long the projects will take and how much they'll cost. Team members and company leaders must be able to tell the truth about projects in order to do well on this metric.

- **Time spent in phases:** Knowing how long similar projects in other companies usually spend in the different phases of the development process can give you benchmark numbers, which help you assess whether a particular project is spending too much time in one phase. If it is, you can take corrective action. For example, you might find a study that says companies of a size similar to yours take five months to move from ideation to funding approval. If your team is taking nine months, you need to look at why you're exceeding the norm. Benchmark numbers also can help you set targets in an attempt to reduce overall cycle time.

    Cycle time is a *dependent variable,* which means you can't reduce it directly. What you can do is spend enough time upfront to ensure clear product definition, fully resource your teams, and have clear review criteria and practices in place. Take a look at the recent Product Development and Management Association (PDMA) study on its Web site (www.pdma.org) for more.

- **Percentage of products that meet or exceed goals set at the Feasibility Review:** The higher the percentage, the better. This metric indicates that teams are spending sufficient time and effort to plan well in the early part of the process, and also that projects are well supported in the NPD pipeline.

- **Value and average value of programs in development:** This metric is a summary of the net present value (NPV) of each project plus the total value of all projects your team has underway. The total should equal the growth objectives for the corporation.

- **Percentage of product ideas that meet or exceed goals:** Can you believe that many companies don't go back to check whether their new products have met the targets they set at the beginning of the projects? Yikes! How can you get better if you don't know how you're doing? This metric focuses on goals stated in the original business plan, and typically looks at projects after one year in the market. The percentage should be high — at least 80 percent— and moving toward the desired goal of 100 percent. These goals are easily identified and measured. Did development time and costs come in as projected? Did you sell the number of units you projected for the first quarter, six months, year? Did your gross margin and net margin results come in as projected?

✔ **Investment per product:** You calculate this metric as follows:

Total dollars of manpower + cost of development equipment and supplies + cost of tests + launch and promotion costs invested in new product development ÷ the number of products commercialized

The final number should drop over time to show increased efficiency in the development process.

✔ **Percent of management time devoted to NPD:** Most research shows that when management puts skin in the game, its development processes improve. Managerial involvement is most important when your processes are new; it becomes less important when the processes have gone through many cycles of improvement. The best scenario is for management to get into the habit early and stay with the effort, even after the processes start to work well.

This metric isn't a call for management to get involved with the technical or project-level activities of the team. It's a call for management to support the practices that lead to product development success.

✔ **Number of ideas entering the Idea/Concept Screen:** You want to have a high number of ideas for this metric. If project reviewers have too few concepts to review, they can't select a group of projects that meet your strategic criteria.

The best way to determine how many ideas you should be generating is to start keeping records of how many ideas you currently feed into the screening process, how many ideas make it through each phase, how many of these ideas go to market, and how well you're achieving your new product revenue objectives. Benchmarks on number of ideas required to achieve commercial success are available. The PDMA Foundation has published material on this topic and offers benchmarking services for specific industries. One study of multiple industries indicated that out of 100 ideas generated, about 70 cleared the idea screening process, around 50 cleared the business case screen, about 35 completed development, and around 25 reached commercialization. Probably less than ten were financially successful. (See Chapters 5 and 6 for more advice on how to increase the number of ideas and for basic info on the Idea Screen.)

✔ **Comparison of products in development to portfolio criteria:** Your team should be able to map the products you have in development against your portfolio criteria to find out whether the next crop of products to hit the market will fulfill such targets as risk versus reward, product line enhancement, "strategic buckets," and so on. See Chapters 3 and 11 for more on these terms and targets.

The company's strategic team should review this comparison frequently. New opportunities will show up, your company's strategic focus will shift, and some projects will under- or overperform. Also, in order to keep the products in development and the portfolio criteria matched up, the review judgments of individual projects need to be tied to portfolio criteria.

# Ten (Divided by Two) Metrics to Make Sure Your NPD Efforts Are Paying Off

An organization's executives want to extract maximum value from their company's investment in new product development. They want assurance that their spending falls in line with business strategy, that the projects in development are in sync with business objectives, and that their investments will help the corporation meet its revenue and growth goals.

Corporate product developers use a balance of financial and strategic metrics to assess the health of their new product efforts and to ensure that their company's investments are helping them meet growth goals. We outline these metrics in the list that follows:

- **Percent revenue and/or number of new products launched in the past XX years:** Companies in fast-moving industries, such as telecommunications, may set a target as high as 50 percent of revenue coming from products introduced in the past, say, three years. Companies in older, more slow-moving industries, such as specialty chemicals, may set a target of 15 percent, or even less, introduced in the past five years. Not meeting these targets is an indication that the NPD process isn't performing as desired, and an examination of *process* metrics is in order. (That is, go back one step to the metrics in the previous section!) Even doing better than plan is cause for investigation. Exceeding targets should lead the team to determine why — is it because older products are delivering lower-than-expected revenues, is there something changing in your target markets? And if you're doing something really great, you want to know so you can make sure you keep doing it.

  Not many companies depend on the number of new products they launch as a target, because the profitability of each product varies greatly. Also, that target is very open to gaming — for instance when product developers make minor tweaks and list the projects as "new products."

- **Investment in new products as a percent of sales:** By comparing the investment in NPD to sales, and finding out what percentage of sales it represents, companies can track how well they're allocating their innovation dollars. For example, say an ice cream company sees sales rising at 10 percent a year, but new flavor development costs as a percent of new sales is rising at 20 percent a year. This would result in a lower overall profit margin. Perhaps the cause is too many new flavors going into the same-sized market, so the same number of people are buying the same amount of ice cream, just buying more different flavors. In this case it may make more sense to cut back on flavor development and invest in a larger distribution network.

  This metric also helps management assess its commitment to new product development. For example, when the percentage is too small, the company knows it isn't putting its weight behind developing new products. In order to have a healthy new product effort, a company must reinvest some percent of its sales into future products. A good approach is to find the average for your industry, and the average for the leaders in your industry, to be sure that your company isn't shortchanging its NPD efforts.

✓ **Investment per product versus sales revenue:** The ideal trend is for your company's investment per product to decline, which shows that your sales revenue per product is, on average, increasing. You get the ratio as follows:

(The investment per product × the number of products) ÷ the total sales revenue

Take the ice cream company from the earlier bullet and change a few things. Instead of sales rising at 10 percent, say they're rising at 20 percent a year, and development costs are rising at 10 percent a year. The decline in development costs leads to increased profit margin. Maybe it happened because you reused some research, or you just got more efficient in market testing flavors. Whatever the reason, the improvement becomes even more valuable on a dollar basis as sales revenue grows — and your job becomes more secure!

✓ **Shareholder Value Added (SVA):** Overall, this metric gets at the point of developing new products: You use some of your corporation's resources to increase shareholder value. Again, using the ice cream vendor, you might say that as a result of a more efficient NPD process, you see an improvement of 5 cents a share in annual profits. If the ice cream company is getting a share price to earnings multiple of 18, you just added 90 cents per share to your company's market value. If the old stock price were $9 per share, and now it's $9.90 per share, you just got a return of 10 percent on whatever shares you own, maybe more if you have stock options. That new Mercedes is closer than you thought!

By pinpointing how new product development adds to shareholder value in different parts of your company — different business units, for example — you can focus your resources to increase value.

Too many companies examine financial metrics only at the company level. Co-author Robin calls this "across the boardism." As in the previous example, we recommend that companies divide their corporations into chunks and compare metrics to see where they're using resources effectively.

✓ **Net Present Value (NPV):** This financial metric focuses on the cost of capital — on what it costs to develop products in these terms.

Executives are more interested in the NPV of the entire portfolio of new product projects, along with the NPV of the portfolios of different business units. A comparison between business units can help members of management see where the company is making wise investments.

Executives shouldn't rely too much on financial and strategic metrics without understanding how they link to process and team metrics. When they do, they may put in motion interventions that don't promote good project work or good processes. For example, executives who must drive to meet quarterly projections may cut development resources, particularly in the front end. They think, "That won't deliver anything for several quarters or more anyway." This thinking sends the whole system into a tailspin from which it may never recover. We give only five metrics in this section to underscore the fact that you shouldn't rely too much on financial and strategic information alone.

# Seeing Ten (Or Fewer) Measures at a Glance with Dashboard Metrics

*Dashboard metrics* refers to the process of collecting a group of performance metrics and displaying them in a simple, easily grasped set of graphs or visual representations. Think of the dashboard of a car: You have a speedometer, maybe a tachometer, an odometer, a gas gauge, an oil light, and so on. With a dashboard metric, an executive might have on one page a graph that shows rate of increase for sales (speedometer), a bar graph showing monthly percent of sales spent on NPD (tachometer), a line chart showing total revenue for the year (odometer), and an overview of corporate resources devoted to NPD (gas gauge). The oil light (you know, the one they call the "idiot light") goes on if too many projects come in late to market. Some cars now have GPS to help the driver figure out where she is. That may be the portfolio map that shows what kinds of products are in development. One glance at this page would give a busy executive a quick idea of how the company is doing.

Product developers came up with these metrics for a few reasons:

✔ They enable development teams to see the all-important financial metrics along with operational, process, and statistical metrics. This takes some of the focus off the financial output taken by itself, and it provides clues to why the company may or may not be achieving its targets.

✔ They push companies to select a few key metrics so they don't drown in a sea of them.

✔ They help teams see, at a glance, the links among the different levels that need to work together.

To build a dashboard — sometimes called a *scorecard* — you choose the categories of metrics you want to track.

Dashboards almost always include financial measures, which let you see how well your development team is accomplishing the corporation's objectives.

You also should include strategic objectives to help you stay balanced. Companies that don't put enough emphasis on balance may end up filling their product development pipelines with quick hits and short-term projects just to meet quarterly financial goals. Putting different kinds of metrics side by side on your dashboard encourages your company's executives to consider different drivers of success (or failure) at the same time.

The dashboard is a tool. Your company can find many consultants who can help you build a process to track in real time your successes and failures. If you type Dashboard Metrics into your favorite search engine, you'll find plenty of variations. After you construct a dashboard, send it out to be used and ask people for feedback. A few months later, publish a second version of the dashboard that responds to people's suggestions. If you find yourself obsessing over this, give the project away or use some other approach.

# Business Case Outline

$E$very new product project must have a business case that states clearly why the company should invest its scarce resources in the project. The business case provides the basis for judging the success of a product in the market. The NPD team, with the help of the functions and departments, prepares the business case for the Feasibility Review (see Chapter 9). During the entire phase/review process, the team updates the business case and presents it at each scheduled review (see Chapter 12).

Here's a template you can use to create a project's business case:

1. **Executive Summary:** This summary provides a one- to two-page overview of the whole business case. Most teams find that it's best to write the summary after they've completed the business case.

2. **Project Overview and Business Strategy:** In this section, the team describes the project, the opportunity that the project represents for the business, and the investment that the team is requesting. The project overview answers the following questions:

   a. **What is the team planning to develop or create?** The answer may be a product with certain features to serve a certain market or a platform to replace a given product line, for instance. Be sure to include information that links product features and functionality to well-understood customer requirements.

   b. **How is this aligned with the strategy of the organization?** The answer should include technology, product, market, brand, growth, and other strategic imperatives. Be sure to describe the relationship of this intended product to the organization's current products, product lines, and product portfolio.

   c. **What resources will the team require?** This answer should include an estimate of employee resources from different functions, expressed in person-years, as well as any known or predicted capital, infrastructure, or other expenses. Use ranges in the beginning and make estimates more precise as the project unfolds.

   d. **What is the project timing?** Include the expected launch date, plus any information the team has about the window of opportunity (for instance, any reasons why the product must be launched in a particular time frame, including seasonal issues, competitors, market trends, and so on).

3. **Market Analysis and Approach:** This section explains the opportunity in the context of the industry, the competitive environment, and clearly identified market segments.

4. **Technology Approach:** Here the team describes the strategy and plans for using or creating technology to meet the customer needs. Be sure to include the relationship of technology development plans to the organization's technology strategy and to highlight any unusual risks or uncertainties.

5. **Manufacturing and Operations:** In this section, the team provides an overview of the processes and systems it will need to produce/manufacture and deliver/distribute the product.

6. **Supply Chain and Partnership Strategy:** Use this section to clearly outline the team's plans for engaging and managing the supply chain and to describe any plans for partnering. Highlight important risks and uncertainties, and show how plans for this project align with the organization's overall supplier/partner strategy.

7. **Safety, Health, and Environmental Impact:** In this section, the team addresses sustainability issues, environmental impact, and worker safety and health.

8. **Legal and Regulatory Requirements:** This section addresses governmental approval processes as well as intellectual property reviews. (Your organization's legal department should be able to help with this part of the case.)

9. **Implementation Plans:** This section describes what has to be done, when, and by whom. Be sure to include commitments by the functions to their roles and responsibilities for systems, operational elements, marketing plans, launch plans, sales programs, training, logistics, and anything else that's critical to the success of the program.

10. **Financial Profile:** In this section, the team should provide a clear financial analysis and an account of its underlying assumptions. Most business cases include estimates of sales units and volume, cost targets, margins, and market share.

11. **Risks:** In this section, the team identifies potential risks, including financial risks, market risks, operational risks, and technology risks.

12. **Assumptions and Scenarios:** The team should articulate its underlying assumptions and beliefs about the future state of the market and the organization, as well as the potential impact of these different future states. Include assumptions about market size, market share, unit forecasts, pricing, organizational support, and so on.

Our thanks to Steven Haines of Sequent Learning Networks for providing this template. For more information on business cases, and for a more detailed template, take a look at www.sequentlearning.com.

# Index

## • *E* •

# Notes

## BUSINESS, CAREERS & PERSONAL FINANCE

0-7645-9847-3

0-7645-2431-3

**Also available:**
- Business Plans Kit For Dummies
  0-7645-9794-9
- Economics For Dummies
  0-7645-5726-2
- Grant Writing For Dummies
  0-7645-8416-2
- Home Buying For Dummies
  0-7645-5331-3
- Managing For Dummies
  0-7645-1771-6
- Marketing For Dummies
  0-7645-5600-2

- Personal Finance For Dummies
  0-7645-2590-5*
- Resumes For Dummies
  0-7645-5471-9
- Selling For Dummies
  0-7645-5363-1
- Six Sigma For Dummies
  0-7645-6798-5
- Small Business Kit For Dummies
  0-7645-5984-2
- Starting an eBay Business For Dummies
  0-7645-6924-4
- Your Dream Career For Dummies
  0-7645-9795-7

## HOME & BUSINESS COMPUTER BASICS

0-470-05432-8

0-471-75421-8

**Also available:**
- Cleaning Windows Vista For Dummies
  0-471-78293-9
- Excel 2007 For Dummies
  0-470-03737-7
- Mac OS X Tiger For Dummies
  0-7645-7675-5
- MacBook For Dummies
  0-470-04859-X
- Macs For Dummies
  0-470-04849-2
- Office 2007 For Dummies
  0-470-00923-3

- Outlook 2007 For Dummies
  0-470-03830-6
- PCs For Dummies
  0-7645-8958-X
- Salesforce.com For Dummies
  0-470-04893-X
- Upgrading & Fixing Laptops For Dummies
  0-7645-8959-8
- Word 2007 For Dummies
  0-470-03658-3
- Quicken 2007 For Dummies
  0-470-04600-7

## FOOD, HOME, GARDEN, HOBBIES, MUSIC & PETS

0-7645-8404-9

0-7645-9904-6

**Also available:**
- Candy Making For Dummies
  0-7645-9734-5
- Card Games For Dummies
  0-7645-9910-0
- Crocheting For Dummies
  0-7645-4151-X
- Dog Training For Dummies
  0-7645-8418-9
- Healthy Carb Cookbook For Dummies
  0-7645-8476-6
- Home Maintenance For Dummies
  0-7645-5215-5

- Horses For Dummies
  0-7645-9797-3
- Jewelry Making & Beading For Dummies
  0-7645-2571-9
- Orchids For Dummies
  0-7645-6759-4
- Puppies For Dummies
  0-7645-5255-4
- Rock Guitar For Dummies
  0-7645-5356-9
- Sewing For Dummies
  0-7645-6847-7
- Singing For Dummies
  0-7645-2475-5

## INTERNET & DIGITAL MEDIA

0-470-04529-9

0-470-04894-8

**Also available:**
- Blogging For Dummies
  0-471-77084-1
- Digital Photography For Dummies
  0-7645-9802-3
- Digital Photography All-in-One Desk Reference For Dummies
  0-470-03743-1
- Digital SLR Cameras and Photography For Dummies
  0-7645-9803-1
- eBay Business All-in-One Desk Reference For Dummies
  0-7645-8438-3
- HDTV For Dummies
  0-470-09673-X

- Home Entertainment PCs For Dummies
  0-470-05523-5
- MySpace For Dummies
  0-470-09529-6
- Search Engine Optimization For Dummies
  0-471-97998-8
- Skype For Dummies
  0-470-04891-3
- The Internet For Dummies
  0-7645-8996-2
- Wiring Your Digital Home For Dummies
  0-471-91830-X

**\* Separate Canadian edition also available**
**† Separate U.K. edition also available**

WILEY

## SPORTS, FITNESS, PARENTING, RELIGION & SPIRITUALITY

0-471-76871-5

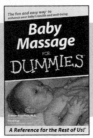

0-7645-7841-3

**Also available:**
- Catholicism For Dummies
  0-7645-5391-7
- Exercise Balls For Dummies
  0-7645-5623-1
- Fitness For Dummies
  0-7645-7851-0
- Football For Dummies
  0-7645-3936-1
- Judaism For Dummies
  0-7645-5299-6
- Potty Training For Dummies
  0-7645-5417-4
- Buddhism For Dummies
  0-7645-5359-3

- Pregnancy For Dummies
  0-7645-4483-7 †
- Ten Minute Tone-Ups For Dummies
  0-7645-7207-5
- NASCAR For Dummies
  0-7645-7681-X
- Religion For Dummies
  0-7645-5264-3
- Soccer For Dummies
  0-7645-5229-5
- Women in the Bible For Dummies
  0-7645-8475-8

## TRAVEL

0-7645-7749-2

0-7645-6945-7

**Also available:**
- Alaska For Dummies
  0-7645-7746-8
- Cruise Vacations For Dummies
  0-7645-6941-4
- England For Dummies
  0-7645-4276-1
- Europe For Dummies
  0-7645-7529-5
- Germany For Dummies
  0-7645-7823-5
- Hawaii For Dummies
  0-7645-7402-7

- Italy For Dummies
  0-7645-7386-1
- Las Vegas For Dummies
  0-7645-7382-9
- London For Dummies
  0-7645-4277-X
- Paris For Dummies
  0-7645-7630-5
- RV Vacations For Dummies
  0-7645-4442-X
- Walt Disney World & Orlando
  For Dummies
  0-7645-9660-8

## GRAPHICS, DESIGN & WEB DEVELOPMENT

0-7645-8815-X

0-7645-9571-7

**Also available:**
- 3D Game Animation For Dummies
  0-7645-8789-7
- AutoCAD 2006 For Dummies
  0-7645-8925-3
- Building a Web Site For Dummies
  0-7645-7144-3
- Creating Web Pages For Dummies
  0-470-08030-2
- Creating Web Pages All-in-One Desk
  Reference For Dummies
  0-7645-4345-8
- Dreamweaver 8 For Dummies
  0-7645-9649-7

- InDesign CS2 For Dummies
  0-7645-9572-5
- Macromedia Flash 8 For Dummies
  0-7645-9691-8
- Photoshop CS2 and Digital
  Photography For Dummies
  0-7645-9580-6
- Photoshop Elements 4 For Dummies
  0-471-77483-9
- Syndicating Web Sites with RSS Feeds
  For Dummies
  0-7645-8848-6
- Yahoo! SiteBuilder For Dummies
  0-7645-9800-7

## NETWORKING, SECURITY, PROGRAMMING & DATABASES

0-7645-7728-X

0-471-74940-0

**Also available:**
- Access 2007 For Dummies
  0-470-04612-0
- ASP.NET 2 For Dummies
  0-7645-7907-X
- C# 2005 For Dummies
  0-7645-9704-3
- Hacking For Dummies
  0-470-05235-X
- Hacking Wireless Networks
  For Dummies
  0-7645-9730-2
- Java For Dummies
  0-470-08716-1

- Microsoft SQL Server 2005 For Dummies
  0-7645-7755-7
- Networking All-in-One Desk Reference
  For Dummies
  0-7645-9939-9
- Preventing Identity Theft For Dummies
  0-7645-7336-5
- Telecom For Dummies
  0-471-77085-X
- Visual Studio 2005 All-in-One Desk
  Reference For Dummies
  0-7645-9775-2
- XML For Dummies
  0-7645-8845-1

## HEALTH & SELF-HELP

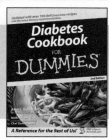

0-7645-8450-2

Dieting FOR DUMMIES

0-7645-4149-8

**Also available:**

- Bipolar Disorder For Dummies
  0-7645-8451-0
- Chemotherapy and Radiation
  For Dummies
  0-7645-7832-4
- Controlling Cholesterol For Dummies
  0-7645-5440-9
- Diabetes For Dummies
  0-7645-6820-5* †
- Divorce For Dummies
  0-7645-8417-0 †

- Fibromyalgia For Dummies
  0-7645-5441-7
- Low-Calorie Dieting For Dummies
  0-7645-9905-4
- Meditation For Dummies
  0-471-77774-9
- Osteoporosis For Dummies
  0-7645-7621-6
- Overcoming Anxiety For Dummies
  0-7645-5447-6
- Reiki For Dummies
  0-7645-9907-0
- Stress Management For Dummies
  0-7645-5144-2

## EDUCATION, HISTORY, REFERENCE & TEST PREPARATION

C.S. Lewis & Narnia FOR DUMMIES

0-7645-8381-6

Genetics FOR DUMMIES

0-7645-9554-7

**Also available:**

- The ACT For Dummies
  0-7645-9652-7
- Algebra For Dummies
  0-7645-5325-9
- Algebra Workbook For Dummies
  0-7645-8467-7
- Astronomy For Dummies
  0-7645-8465-0
- Calculus For Dummies
  0-7645-2498-4
- Chemistry For Dummies
  0-7645-5430-1
- Forensics For Dummies
  0-7645-5580-4

- Freemasons For Dummies
  0-7645-9796-5
- French For Dummies
  0-7645-5193-0
- Geometry For Dummies
  0-7645-5324-0
- Organic Chemistry I For Dummies
  0-7645-6902-3
- The SAT I For Dummies
  0-7645-7193-1
- Spanish For Dummies
  0-7645-5194-9
- Statistics For Dummies
  0-7645-5423-9

# Get smart @ dummies.com®

- **Find a full list of Dummies titles**
- **Look into loads of FREE on-site articles**
- **Sign up for FREE eTips e-mailed to you weekly**
- **See what other products carry the Dummies name**
- **Shop directly from the Dummies bookstore**
- **Enter to win new prizes every month!**

**\* Separate Canadian edition also available**
**† Separate U.K. edition also available**

Available wherever books are sold. For more information or to order direct: U.S. customers visit www.dummies.com or call 1-877-762-2974.
U.K. customers visit www.wileyeurope.com or call 0800 243407. Canadian customers visit www.wiley.ca or call 1-800-567-4797.